THE WARRIOR STATE

THE WARRIOR STATE

HOW MILITARY ORGANIZATION STRUCTURES POLITICS

EVERETT CARL DOLMAN

First published in 2004 by
PALGRAVE MACMILLAN™
175 Fifth Avenue, New York, N.Y. 10010 and
Houndmills, Basingstoke, Hampshire, England RG21 6XS
Companies and representatives throughout the world.

PALGRAVE MACMILLAN is the global academic imprint of the Palgrave Macmillan division of St. Martin's Press, LLC and of Palgrave Macmillan Ltd. Macmillan® is a registered trademark in the United States, United Kingdom and other countries. Palgrave is a registered trademark in the European Union and other countries.

ISBN 1–4039–6661–3 hardback

Library of Congress Cataloging-in-Publication Data

Dolman, Everett C., 1958–
    The warrior state : how military organization structures politics / Everett Carl Dolman.
        p. cm.
    Includes bibliographical references and index.
    ISBN 1–4039–6661–3
        1. Civil–military relations. I. Title.

JF195.D65 2004
322'.5—dc22   2004046081

A catalogue record for this book is available from the British Library.

Design by Newgen Imaging Systems (P) Ltd., Chennai, India.

First edition: December 2004

10 9 8 7 6 5 4 3 2 1

Printed in the United States of America.

For Those Who Serve

Contents

CHAPTER ONE

MILITARY SERVICE, CITIZENSHIP, AND THE INTERNATIONAL ENVIRONMENT

Political freedom begins with military service. This plain statement could have passed unchallenged as late as a century ago. From early Greek philosophy through the Enlightenment, the notion that those who fight for the state inevitably rule it was not only politically deterministic—it was morally just. Military service in support of state and society obliged certain social rights that eventually became codified in the form of government.[1] Early modernists would extend these beliefs to their maximum practical application. Liberal democracy they insisted, with its principled goal of the complete dispersion of social rights, was possible only with *universal* military service.

By the latter half of the twentieth century, however, these notions were systematically abandoned. With the rise of the totalitarian state and the evolution of total war, military participation became viewed instead as the foundation for an insidious and pervasive model of government control. The state created its armed forces and they, in turn, supported the state. This spiraling process ended in the renunciation of all political power for the individual, its concentration instead in the political Leviathan of pervasive and tyrannical government. In a likewise determinist corollary, adherents of this alternative stance could assert that the larger and more powerful the military, the more authoritarian the state.

These views, the classical and the contemporary, are diametrically opposed. They should not be able to coexist, at least not in the abstract realm of theory. Yet both do, along with mountains of real-world evidence in support of each, and so we are left with a curious conundrum. Long-established guidelines demand that when such a theoretical impasse is evident, the divergence must be explained away or rectified. The effort to do so here begins with a pair of interrelated questions. First, has there been a change over time in the influence of military power on politics? In other words, could the classical view have been valid in previous eras, but has given way to the contemporary one in modern society? Second, has one position always been correct, simply misperceived? Did the classicists have it wrong, even in their own day, thus the contemporary antimilitary views extend back through antiquity, or can the classic case be made today that military forces are for the most part liberalizing?

A yes to both questions is logically impossible. A yes to *either* question simply adds voice to one or the other's chorus. A rectification (more accurately here, a reconciliation) requires that the simple answer is no—to *both* questions. Rather than make a case for one view over the other, or for an evolution of political influence that would have to argue that the fundamental nature of military service has somehow changed over the last century, the effort here is to find an explanation for the enduring and simultaneous existence of both views.

Background and Assumptions

That military forces have influenced the formation and political development of every Western state is nowhere seriously challenged. Social organization beyond the family sprang from the perceived need for external protection, and the maintenance of military power is traditionally one of the largest fiscal and resource drains on government. That this influence today might be in any way socially or politically positive, however, is in most cases harangued. The now conventional wisdom appears to be that the health and normal progression of (at least) the liberal state is at severe risk from military forces. Especially for state structures whose legitimacy is founded on popular participation and representation, the military is seen as notoriously corrosive. David Apter expresses this view tersely, and with typical conviction: "The military is a particularly important *obstacle* to democracy."[2] Military force is vestigial, goes this line of thought, an unwanted relic of an earlier yet persistent age that the republican or democratic state forever struggles to overcome. It is blight, a disease that the state must fend off and to which, if possible, it must develop immunity.

Unfortunately from this dominant perspective, there seems to be no ridding the state of its pernicious affliction. Modern military forces are the unwelcome but undiscardable remnants of a frightful state system that remains locked in constant war or preparation for war. The state's military power is still its only sure guarantee of sovereignty in this hostile interstate environment. To give up such power unilaterally is but to betray oneself to one's enemies. Negative sociopolitical influences of the military must therefore be accepted as an unavoidable evil of state development, residue of an embarrassing history of violence to be done away with as soon as the future-perfect world of perpetual peace makes its belated appearance. The practical problem for states, in the meantime, is how to limit the negative influence of the military domestically while optimizing its power externally.

The preceding view is based upon an incongruous and absurd notion—that the military is somehow unitary in nature. That we so commonly use the definite article when describing it shows a bias toward treating a state's military as an unvarying, homogeneous actor. Modern militaries do not speak with a single voice, do not influence political decisions in a consistent manner, and do not exert equal pressure on state development. One can no more accurately state that *the* military is always a threat to liberty than one could claim that *the* government is always an inefficient protector of rights, or that *the* people will always oppose war. Too many variables and contexts exist for such blanket statements to be valid.

Differences within and among militaries and their consequent influences on the state are founded primarily on strategic and operational necessities, cultural and social values, and organizational structure. Just as state political structures run the gamut from autocracy to democracy, military organizations are very much diverse.

They can be rigidly hierarchical or loosely decentralized, inclusive or exclusive, offensive or defensive. They can consist of professionals on permanent duty or primarily part-time militias on call as needed. Their force structures can be predominantly land, sea, or air and space-based. We quickly see that military forces are structured differently over time, from place to place, and within their own organizations from top to bottom. It is this basic observation, that organizational differences within military forces substantially determine the strength and direction of the military's political influence on state development toward, or away from, political inclusion with citizen-based rights, which inspires this book.

Accordingly, the initial and animating assumption is that a state's military forces shape its political structures and the institutions of its government. Broadly declared, the argument has rarely been disputed. Areas of contention include the primacy of its influence, whether militaries influence states to a greater degree than states influence militaries, and the direction or tenor of that influence—toward or away from which kind or type of political structure (authoritarian or democratic).

For the most part, military factors have primacy of influence. That is to say, the tendency of military organization to have a subsequent impact on political organization and development is greater than the reverse, political structure's impact on military organization and development. While there are numerous cases when the state has consciously shaped the military for specific political or social ends (several of these are described in subsequent chapters), these efforts repeatedly follow profound structural change in society rooted in the effects of a prior need-based military reorganization. Here the case will be consistently made that while the impact is dynamic and mutual, *the influence of the military on state or political organization has generally been greater*. The phenomenon is so strong, and occurs so regularly, that once identified it cannot be ignored.

The opacity of military influence is in part explained because its primary effects are structural rather than agent-based. Modern study of the civil–military relationship tends to focus solely on the problem of direct intervention by the military into affairs of the state—the military *coup d'etat* or so-called *praetorianism*. Personalities and unique cultural and geopolitical factors dominate analyses. To be sure, direct military intervention is a distinct problem in authoritarian states and fledgling democracies, especially in less developed countries, but its overall importance is magnified by a regionally myopic and short-term outlook. The larger and more profound military to society influence, appreciated by classic theorists, is passive and indirect, affecting political structures through gradual sociological transformations in the population. Those changed are often unaware of its directing influence; and so they are receptive, tending to internalize the changes readily. Moreover, those acting on behalf of the state may be unable to modify or reform the military to their desired mode, even when they recognize a negative or undesirable influence on their political structures. The exigencies of war, the juxtaposition of competing states and their relative military power, and contemporary dominating military technologies and strategies can compel a state to accept an unwanted military organization in order to survive.

Analyses that present mono-influential trajectories of state or military development must always be flawed, yet this is the typical method. For most of those who study the problems of war and tyranny, the impact of the military is assigned a negative role in the development of agreeable governmental forms such as democracy or republicanism, and conversely, a positive role in the appearance of disagreeable ones such as absolutist autocracies and dictatorships. The explicit focus of these studies is to find means for mitigating the most damaging influences of politico-military interaction. Sporadically we find classical theorists like Machiavelli who will reverse the force's polarity, and assign always positive democratizing or republican influences to certain types of military forces, but this view is in the distinct minority. The rise and development of military forces across time is too varied and rich, however, for such simple, mono-influential theories. The alternative presented here is that the tenor and direction of influence are not uniform, but are instead dependent on the structure and organization of the armed force.

Note that this theory does not dispute the well-documented historical role of militaries supporting authoritarian governments and opposing democratic ones. Through most of recorded Western history, and currently in most of the non-Western world, militaries have been organized in a manner that sustained authoritarian political control. During several recognizable and separable periods in European and American history, however, military influence had a decidedly opposite impact. Without exception, wherever increasingly inclusive republican or democratic regimes have spontaneously emerged (i.e., rose to power internally and not as a result of external imposition), radical changes in military organization and structure can be shown to have shortly preceded radical political change.

When the military has had a positive (supporting) role for authoritarian government, its organizational structure has been very different from when it has had a positive influence on republican or democratic ones. In order to make the case, Western military organizations in various historical periods will be isolated and examined to determine structural differentiations that contribute to these exclusively different influences. These examples will be employed to directly dispute mono-directional hypotheses, such as the more militarized the state the more likely it is to develop an authoritarian political structure.[3] To the contrary, massive militarization appears instead to have had a very strong correlation with *both* the emergence of absolutist monarchies in seventeenth- and eighteenth-century Europe *and* the development of mass participation political structures in the eighteenth through twentieth centuries in Europe and North America. Of particular interest and importance, fully discussed in the following chapters, the mass military mobilizations of the modern era directly preceded the mass political mobilizations of modern liberal democracy.

Military Structure and the Democratic Peace

One of the outcomes of this analysis should be a determination of which military organization characteristics are consistent with the promotion of authoritarianism, and which are consistent with the promotion of political participation. The emphasis is on the latter. Since the abolition of military forces is a remote near-term possibility, the practical payoff is the potential restructuring of existing military institutions to maximize their positive impact on liberal democratic government.

In the process, I investigate a decidedly contentious premise. Military factors traditionally considered destabilizing in the international environment (to include large, well-trained armed forces organized for offensive or out-of-country operations) have, at critical junctures in the Western experience, had a distinctly positive impact on the emergence and maintenance of the liberal democratic state. If this is indeed the case and liberal democracy can be shown structurally and normatively to produce interstate peace, then the preferred policy of peace-desiring states should be to promote and implement military reform at home *and abroad* that most efficiently generates democratic structures and values, regardless of intuitive fears of international instability. In short, if liberal democratic states do not go to war with each other, then the size, proficiency, and strength of their military forces should not be a security dilemma issue.

Mounting empirical evidence indeed points to the proliferation of modern liberal democracy as a pacifying force in international relations. Although the phenomenon was first empirically described by David Singer and Melvin Small, it was Michael Doyle who provoked a storm of activity with his attempt to tie the observation to Kant's claim that liberal democratic states would be naturally less prone to war.[4] Tests of the hypothesis showed that democratic states appear just as likely to engage in war as any alternative politically organized state, but what remained intriguing, and promising, was the empirical evidence and rationale that democratic states do not go to war *with each other*.[5] Even where they have had considerable conflicts of interest, liberal democracies appear content to resolve common disputes with rare resort even to the *threat* of military violence. As more states democratize, these observations lead to the promise of an ever-widening democratic zone of peace, ultimately encompassing the globe and presaging an era of international cooperation and stability. When all states are democratic, war will be a social relic.

If mutual liberal democracy is in fact a sufficient precondition for interstate peace, then democratic peace theory provides both the means and end for a stable and pacific world order. Any policy that efficiently enhances the process of democratization in authoritarian and developing states will generate pacific interstate results, and should be thoughtfully considered. For many traditional peace theorists, however, who concentrate on eliminating war by reducing and eliminating the military capacity to engage in combat, neo-Kantian peace theory appears fully complementary. Since war is the problem democracy corrects, they presume the tools of war are by association antidemocratic. Reducing or eliminating arms promotes peace and decreases external threats, so the argument goes, which in turn fosters domestic development of individual liberty. William Thompson makes precisely this point as he argues peace causes democracy, not the reverse.[6] Moreover, when all states are democratic there will be no need to maintain the military forces necessary to prosecute war, and all states will be able, if not compelled by socioeconomic necessity, to complete any remaining process of disarmament.

Most international realists contend instead that the democratic peace is a coincidental facade, that democratic states have not gone to war simply because traditional power politics inducements have not yet presented themselves.[7] They argue it is not armed force that destabilizes; it is the attitudes and perceptions of the potential wielders of weapons that matter. States must anticipate increasing competition and expect democratic states to act as any other power-optimizing state, regardless of domestic governing arrangements, when presented with an overwhelming incentive to press a military advantage. Stable peace, wholly desirable but fragile, can be obtained only via balancing strategies based on mutual positions of strength. Democratic states may be especially vulnerable in a less militarized world, since their societies tend to be more open, mobilization is public and difficult, and they are thus susceptible to first-strike attacks.[8] Under these conditions, all states should avoid eliminating or unduly weakening their armed forces. To do so would be an invitation to war.

The concerns of the realists are well argued, and cast a wary doubt on the abundance of empirical evidence cited by the neo-Kantian peace proponents. Nonetheless, the data is compelling, and I therefore accept as an *analytical assumption* the proposition that liberal democratic states do not go to war with each other. Should events one day demonstrate that liberal democratic states can and do war with each other (and at a rate approaching that of nondemocratic states), then the fundamental argument that follows is moot. Also accepted is that stable interstate peace is the goal of both liberal and realist theory.[9] Here, the means of one school (realist military preparedness) are reconciled with the means (liberal democratization) and end (global peace derived from the condition of full democracy) of the other. The point of harmonization is democracy itself. To be precise, democracy causes peace, but what conditions cause democracy?

The bulk of democratization theory correctly emphasizes socioeconomic factors, and my analysis is intended to add to, not contradict, this significant body of established theory.[10] I contend that a powerful and too-often overlooked contributing factor in the spontaneous emergence and healthy maintenance of stable liberal democracies is a competent military structure that promotes citizen activism. The paradox that maintaining effective means for war is the best guarantor of peace has been staunchly defended by balance of power realists and relentlessly attacked by pacificist idealists. Based solely on calculations of capacities for war, there appears to be no compromise solution. When such an impasse is evident, it often proves beneficial to change venue. I propose shifting the argument from issues inherent in the security dilemma to the role of military forces in shaping social and political institutions, fully engaging state-making and civil–military relations literature in the process. I contend that under a precise (and historically rare) set of organizing conditions, military forces can both promote democracy and enhance deterrent policies. I further assert that despite a requirement for specific military preparation, war proper is neither necessary nor beneficial to the process of democratization. In this manner, the means of both liberals and realists are supported en route to a common goal.

The most perplexing concern regarding democracy and peace remains. Although state-of-the-art international relations theory posits that liberal democracies are impervious to war in their mutual interactions, the historical record points to the conclusion that some interaction with war has been a necessary if not sufficient precursor of liberal democracy. I am confronted with the unsatisfactory observation that war or intense preparation for war precedes every Western example of successful liberal democratization, yet liberal democracy only rarely follows war or its preparation. If war or preparation for war is to have a causal impact on political institutions, especially on democratic ones, then it follows that there must be a critical intervening variable. My analysis places military organization—differentiated by levels of preparation, locations of mobilization and recruitment, strategy and tactics, and training and professionalism—at the center of this puzzle.

Ultimately, I ask democratic peace theorists to take a leap of faith. Their trust in the premise that liberal democratic states do not war with each other must be so tenacious that they can accept the continued presence of large, disciplined, and proficient military forces in the international system. The natural tendency of properly designed and managed militaries to promote democratic attitudes and structures, I argue, enhances the process of democratization and maintenance of democratic institutions. The natural inhibitions of stable democratic states to mutual armed conflict will ensure these forces are used only to combat authoritarian states. Realists should find this solution fully compatible because if the neo-Kantian peace should break down, democratic states will not have sacrificed military readiness to a utopian ideal. Thus, my goal is to identify a military structure that is both combat-proficient (to satisfy realists) and at the same time promotes democracy and interstate peace (for the idealists).

Military Organization and the Liberal State

The occurrence of both democratic *and* military values in a single state may initially appear to embody a contradiction of the first order. The first is choice-dominant, via the necessity of electoral processes, the latter harshly obedient. There is ample evidence, however, for a very close and sequential evolution of certain characteristics of military organization and democratic values, and this relationship has had enormous impact on the emergence of the modern, liberal democratic state. So important, in fact, the question that must arise is whether or not the truly democratic state can spontaneously emerge—much less maintain itself—without the democratizing influence of the properly organized military to nurture it. Current sensibilities tend to recoil from any suggestion that positive social and political liberalization might be correlated with military undertakings, yet nineteenth- and early twentieth-century European intellectuals were shrewdly aware of a strong relationship. By making the case that military action inspires political liberalization, an obvious argument for the necessity of military force in the development of modern democracy is plain. In a world of violent and predatory competing states, without the military to inspire and then protect the democratic ideal, the democratic state cannot solidify. Its enemies would simply overwhelm the nascent state. This is exactly what happened in the case of the First French Republic, whose mere existence so threatened the monarchial international order that virtually every state in Europe allied to overpower it.

It was precisely this structural argument that so convinced the neoclassical economic and social theorists. German social historian Otto Hintze argued that in fact *all political associations sprang from the need for collective defensive or offensive action.*[11] To paraphrase Charles Tilly, war made the state, and *then* the state made war.[12] Hintze charted the concurrent rise of representational democratic government with absolute growth in the size of military organizations, and associated this relationship to a recurring historical pattern. Central to his argument was the assertion that those who fight for the state ultimately will rule it.

Hintze used examples from primitive societies, where all able-bodied males were members of the warrior class, and from the record of Greek and Roman antiquity, where the citizen-soldier became the predominant model in participatory governments. The subsequent decline of representational ideals and a corresponding decrease in the size of armed formations in the so-called Dark and Middle Ages were further illuminating, but the record of the modern European era showed the strongest positive parallel between military and state organization. With the passing of the Age of Chivalry, when knights on horseback were proven inferior in battle to masses of organized infantry, the population of armies by necessity grew. As their size increased, their recruitment bases expanded. The nobility, who fought in exchange for political status from their sovereign, supplemented by mercenaries who accepted cash payment for their services, could no longer fill the ranks of effective military formations. The state looked toward militias of guildsmen, landed peasants, and merchant-privateers to augment its armed forces.

In order to meet increasing threats from neighboring states, ever-larger portions of the population were needed to take arms in defense of the state. Whether volunteers or conscripts, in return for military service their rulers were compelled to reciprocate by granting or endowing those individuals with franchise in the affairs of government proportional *to* that service. In an added benefit, franchised soldiers were often more militarily effective than mercenaries. When an individual has attained certain rights and privileges, he could be relied on to fight with greater spirit than their mercenary or forced-service counterparts, an argument forcefully made by Machiavelli in *The Art of War*.

The most spectacular example of the growth of popular military force occurred when Carnot and then Napoleon manipulated the liberation enthusiasm of the French Revolution to fashion the largest citizen-army the world had ever known. The base of that growth was a national political awakening that rose from the "two-sided education" of military service, planting in the soldier's mind an image of the state as "an affair not merely of the rulers but of the ruled and being conceived of as a community."[13] Faced with the threat of emancipated and armed throngs on their borders, rival European powers were forced to follow the French model and recruit thousands of previously disenfranchised into their own armed forces.[14] In order to increase the loyalty of these masses, as well as their combat effectiveness, these amateur warriors were promised limited rights of citizenry. In this way, the anticipated need for military forces of modern scale bankrupted feudalism and led to the emancipation of the European population from serfdom.[15]

Perhaps the most important political lesson of the French Revolution was its subsequent embrace and incorporation of militarism. Despite the obvious fact that liberating the masses created the Republic, it also became its downfall. The *Grand Armee* was refashioned into an imperial tool of the ambitious Jacobins.[16] Fisher Ames's famous pronouncement that "a democracy cannot last" is based in his belief that the inevitable result of democracy, by its very nature military in character, must be mob rule, which "*dictates* that its next change shall be into a military despotism."[17] The leaders of the Revolution, after seizing power, found that a disciplined force is much easier to control and manipulate than a free mob, and quickly organized the people into formations of national guards. An army thus formed, says

Ames, is a "democracy in regiments and brigades," and such "a military government may make a nation great, but it cannot make [its people] free."[18]

The story of the rise of the modern citizen-army prompts another lesson. By arming the population to defend it, the state provides the masses with the power to overthrow it. A newly armed citizen-military may pose a greater menace than any foreign threat to the continued existence of the exclusionary or autocratic state. Alfred Vagts describes the nineteenth-century Liberal–Tory argument in England as mired in precisely this quandary—would the continually armed masses gravitate toward militarism and thus become a threat to (Liberal view) or protector of (Tory view) the institution of political liberty?[19] The debate posed yet another fundamental question of sovereignty for the state. If arming the population decreases the threat of foreign invasion but increases the likelihood of rebellion, and, conversely, disarming the population, while suppressing the tendency for revolt, invites foreign adventurism, how can the liberal state preserve itself?

Hintze offered a structural explanation. The military is customarily understood to have two primary roles: defense of the state from external threat and defense of the government from internal rebellion. The former role is conducive to liberty and democracy, for it protects and nurtures society. Without a military force to shelter it, democratic society would fall prey to neighboring expansionist authoritarian states. The latter role is obviously not so conducive, as the military becomes a tool of oppression. Hintze therefore believed that a military structure dominated by the army is prone to succumbing to the latter role, but one dominated by the navy is not. This was, in Hintze's view, simply because the navy is not organized to occupy territory. For this reason, nations that have traditionally relied on naval power for state security (e.g., Britain and the United States) developed relatively more democratic and enlightened constitutions than their land-power contemporaries.[20] Problematic for political idealists, however, is that militarily influenced governing structure was for Hintze geopolitically determined. Reliance on a navy is not possible in a land-locked state surrounded by hostile powers. The good political fortune of Britain and the United States came from their isolated island and continental positions, not from any conscious decision to pursue liberal leaning naval over land power.

The macro view of military–democratic interaction, in which the structures of one institution affect the evolution and organization of the other, readily transforms into a micro view, where a spiraling interaction of individual rights conferred and rights demanded takes place. The military veteran, armed and now steeled in battle, will demand more rights or privileges and greater access to the decision-making process than previously granted by the state. The government cannot ignore these demands, as the combatant has the potential power to take those rights by force, and these demands will continue until the combatant feels completely enfranchised.

Military Experience and Democratic Values

The interactive path to franchise through military service is commonly accepted. The notion that a military veteran should enjoy full rights of citizenship is "an implicit social contract" virtually universal in the modern democratic state.[21] Yet more than just the right to vote (franchise) is embedded in the journey toward citizenship. Equality is the ultimate goal. During the U.S. Civil War, Joseph Glatthaar writes that "colored" volunteers enthusiastically enlisted to aid in the fight to abolish slavery. After having fought gallantly, they let it be known that "their ultimate goal had been equal rights with whites."[22]

Reward for service rendered is a simple enough notion, with long-standing precedent. It is also often viewed as a morally suitable method for granting political inclusion—a test of worthiness in exchange for franchise. Proof of residency, poll taxes, property qualifications, and competency exams have all been employed or proposed to gauge electorate responsibility. Qualifiers such as these have been routinely recognized as acceptable within a democratic society as long as they are applied in uniform fashion. The most basic, the requirement that a citizen must reach a specified age of maturity before being recognized responsible enough to cast a ballot, is not seriously challenged. The citizen who meets community-defined standards of responsibility to, or a vested interest in, the welfare of the body politic is thought more likely to participate responsibly when political privilege is exercised. The use of military service as society's test of worthiness goes well beyond the quibbling inconvenience of these slight qualifiers, however. It requires real sacrifice, perhaps even the ultimate forfeiture of personal liberty—death.

This characterization of the military identifies a pivotal ingredient in the evolution of the democratic state. In a direct metamorphosis, the transformation of soldier to citizen has had a leveling effect on society. Individuals too disadvantaged to find respectable vocations within the community have used military enlistment as an outlet for upward social mobility. It is the employer of last resort.[23] This function is reinforced by the military's accepted policy of recruiting at the social margin.[24] In the United States, the issue has been argued since at least the 1814 draft debates, when proponents of James Monroe's conscription scheme averred that an all-volunteer force must necessarily cull its recruits from the "dregs of society."[25] Alfred Vagts contended this requisite "civilization" of the army was precisely the action that necessitated the dismantlement of European monarchical systems, as it led to the "intermixture and equalization of the classes."[26]

Social equality does not come easily in a stratified society. It is one thing to desire integration and another to implement it. Here, too, the military has certain organizational advantages. Its rigid disciplinarian and hierarchical structure can be tapped to transform the armed forces into a laboratory of social engineering. Liberal reformers, for example, have been able to dictate equality measures to the military that civilian society has been unprepared or reluctant to accept. When it became apparent during World War II that the second-class citizenship of black Americans was a national embarrassment, moreover that it was a cancer on free society, civilian government stepped in to enforce the process of integration.[27] The first arena of social change was the military. From 1939 to 1953, the United States moved from a policy of restricting and segregating black Americans to one of equal opportunity and integration.[28]

By 1951, American military forces had just begun the process of true desegregation, and progress was slow. When the Korean War swelled the ranks of new recruits, an external catalyst energized the process. Black and white soldiers were sent into battle for the first time together, and the measure of competency quickly became not skin color, but courage under fire. Having experienced relative equality in the military, black Americans returning to their homes in the 1950s could not reconcile their previous classless positions with civilian society's racist contempt. It is neither coincidental nor insignificant that President Truman's Executive Order 9981 (1948), which dictated the integration of the armed forces, preceded the landmark Supreme Court school segregation decision *Brown vs. Board of Education* by six years. Truman's order and its rapid compliance within the armed forces was undoubtedly a primary stimulus for the modern civil rights movement.

Whereas most minorities defined by race or class have had the advantage of military (combat) service to press their claims and polish their credentials for full citizenship, women have traditionally been denied this avenue toward equality. Sue Berryman is explicit: "If women are equally subject to the draft and combat duty, those in power have substantially less moral basis for denying women full political and economic rights in the society."[29] Even with only partial access to combat duties, however, the positive impetus for democracy inspired by military service is noteworthy. Binkim and Bach observe that women in the armed forces can already achieve a social status "far superior to many of their civilian peers."[30] The surety in their status that women gain from "egalitarian principles" within their admittedly proscribed military roles make it "conceivable that upon completion of military service, women might be more inclined to participate in the political process."[31] In the present work, an explicit argument is made that preventing women from serving in combat, and limiting their liability exposure by not requiring them to register for the draft places them in a patronizingly subordinate political position. Symbolically, if not in fact because of these limitations, men are called on to protect and care for women in time of greatest state crisis. It is the perpetuation of patriarchy. Women are not *allowed* to defend themselves or their country, and for this reason they remain second-class citizens. Saying to women that they cannot serve their country in the capacity most historically recognized as a path to citizenship, even if they are fully qualified and capable—simply because of a factor of their birth—is wrong.

Unfortunately for society's minorities, the attainment of upward social mobility through the military is not an automatic function of participation. It requires not just equal service, but exceptionally valorous service *on the battlefield* or, in times of peace, in the most difficult military endeavors. Cameron and Blackstone reveal that during the 1960s, when 11 percent of the U.S. population between 18 and 21 years of age was black, and just under 10 percent of total service personnel assigned to the Vietnam theater of operations were black, a full 20 percent of combat forces and 25 percent of elite combat troops were black.[32] The most dangerous and difficult jobs had been sloughed off on minorities. Stating, "the moral dilemma is obvious," Berryman noted that by 1983, when the American military no longer relied on conscripts but had become an all-volunteer force, 29 percent of all U.S. combat troops were black.[33] The apparent fact that minorities were shouldering an unfair burden in the defense of democracy, she declared, should enhance their rightful claim to full citizenship.

It is a dilemma that won't go away. When a social group is attempting to gain political equality, its members must serve the state not *as well* as the rest, but better. In the military, it seems that recruits from disenfranchised or politically subordinate groups must be twice as valorous to be considered minimally acceptable. There is no solution to this problem, and perhaps there should not be. The extraordinary service of Japanese Americans in World War II, who won more medals of valor per man than any other unit, is a case in point. Their exemplary service assisted in breaking down social barriers that were sure to have remained after the war had these great Americans not been able to *prove* their worth and loyalty. The legendary perform- ance of the Tuskegee Airmen, whose distinctly painted fighter aircraft became a visual blessing to weary bomber crews anxious for escort protection, did more than polish the credentials of an entire social group for society. It effectively *demanded* equality, not based on equal service, but on the basis of *exceptional* service. Such a demand cannot be ignored.

The military path to citizenship is not without its own slippery slope. The problem with supporting the notion that veterans should have the *right* to vote, directly due to military service, is the potential that the idea will be perverted into the principle that only veterans are *worthy* of franchise. Such a position is an insult to the patriotism of every civilian who has not served in the military. Surely *battle* cannot be the only test of value, loyalty, and love of country. Still, it is undeniable that service men and women have a morally superior position to argue such a point should they wish to do so. This is because the soldier acknowledges upon entrance that he or she willingly relinquishes the rights and privileges of a free citizen (the soldier becomes subject to military law and discipline, a much harsher and restric- tive code than that covering society at large) in order to guarantee those same rights and privileges for the civilian who is not bound to make such sacrifice. In this way, the simple act of enlistment becomes an expression of community altruism. A life is offered for the state, the highest sacrifice for the common good.

Yet most of us who protest the service-only path to citizenship might grudgingly admit to a lesser point. *Some* qualification for suffrage measured by civic responsi- bility is rationally desirable. Without it, the masses will rule through passion and not foresight. Plato understood that unqualified and universal democracy is no more than mob rule. How effective is democracy without sacrifice? What is the value of a slothful populace's decision to vote itself bread and circuses, or the usefulness of the decision by mice that vote to bell the cat?

These admonitions aside, it is this potential notion of supra-worthiness of soldiers that is incompatible with the truly democratic state, and is the point of entry for a theory of military organization that can unravel the positive influence it has so far shown for the liberal state. Although certain military organizations have demonstrated a capacity for positive reinforcing effects on the establishment and maintenance of democratic values in society, it is simply not credible to argue this is the *only* way such qualities of political freedom can be sown. While on the one hand, military service can be shown to have positive effects in specific situations, the military does indeed have the dubious and paradoxical trait of being one of democracy's greatest challenges. Power is a tenuous and corruptible force, and a strongly elitist military can quickly slip from a socially egalitarian to an authoritarian vector. The ultimate expression of this kind of change is the military coup—a staple of twentieth-century politics. It is the fear of this illegal transfer of power from civilian to military control that is the moral basis for much of the military suppression argument evident in current assessments of state development.

Militarism is the name given to the circumstance of military dominance of politics, society, and culture. The conditions necessary for the emergence of military elitism are present in several modern state institutionalized practices of the modern state, nowhere more clearly than in its overreliance on veterans in the civil service. Hintze remarked with some trepidation on the almost universal habit of veterans to entrench themselves in civil service positions upon retirement. In this way, the looming specter of "[m]ilitarism still pervades our political system and public life."[34] This phenomenon arises in general because the hierarchical organization of the modern state bureaucracy lends itself to attracting ex-military personnel. The modern bureaucracy may be most efficient as a military-style organization, but in Hintzian terms, it can be argued that the use of military retirees pressed the development of bureaucracies in that direction. The military retirees functioned in the manner they had become accustomed to, and perhaps the bureaucratic organization evolved differently than it might have. With the establishment of a separate, veteran-dominant civil service, the traditional egalitarian emphasis of the military on society is placed in doubt. The creation of a privileged or simply separate class of veterans offsets the crux of the argument, that the military instills democratic values by intermingling the classes. The soldier, who has been appropriately trained to feel superior in war, may in peace search out other social groups within the community to dominate. The stratification of society that leads to militarism and forces the decay of liberty is in this manner debuted.

Yet for the military to dominate, society and the state must provide a suitable environment for the transfer of power. The government must be prone to totalitarianism and society must be conditioned for it. With this logic in place, Samuel Huntington argued that an effective defense against militarism is a constitutionally entrenched and fully mature democracy.[35] Class-dominant authoritarian society requires at a minimum rigid stability in the existing social order. This stability can be created by the military, or destroyed by it. The practice of accepting any and all residents into military service, removing restrictions to professional mobility within that service, and concentrating on the challenges of external military threats (vice internal social status), blunts the formation of an elitist social order within the state.

CHAPTER TWO
ARMS AND STATE

For who ought to be more faithful than a man entrusted with the safety of his country and sworn to defend it with the last drop of his blood?

Niccolo Machiavelli, *The Art of War*

The study of war has been aptly dubbed the "dismal science."[1] Its grisly calculations of blood spilt and lives lost make it appear a callous investigation in the academic disciplines of history, philosophy, law, and, of course, all the social sciences. It is the most passionate of social activities, yet it is eminently suitable to scientific inquiry, never separated from the violence and ardor that describe it, nor unduly biased by them. Objectivity is essential when dissecting this most cruel pursuit.

Carl von Clausewitz, perhaps the only true philosopher of war, stated "no one starts a war—or rather, no one in his senses ought to do so—without first being clear in his mind what he intends to achieve by that war and how he intends to conduct it. The former is political purpose; the latter its operational objective. This is the governing principle which will set its course, prescribe the scale of means and effort which is required, and makes its influence felt down to the smallest detail."[2] For all its destruction, war is a most rational activity. The study of it must be impartial and coherent.

It must also be guided by theory, and in this, Clausewitz again shows the way. He first attempts to grasp the meaning and purpose of war with a constitutive theoretical definition: "War is thus an act of force to compel our enemy to do our will,' and as such, it is 'but a duel on a larger scale."[3] This is consistent with Clausewitz's insistence on the functional nature of war, but the duel writ large motif is unsustainable. Since the opponent presumably does not wish to succumb, both sides will use all of the capacity and effort available to them. In theory, every war is total war. Because theory is the realm of the abstract and the extreme, concepts there must be tested against reality. Clausewitz could find no evidence of war so complete that it could be called total, extracting all possible resources from the state and culminating only in the complete, utter, and permanent destruction of all opposition. War, in history, has always been limited. Such limits dictate that it is subordinate to external physical and moral influences, and the primary limiting factor is political purpose: "We see, therefore, that war is not merely an act of policy but a true political instrument, a continuation of political intercourse, carried on with other means."[4]

This emphasis on the political means and ends of war narrows the scope of definitions, and highlights the connection between arms and state.

Theory

Before settled agriculture, when nature provided a limited population with abundance, property in hunting-gathering society was understood to be *communal*. Men hunted together in tightly knit groups, and whatever they killed was shared among all members of the tribe. Hunters worked diligently to gain individual honor, and the whole tribe reveled in their accomplishments. Bravery, audacity, and weapon skills were the admired attributes. So long as game was relatively plentiful, the system worked well and relations between tribes were relatively nonlethal.[5] As populations increased, food became scarce, and the skills of the warrior-hunter were highlighted. Those who could provide meat when little is available were venerated. Those who could take meat from others outside the tribe when food was impossible to find were revered.

Over time, tribes transitioned to agricultural activities to maximize calorie production. The move made way for the rise of agrarian economies and nascent political structures and from there to modern civilized economies and governments. It seems likely that in this era favorable climate changes prompted an increase in human population relative to the sustainable carrying capacity of hunter-gatherer society. As food became harder to find naturally, the return on hunting-gathering became significantly less than that for settled agriculture. In other words, the amount of work needed to feed oneself and one's family in a world of *abundance* is not great. Simply go out and take from nature what is readily available. Settled agriculture, on the other hand, takes a great deal of time and drudgery; turning soil, planting, monitoring growth, harvesting, processing, and storage. One changes over to it only in a world of *scarcity*. While agriculture could not, at least initially, produce the *variety* of consumables that following the herds and seasons could, it did allow for storing more food as a hedge against famine than that for nomadic wandering.

Still, the return on agriculture might never have successfully competed with that of hunting-gathering if the fruit of that arduous labor could not be guaranteed. Imagine spending an entire season at an oasis or fertile bend in a river, toiling daily to bring a crop to harvest and winter storage, only to have it looted by the first wandering band to come by. Until some protection is in place, some semi-reliable guarantee of the farmer-herder being able to maintain the product of labor, the incentive to move to settled agriculture is extremely limited. This protection is not possible in a world where the notion of individual ownership, or the right to posses a thing based on the labor expended to produce it, is subordinated to group or collective ownership.[6]

The transition happens like this: Individuals initially attempted to protect their property by the force of their own arms, although this is extremely inefficient. The primitive farmer would spend the bulk of his time monitoring the landscape for incursions of others who might steal his property, but even if he was able to identify their approach, he could not prevent its theft if he is outnumbered. He could build fences and walls, and train himself in the use of weapons so as to increase his combat power, but this has natural limitations as well, and takes even more valuable time away from production. He may also have to forego fishing, hunting, and gathering at any distance, to supplement his diet, for he cannot spend extended time away from his fields and cached property. His family will be of great value to him in these pursuits, and the larger the better. But as his family swells in size, increasing the amount of food that *can* be produced, it also increases the amount of food that *must* be produced. He is now even more vulnerable to disruptions in the food supply. It is not difficult to imagine that this primitive farmer (and his family) will spend 75 percent of his time in nonproductive activity (i.e., activities not directly related to the production, storage, and processing of commodities) to ensure that his wealth is maintained.

Imagine now that there are 100 of these primitive farmers along a river or at an oasis. They must protect themselves not only from wandering bands, but also from less scrupulous members of their community who might filch their belongings while they sleep or otherwise let down their guards. One of these farmers has an idea. He goes to all the others, persuading them one by one that they would be better off if a compact could be devised that would allow most of the farmers to tend solely to productive activities while a minority of them give up their land-tending duties and specialize in protection. Since their primary concerns are not just protection from external enemies, but also from internal criminals, policing and administrative functions (including but not limited to monitoring, arrest, adjudication, and incarceration) will be assigned. The community agrees. Twenty-five of the farmers become a militia, to receive 25 percent of the remainder's production in exchange for their service.

The new army spends all of its time training and monitoring, building walls and other defenses, and occasionally fighting. As the immediate threats abate, it is logical to assign long-term social protection programs to the leadership of this group. Such things as canal and granary construction require an organization scheme not dissimilar to creating large defensive bulwarks. Leadership hierarchies and specialization emerge. Experience is gained that replicates itself.

Those assigned as farmers now spend 100 percent of their labor time and effort in productive activities, and immediate productivity gains are realized. Whereas before, 100 farmers were 25 percent productive, now 75 farmers are 100 percent productive. If one farmer can produce 100 units of value at full production, then the total productive value of the whole increases from 2,500 units to 7,500 units. If the value is evenly distributed among all members of society (25 percent or 1,850 units are distributed to the protectors as a form of tax), each member has now more than doubled his personal wealth. Moreover, the probability of being able to keep that wealth has gone dramatically up, as the protecting militia is more able to ensure the gains of the majority than a band of unorganized individuals. A compact has thus been devised that allows the bulk of society to pursue industry while a defined minority protects and administers the whole. The minority does not produce goods, but it does provide the leadership necessary to engineer and coordinate public works, and it accepts personal liability in conflicts with other societies. For these functions the minority is permitted to extract resources from the productive majority. The infant state is born.

The model just presented allows for the probability that over time, the section of society chosen to defend the majority will become ensconced in its position. Social classes have been created at the outset of civilization, and these will become hereditary—farmers passing land to their offspring, and soldiers passing on their weapons. Eventually, the warrior class will demand a greater share of the community's production in exchange for its services. The farmers are in a poor position to refuse, for the minority has been honing its martial skill, and the majority can be forced to do its will. Here, then, is the animating proposition of *Warrior State*. The transition from warrior-hunter culture to the agrarian bureaucratic state came at a stiff price. Individuals traded the right to influence political decisions in return for a guarantee of economic stability and of safety from neighboring societies and natural deprivations (war, of course, but including drought, flood, and famine through communal granaries and other public works administered by the state). This is the *authoritarian bargain*, in which protection was negotiated with the would-be ruling group. The majority might have presented the covenant in these terms: "if you will protect and administer us, we will provide you with a fair share of our gains." In this vision, the state people come together voluntarily. Administration and force protects one individual from the violence of others, and allows for the maximum level of accruable wealth.

This rather benign view has its insidious side. If laws make people free to pursue wealth without interference, then the more laws the better. Government is good. More government is better. Unfortunately, the history of government has not been as agreeable and cooperative as the mode implies. Indeed, so foreign to the individual's *natural* predisposition is rule by government that some social contractarians argue that the state could not have been freely and amiably created. Rather, it was established by the strong to exploit the weak. In this view, the most radical of which is Charles Tilly's conception of the state as a protection racket, the blessings and abundance of nature are taken away from the individual by the *predatory state*.[7] The warrior-hunter class, preferring leisure to community work, bullies the majority of people to accept their leadership and forces them to pay tribute. Hardworking farmers, cheerfully tending their fields, bothering no one and expecting no hindrance of their activities, are accosted by this minority band of warrior-thugs. They could slay the farmers and take all their produce, but they are smart enough to realize that this would be killing the golden goose. A better deal is for a continuous payment, a percentage of the farmer's production now and on a regular basis hereafter. They offer an arrangement: "we will fight for you and keep you from harm if you swear allegiance and pay tribute to us." The farmers might protest that they need no protection, "who would be so disagreeable as to threaten his livelihood?" "We would," say the thugs, and the cycle is complete.

Having established themselves as the local area protectors, the minority must fulfill their end of the deal. They must ward off other would-be ruling gangs and encourage commerce so as to sweeten their take. As such, the predatory state model is extremely clever, and a very persuasive analogy. It would seem the weaker of the two models for initial contracting, however. No matter how the neoclassical economist might like to show that a mugging is a free exchange between bargaining agents, the mugger's terms, "your money or your life," are not, and can never be, a free choice. It is coercion, plain and simple.

With the predatory state, as in a mugging, the contract is bound by the threat of immediate violence. If the threat is not credible, or the threat is removed, the contract is broken. If the predatory state does not constantly apply force to the population, it will quit the arrangement as soon as the protectors are out of sight or an alternative protector makes its services available. On the other hand, the advantage to the free contract model is that the majority will not attempt to leave or hide revenues if they believe the arrangement is mutually beneficial. It is simply more profitable in the aggregate, and allows the generations of time necessary to ensconce the hereditary state.

Beyond the necessities of defense, when the community decides to go to war and attack another group offensively, the contract model is even more persuasive. While it seems *possible* that a dominant individual or subgroup could coerce others to *effectively* participate in limited organized offensive combat engagements, it is even more difficult to conceive of this organization maintaining itself in the absence of the dominant individual or group's continued coercion. In addition to the likelihood that unwilling but coerced warriors would make poor raiders, when the hated oppressors go off in search of plunder, those left at home would be liable to rebel or leave. Until the advent of state bureaucracy, *universal direct and continuous* coercion was probably not cost-effective, and impossible to maintain. Imagine the coercive bargain that must come before a group of warriors goes out to fight and loot another: "let us all go and risk our lives for plunder, and when we have seized all those goods, give them to me and my associates. If you don't, we will kill you." It is a demand for active participation, with little or no reward. It is a mugging. As a foundation for continuing and stable social intercourse, it is absurd.

Hence the model of state formation based on the free contract of participants is much more likely the foundation for the modern political state. It provides for the creation of institutions necessary for the state to develop a continuing public power, including such notions as social justice through equitable distribution of wealth or spoils and authority for group leadership based on capacity for organization over force. Here the bargain is stated: "Join us in this enterprise of organized attack and loot and you will receive a share of the plunder based on your participation. Accept our leadership as the most efficient means of achieving such riches." Coercion does not persist in the absence of the coercer. Contracts, built on experience and trust, can and do persist.

Hence, the contract position of state development posits that the first extra-family social organizations were the result of free covenant among relative equals. The first decisions to go to war were contracts of trust regarding the active participation of all and an equitable distribution of spoils. Whereas the contract position allows for the long-term incorporation of masses for offensive action based on motives of greed and honor, the coercion scenario is suspect because it does not allow for the development of a legitimized or enduring public power that outlasts the institutions of force. When the coercive element is lifted, the primitive social organization disintegrates. The contract method of state formation allows for the repetition of voluntary participation actions that, over time, become institutionalized and legitimized as norms.

Once the contract society has managed to establish a legitimized and stable state it *then* becomes susceptible to displacement by the coercive element within it that can harness the previously institutionalized apparatus of government for its own use. All too often, this element is the warrior or military social group, but it can also be a religious cult or economic/business cartel. Eventually, all primitive contract states become coercive through usurpation of the legitimized state apparatus. At least I can find no examples to the contrary.

Free contract or protection racket, the result is the same. A minority of warrior-hunters assumes control of the organization of the whole, and attempts to permanently ensconce itself in power. However it happens, the initial decision to specialize and stratify is the beginning of the civilized state. Coerced or negotiated, the communal lifestyle of primitive socialism is superseded. So long as the rulers hold their end, the authoritarian bargain stays in effect, social stratification is maintained, and personal safety and public prosperity is possible. The *democratic moment* comes when the class-stratified state can no longer protect its interests. It is threatened with dissolution from outside forces. The privileged class recognizes it can no longer maintain itself in power without expanding military capacity to counter the impending threat. It must incorporate previously exempt groups into defense of the state, and these groups become physically liable for the well-being of the state. The original contract is overcome by events, and is no longer valid. Unless it can be demonstrated that the impending consequences are far worse than the existing political order (in other words, if the government is overthrown and a new one takes its place, it will be substantially more brutal or oppressive than the old one), the group entreated for supplementary military service will demand a reward or payment for its participation. If this payment includes political rights, the subsequent political order (presuming military success) will be more inclusionary.

This model of transition to political authoritarianism and back to dispersed or decentralized political inclusion is the main argument in the following analysis. Military-based authoritarian rule, the most common political structure in history, evolves from the primitive contract and is dependent on its perceived ability to protect and administer the social mass. So long as the perception of safety from *external* threats is maintained, the subordinated individual will tend to remain politically inert. When the authoritarian state can no longer meet the challenges of the interstate environment, and is compelled to expose the individual to military liability, it must reciprocate with a dispersion of economic wealth or political authority. This process, it will be shown, broadly describes the emergence of modern liberal democratic or politically inclusive states from a previously authoritarian or politically exclusive governing structure.

War and the State

This inquiry is not generally concerned with the *causes* of war. That war or the threat of war exists is evident. It is preparation for war, not the event itself, which is the focus here. Indeed, war plays a minor if not insignificant role. It may even be confounding, as war tends to disrupt socioeconomic tendencies that are fairly well traceable in its absence. In establishing the relative impact on political development of certain types of military organization, the only roles war is given are spurs to military mobilization and innovation, an affirmation of the effectiveness of various organizations relative to competing ones, and as a wild card—those innumerable elements of Clauswitzian friction that tend to frustrate the best-laid plans.

Does military organization for war matter in sociopolitical context? If so, has it helped or hindered the rise of the state? The dichotomy of arguments is uncomplicated. War and organization for war have either been essential in the progression of civilization in general, and the modern state in particular, or they have not. With notable exceptions, the vast majority of historians, philosophers, anthropologists, and social scientists who examine this question have concluded that war has indeed been a critical factor in state and social progress, but are unevenly split on the role that war has had—positive or negative. Although a complete denial of the role of war in the process of social development is impossible to find, contrary positions held by theorists who deny the *positive* or constructive role of war are illuminating.

Arnold Toynbee asserted that war has been the proximate cause of the breakdown of every past civilization.[8] War, in his view, can have absolutely no constructive capacity. It is a tool of destruction only. Any short-term gains one state realizes (at the expense of another) will ultimately be negated in a later conflict. The progress of modern civilization, it can be inferred, will ultimately be wiped out by war. In an age when the mere presence of nuclear weapons can threaten the survival of an entire planet, Toynbee's claim is not unreasonable, and part of it is accepted here. War *is* violent and destructive. Any advance or progress made by civilization can be overturned in war. Therefore *war proper* is not the focus of this study. Its impact is indiscriminate, and in the long term, universally undesirable.

To the contrary, Arthur Marwick argued that war *could* have a positive impact.[9] War is an abnormal circumstance, a kind of artificial crisis that, if extended, can produce severe changes to extant macro-social relationships. The effect of war is to radically shake up the existing social order and create unexpected circumstances. Outcomes are not deterministic or accretive (there is no progression noted), but Marwick concludes that war itself is the catalyst for change, while preparations for war are simply continuations of existing patterns of interaction. In a complementary analysis, Bruce Porter declares, by "weakening or destroying traditional political structures, or by compelling internal reforms, war creates conditions conducive to change and political modernization."[10] Porter maintains that as the scope and scale of war increased, the inevitable trajectory of political change has been toward the modern democratic form of the welfare state. This trajectory occurs because of the dual requirement of state resources to prosecute war and the endowment of benefits (or payments) to citizens who participate. Porter is explicit in his insistence that war itself is the catalyst for political change, and certainly *not* "defensive preparations" or other organizing for war.[11] War compresses developmental time and creates a social crisis that is extremely difficult, if not impossible, to duplicate in peacetime. In a well-argued counter, John Nef claims all the progress implied or stated by war theorists is exaggerated, and insists it is societies' attempts to *limit or deny war* that have been the true engines of social progress, not the efforts to make war.[12]

Toynbee clearly denied the positive role of war in human progress, but emphatically *did not* deny the immense if perverse role of war in shaping human history. In fact, war and the preparation for war have been so intrinsically involved with social and political development that several theorists have been willing to note that *any* good associated with civilization *must* be accepted as an outgrowth of war, just as the bad is derided. Lewis Mumford, although he lamented the role of military organization in "creating a dehumanized response," credited the "general indoctrination of soldierly habits in the seventeenth century [as] a great psychological aid to the spread of machine industrialism."[13] Mumford directly credited the "pressure of military demand" with hastening and maintaining factory organization.[14] German economist Werner Sombart claims the modern economic system is a direct outgrowth of the need for supplying war, and that the modern condition of abundant wealth and potential for mass economic freedom could not have emerged without military necessity.[15] William McNeill, in a sweeping narrative, traces the development of state structures and social relationships to military innovations such as gunpowder and techniques of siege warfare.[16]

J.F.C. Fuller may have put forward the most extreme position. He argues that it is the military search for battlefield advantage through superior weaponry that drives advances in technology.[17] Society then benefits from applying military technology to civilian use. In a direct counterargument, J.R. Hale instead asserts that it was the increasing attractiveness of peace as an economic boon (through trade, commerce, etc.), and not the search for war technology, that was decisive in shaping the European state and state-system.[18] Peace in the modern state-system, perhaps for the first time, was so much more profitable than war that the modern nobility's desire for conflict was appropriately tempered.

John Ellis contends it is the ever-expanding technological and industrial base that drives the expanding violence of war and through this mechanism drives societal changes.[19] Industry and technology, rather than being spurred by wartime necessities, create surplus capacities that must be tested and even depleted in some fashion. Society pays for its economic progress and wealth with blood. For Marxists, the argument is intuitive. Rosa Luxembourg (in attempting to answer the implicit question: "Why hadn't Marx's revolution already come to industrial Europe?") responded that capitalists could forestall their inevitable demise by burning off excess production (as well as the most active revolutionaries) in the nonproductive cauldron of war.[20]

With a recognition that war and organization for war appear to have had some positive influence in the development of the state, come suggestions that war is somehow necessary for progress or otherwise ennobling to the human condition. Heinrich von Treitschke was able to combine these perverse notions with ease: "war is both justifiable and moral, and [the Kantian] ideal of perpetual peace is not only impossible but immoral as well."[21] Von Treitschke saw war as the separator of humanity from the animals, a part of the historical capacity that let one generation accumulate wealth and experience from the last, and the psychological temper that kept people dignified and civilized. Benito Mussolini would echo von Treitschke's sentiments 60 years later; "War alone brings all human energies to their highest tension, and sets a seal of nobility on the peoples who have the virtue to face it."[22]

To acknowledge that military organization and war have provided an impetus toward progress is far removed from the logical leap required to assert that they are *required* for progress. To recognize that the military stresses such virtues as bravery, loyalty, and honor is to acknowledge and appreciate their place in military operations and discipline, but to then deny their universality or suggest the only source of these virtues is military service is ludicrous. Military organization *can*, if properly controlled and restrained, promote progress and social development. It can also destroy the trappings of progress, and reduce combatants to savages. War tears down, destroys, and obliterates. It builds nothing. It may be a *catalyst* for change, even an *arbiter* of change, but as its outcomes appear random, it cannot be a *causal variable*.

With these and many other works, the role of the military and organization for war in forming the modern state has been overwhelmingly affirmed. With significant caveats and dissenting opinions, military organization has had both negative and positive impacts. Whether one views the current place of global social development and civilization in a negative or positive light no doubt shapes one's judgment.

Max Weber stated the case flatly: "The basis for democracy is everywhere purely military in character."[23] He consistently identified the interrelationship between the growth of armies and their requirement for military training and discipline with the rise of modern democracy. Otto Hintze's observations on this issue are subtler, and begin with the comment: "The form and spirit of the states' organization will [be] determined primarily by the necessities of defense."[24] According to Hintze, relations between state and military organizations are a continuous and adaptive historical process, placed in the context of the positional ordering of the state system—commonly called the balance of power.

Charles Tilly chides those who both ignore and those who overemphasize the role of the military and of warfare. In a pointed comment on political rights, he asserts: "Extensions of the suffrage, for example, do not follow from the pace of state making alone, or from the pattern of mobilization alone, but from an interaction between the two processes."[25] Tilly's argument is masterful, and portends the fuller treatment of the mobilization and suffrage relationship covered in this study. Notwithstanding his precautionary statement, Tilly describes a complex causal chain in assessing the military impact on state making, and insists: "*Preparation for war* has been the great state-builder."[26]

Propositions and Arguments

Military force can be organized in a myriad of fashions, but about ten broadly conceived organizing principles capture the determinist influences (discussed in full below). Each has the capacity to influence the liberalization of political development positively or negatively. Each of the ten should be viewed as a single piece in the overall construction of a complex theory. In other words, *no one organizing principle fully accounts for the military impact on sociopolitical structures*. Each can be isolated and analyzed in terms of its tendency to produce political outcomes, but no single principle determines the level of authoritarian or democratic sway in political institutions. Nonetheless, a predominance of these principles weighted toward one governing style or the other will tend to push the political structures of the state in that direction. If *all* are aligned with pro-democratic influences, the liberal democratic state may not inevitably result, but the purely authoritarian state cannot survive. The converse is also valid. All principles aligned with pro-authoritarian influences may not create the totalitarian state, but liberalizing movements within it will be stillborn.

Before proceeding, two caveats apply. First, the ten principles that follow are not an authoritative or comprehensive inventory. It may be that several of these should be combined. It may be that new ones will emerge. There is clearly no power in or commitment to the number ten, though it seems likely that more rather than less distinction will be beneficial. Second, all of these principles will need to be modified over time, as additional historical insight is incorporated. This is a first cut, and while robust, it is quite open to adjustment and revision.

Preparation for War
As preparation for war increases in scope and scale, existing social and political institutions will be stressed, promoting short-term consolidation of authority, and long-term growth of participatory values.

Preparation for war initially has a centralizing effect. Power is gathered to the political center and authority relationships are at first strengthened.[27] Patriotism, idealism, and fear motivate individuals to sacrifice liberty in favor of security, at least for a time. If war or periods of mobilization are brief, and the outcome of battle satisfactory, then the status quo will generally remain. The time frame is to some extent technologically and spatially defined. As speed of communications and movement increase, and as the size of the area under strain is enlarged, the time from increased authoritarian impetus to a liberalized one decreases. This may appear quite counter-intuitive at first, but if mobilization is widespread, preparation for war is prolonged, and economic activity is disrupted over an extended period, then existing social and political institutions will become strained. Reorganizations within the military and state will be unavoidable. As forces grow, direct control becomes inefficient. Independent jurisdictions will proliferate as the center loses capacity for control.

When preparation for war is limited or absent, government can divert resources otherwise dedicated to external defense into internally focused police powers, which can coalesce into authoritarian tools for repression of the majority. When the center finds no external threat to its power, it is free to increase its dominance over its population. Where an external threat is active, extended or frequent periods of *inconclusive conflict* can cultivate military reforms that in turn reinforce democratic values.[28] The longer and more deeply the state relies on its population for support, the more agitation for political inclusion in decision-making process will transpire. In this condition, a battle or campaign that fares poorly could trigger democratic reform.

If war does not occur, pressures for dispersion of political authority will mount. How long the state can stave off a rebellion is indeterminate; highly dependent on the nature of the foe. If war does occur, the outcome is critical. A perceived victory might legitimize the state, thereby rationalizing the hardships of preparation, or it could embolden the combatants to seek compensation for their efforts. If military forces performed poorly, and especially if the war is lost but the state remains viable, the military is susceptible to active reform by the state. In both winning and losing the prolonged war, the extended disruption of normal activity prompts new social and political relationships. This is because war does not distinguish between tearing down authoritarian or democratic institutions. It tears them all down.

The capacity of war as a catalyst is in continuous social upheaval that eliminates the tendency toward centralization of power in more stable states. The bureaucratic entropy of political systems, if one accepts Olson's thesis, is not possible in a society constantly rent with violence.[29] On the other hand, in highly decentralized states and regions, warlords and warrior-kings have often used organization for war as a pretext to increase local dictatorial capacity, making the foreseen result of democratic institutions highly suspect in the short term.

Implicit within this argument is a distinctly unsavory proposition. It would seem war or the effects of war may be a precondition for democracy or democratic institutions. While it is quite impossible to ignore the prevalence of war and political response to war on political development, war itself has no correlation to long-term political organization. It is organization for (and in) war that appears to be the common foundation precedent to participative government. To be sure, warfare has been so historically endemic it could be correlated to any political phenomenon. But, this would be a misreading of the principle. In a world where war is *constant*, all *consistent* outcomes will correlate to war. Constants do not explain variables.

But war has not been conducted indistinguishably nor evenly distributed through history. Enough variation exists that correlations can be assigned and assessed. If war itself were the catalyst for change, then a statistical correlation describing a significant *rise or fall* in the *number or intensity* of wars and the rise of the democratic state should be evident in the historical record. Insistence on the efficacy of war for state building appears valid, at first glance. For the period 1850–1990, which saw an unprecedented rise in the number of Western states definable as democracies, the *number* of wars and their *duration* went significantly down—from almost three per year to about five per decade.[30] The *intensity* of wars as measured in raw casualties went up, however, perhaps confounding a pacific-democracy association. More problematic, although an overall decrease in war does come at the same time as a rise in the aggregate number of democratic states; within states the apparent correlation is inconsistent. France and Britain, which far and away participated in the greatest *number* of wars during the period (63 and 54, respectively), developed strong liberal institutions. Russia, the third most active participant in wars (23), remained strongly authoritarian throughout the period. Germany, which had significantly fewer wars (11) than Britain, developed alternately very authoritarian and very democratic governments. Correlations with war and government are extremely tenuous at the level of individual states.

Sweden and Switzerland participated in no wars at all, but both prepared heavily for war contingencies, and both developed strong democratic institutions, strengthening the claim that external threats prompt reorganizations promoting democratic or participatory reorganizations. As states significantly accelerate their *preparation* for war, measured in terms of personnel and supply mobilization, newly institutionalized democratic outcomes follow within roughly ten years, *regardless of whether the state participates in war or not.*

The presence of war does not appear *necessary* for the democratic state to emerge and survive. Preparation for war, and the threat of external challenges, *may be*. A persistent external threat may even be the glue that holds the naturally competitive democratic society together. Factions are more willing to cooperate internally if to splinter would mean exposure to predatory states. The majority may be far more tolerant of the minority if it recognizes a need to incorporate it into the common defense. Elections may be conceded more readily if the minority recognizes its situation would be worse if it defects from the state. It may even be that periodic *threat* of war revitalizes the sense of belonging and nationalism that allows civilized competition and discourse in a diverse democratic society. Without it, the political balkanization of democratic society may be preferable to a continued association of its components.

The dilemma is how to maintain a pacific, nonwar world order in a system of states that are constantly preparing for war. The relevant question is plain: is war more or less likely when potential combatants are prepared for war, or when some or none are prepared? If *some* states are prepared for war, and others are not, would prepared states be compelled to take advantage of non-prepared ones? If *no* states are prepared for war—not the unforeseeable circumstance that no states *would be able* to go to war—some may calculate a capacity to prepare before a potential enemy, engaging in a mobilization race that could be very destabilizing to the interstate system. If *all* states are prepared for war, how many would be willing to risk war with other prepared states? A consensus answer to the last question has not been found, but that mutual preparation could reduce the likelihood of war has evidence in its favor. The nuclear stalemate of the Cold War has shown that mutual preparation may be a stable deterrent to (at least) nuclear war.[31] After a lengthy game theoretic analysis, Frank Zagare concludes that "capability is shown to be a necessary condition for deterrence stability."[32] Scientifically and statistically, peace through strength may indeed be a valid and stable systemic condition.[33] If one accepts that mutually prepared states *may* achieve a stable deterrent, and buttress this with the tenet of neo-Kantian peace theory that democratic states do not war with each other, we gain mutually reinforcing insights for democratic development and international peace.

Scale of Eligibility for Military Participation
As the percentage of military and military-support personnel increases relative to the total population, the rate of liberal or inclusive sociopolitical reform tends to increase. Conversely, as the percentage of military and military-support personnel decreases relative to the total population, the rate of sociopolitical democratic reform tends to erode and can reverse.

The foundational work in this area is Stanislas Andreski's *Military Organization and Society*. Andreski developed an index called the Military Participation Ratio (MPR), or that percentage of society actively engaged in the functions of war, and correlated it to the relative level of individual rights and freedoms in society. Andreski insisted that a strict correlation between MPR and democracy was decipherable, and set the tone for much of the subsequent analysis here: "Which way its influence will be exerted depends mainly on whether the co-operation of the masses is essential for the successful prosecution of war or not. It depends, in other words, on the proportion of militarily utilized individuals in the total population."[34]

Andreski's assessment suggests that a direct correlation between the historically recent global explosion in the number of liberal democratic states and the concurrent pervasiveness of the post–World War I concept of "total war" is discernible.[35] Total war involves engaging every segment of the population to successfully prosecute combat, the maximization application of Andreski's MPR. Most analyses of total war and political development have focused on the militarist totalitarian state's rise to power—less so on its demise—and are understandably biased in their condemnations of total war as a deterrent to democratic development.[36] But their analyses are clouded by a proper abhorrence of the totalitarian state, which is presumed to irreversibly assume power and responsibility in the mobilization of the entire nation to a war footing. The historical sequence of events is rarely drawn out to its conclusion, beyond the fall of the totalitarian state, and so the result of such mobilization is not appreciated.

The *long-term* effect of total war (including its modern manifestation, totally destructive war or nuclear war), which continuously threatens as well as involves every segment of the population, is to entrench participative ideals. As more people are subjected to personal liability in the affairs of state, their interest in participating in the political functions of that state increases. The empirical evidence associating the rise of military participation with the rise of democratic or participatory institutions, as measured in terms of individual franchise, is powerful and compelling. Following each significant rise in the incorporation of civilians into military service, a corresponding rise in the franchised electorate is apparent (figure 2.1). The use of individual case studies is extremely heuristic, but structural analysis isolates

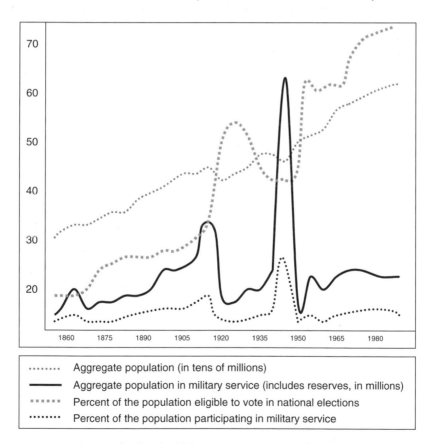

Figure 2.1 Military and political mobilization (Western states, 1860–1992)

comprehensive tendencies of military organization to impact political processes. If a given outcome can be shown to occur repeatedly, *despite varied routes to that outcome*, the specific paths become less explanatory in theoretical terms (though perhaps more interesting in historical ones). For the structural correlations here, data was collected and aggregated for seventeen Western European states, Russia/Soviet Union, Finland, the United States, and Canada for the period 1790–1992.[37]

The most striking observation is the tremendous rise in political mobilization following the massive military mobilizations of the two world wars. Clear are the gradual military buildups before the rapid mobilization spikes centering on 1914–18 and 1939–45. Also evident are increases in political mobilization following military buildups centered on 1860–75, and the Cold War military increases of the 1960s. Political mobilization, which is seen to rise following increases in military mobilization, *clearly peaks within five to ten years* of the two primary military mobilization spikes, and less clearly but still indisputably within ten years of the minor spikes.

Within ten years of the rapid military *demobilization* following both world wars, rates of political mobilization and absolute participation were in decline as well. Although political mobilization never resumed pre-military mobilization levels, the downward trend (after major demobilizations and slowing of increases following more level periods of military mobilization) is plain. Moreover, whenever political mobilization entered a downward trend, reversals were not evident until after military mobilization once again began to climb. This trend supports the idea that some relationship to external threats may be necessary for the continued health of democratic states.

Aggregate military mobilization in the modern era followed a pattern of dynamic growth, with each successive systemic mobilization larger than the preceding one, though the percent of peacetime population under arms has tended to stabilize between 0.02 and 0.04 percent. Political mobilization followed a more distinctly stair-step pattern. Once a new level of political mobilization was achieved, the percent of the population eligible to participate politically tended to remain higher than pre-military mobilization levels. This suggests that military mobilization is extremely important for political mobilization, but military mobilization may not need to be sustained to ensure that higher levels of political participation are kept. In other words, the apparently necessary role of high military participation for the *spontaneous* emergence of democratic liberalism may not be required for its maintenance.

These observations may be peculiar to the era and region under scrutiny, and there is no argument here that military factors *alone* can explain the ongoing dramatic rise in global democratization. The dataset does show, however, that patterns of political mobilization can be reversed and enter a period of decline. Military preparation appears to have a significant role in this as well, through a lost war that subjugates the enfranchised population to an imported or outside power, for example, or through an internal expansion of military power by a distinct and exclusive segment of the whole. In the period under study, individual political participation rights were lost when Fascist Parties assumed power in Italy, Spain, and post-Weimar Germany, and in a number of participatory states including France, Belgium, Holland, Denmark, and Norway when these states were occupied militarily by the Axis powers. Still, the overall pattern does reinforce the notion that military factors are a significant, possibly necessary component in the modern process of liberal democratization.

The development pattern of military mobilization and political participation makes a clear statistical correlation between military participants and political electorates difficult. Even with the rudimentary data under analysis here, a socially significant correlation between total electorate and total armed forces emerges. That correlation increases when controlled using a shift procedure that compares electoral trends to five- and then ten-year-old military ones. More impressively, total active military personnel to electorate percentage rises significantly with a five-year lag and peaks with a ten-year lag. These correlations reinforce the previous observation that the full impact of military mobilization on political structure has peak influence lag of five to ten years—at least in the modern era.

When computing the data, it was interesting to note that the occurrence of war had a very strong *negative* correlation to electorate and electorate percentage. These correlations dropped off with the five- and ten-year shifts, but remained quite strong: the less war, the greater the electorate—or quite possibly the reverse, the greater the electorate, the less war. This negative correlation supports but does not confirm the Kantian notion that highly participatory (democratic) states are less war prone than states with autocratic or less participatory governments (at least in the aggregate). That there are an increasing number of democratic states in the population skews the raw total of war. Democratic states are simply less likely to war with each other. It could be argued that as the military population rises, and as the element of the population likely to engage in war participates in the decision to go to war, they are increasingly less likely to place themselves at risk. When correlated solely for democratic states, the negative ratio is indeed much higher.

The war–electorate correlation also appears to support Brian Downing's notion that the greater the incidence of war, the less likely the emergence of democracy, and clearly refutes insistence on the necessity of war in the rise of the democratic state.[38] Applied to individual states, I was unable to confirm his assertion. Nonetheless, at the aggregate or systemic level, Downing may have intuitively stated an apparent relationship. It must be noted, however, that while the total number of wars decreased remarkably in the period (coincident with the global rise of democratic liberalism), the deadliness of wars has increased dramatically.

Restating the argument, we see that action taken by the state to expand the percentage of armed population, in order to prosecute interstate conflict, effectively empowers the newly armed sectors of the population and structurally forces a compromise or bargain that transfers political rights or powers to them. This association or relationship should be readily identifiable in an examination of military mobilization levels and subsequent expansions or decreases in political participation, and so it is. Nonetheless, military participation alone is not enough to ensure political participation. Massive growth in military formations has been possible without the transfer of political rights, most notably when the nation is called to arms in defense of the homeland (e.g. Soviet Russia in World War II; though one could argue that Khrushchev's relatively liberal rise to power in the 1950s occurred within the ten-year lag). State-sponsored offensive operations can also raise large military formations, but the soldiers may be fighting for booty as opposed to political consideration. Additionally, offensive and defensive operations can be mounted without transferring political privilege if the motivation for war is religious or idealistic. Fanaticism and holy war have slaughtered millions through history, with the reward for service being a place in the afterlife; deferred eternal empowerment instead of immediate political power. Finally, populations may simply be coerced to fight. In this example, the prospect of going to war and taking one's chances in battle must be more appealing than the prospect of being executed for failing to partici- pate, or at least more appealing than the prospect of life under a new government. Such armies of coercion (including ancient slave armies) are notoriously poor in morale. They are militarily successful only when sheer weight of numbers engulfs the enemy. These examples notwithstanding, the relationship between the percentages of population participating in or liable to military activities and the breadth of constitutional protection or political franchise provides the strongest correlations in this study.

Scope of Eligibility for Military Participation
As the scope or breadth of eligibility within the population for military service increases, both individual democratic values and the rate of democratic reform tend to increase. Closely related to the preceding argument, concern here is not only with increasing the total size of the military (scale), but the social location of that increase (scope).

The scope of *military* inclusivity has had profound influence on democratic ideals, and has routinely preceded *political* inclusivity. Martin Edmonds notes, "recruitment is the point at which the civilian world meets the military."[39] Military requirements are slated against political realities and social contexts. Oliver Cromwell, for example, in establishing his New Model Army, was careful to recruit his officer corps from those gentlemen in society who had "a personal *financial*, political, and social stake in its survival."[40] When the state is compelled to signifi- cantly increase the size of its military force to counter an external threat, it generally does so through the admission of previously non-enfranchised segments. These segments then demand increasing enfranchisement as a condition of their service.[41] The trade-off for the state is that, in return for an expansion of participation in the political process, it can expect an enhancement of its military capabilities.

Especially when the state feels *compelled* to incorporate previously non- enfranchised segments of the population into its military structure, the trade for political inclusion can be substantial. Andreski noted: "Significantly, even in Athens it was only when the fleet became the basis of its might that those too poor to afford the equipment of a hoplite, but whose services as oarsman now became essential, gained equal rights. After the Persian Wars, the Athenian State became a sailors' republic."[42] Moreover, when the state is forced to grant political recognition in exchange for crisis support, it is in a poor position to renege on the deal when the crisis is abated. The population is now armed, trained, and dangerous (in the eyes of the state), capable of taking the promised rights—and more if desired—by force. The circle of rights granted and rights demanded in this manner spirals toward democracy. Weber argued the point accordingly: "Military discipline meant the triumph of democracy because the community wished and was compelled to secure the cooperation of the non-aristocratic masses and hence put arms, and along with arms political power, into their hands."[43]

Throughout the Western experience, as will be shown in the case studies that follow, as the scope of military mobilization increases, attempts to rectify social inequities through political legislation can be described as expanding the franchise directly to those groups incurring increasing liability for the security of the state. Although the legislation was not in all cases deliberately directed at rectifying military–social inequities, rectification was the aggregate result. In the Western experience, four distinct periods of political inclusion through legislation are apparent in the modern age, and each begins with a period of increased military activity:

(1) *1860–1900*, centered on the Prussian-model military buildup of national cadre and reserve forces throughout Europe and North America, which resulted in lowered property and income requirements for franchise as vastly increasing manpower requirements became evident. As war continued its transition from the sport of kings to mass public engagements, the requirement for direct military liability was reduced.

(2) *1910–30*, centered on the wholesale incorporation of previously disenfranchised groups into the support and production of national warfare efforts and the unprecedented mobilization for direct combat troops (almost 11 percent of the total population in World War I). This period began in earnest with the spread of political enfranchisement to women and completed the practical elimination of property and income requirements for suffrage, effectively confirming the dual principles of universal military liability and universal suffrage for adult citizens throughout the analysis population.

(3) *1945–55*, in reaction to the mobilization of World War II (over 17 percent of the population was directly involved in combat, the majority of the rest directly involved in military support activities), reestablished suffrage for groups that had been disenfranchised in the fascist preparation and military course of conquest in World War II, and effectively completed the principle of full and equal franchise for women (Switzerland, which did not participate, holding out until 1971).

(4) *1960–80*, centered on a series of unpopular wars that encouraged the incorporation of suffrage to those minorities that shouldered an unequal burden in the combat arms of states engaged in those wars, specifically minority ethnic and racial subgroups and most emphatically young adults (17–21-year-olds routinely conscripted for service but ineligible for franchise). This period also marks the withdrawal of the notion of total war as a practical matter (due to the possibility of global nuclear holocaust), and reestablishes limited war on the battlefield. In this environment, liability is limited to participating segments of the population, and the critical feature of political debate is the equitable distribution of military burden among disparate social groups.

These periods of inclusion are consistent throughout the states under study, whether or not the states actually participated in war. Mobilization and political inclusion requirements of nonparticipating states, as those states perceived them, were uniform with those who participated, once again suggesting the focus on military preparations for war, as opposed to war itself, is the proper focus of study for macro socio-military comparisons. Thus, the historic record clearly shows systemic forces at work in the political mobilization of states. These systemic forces can be found to have military mobilization antecedents, and the repeated demonstration of temporal correlations suggests a strong causal relationship.

Mercenaries versus Citizens
States that rely on indigenous militias will tend to develop more liberal democratic institutions than states reliant on mercenaries. This argument reprises one of the classic debates in military–social philosophy. The academic literature is vast, and the preponderance of evidence is clearly weighted toward citizen-militias as a democratizing force. The current argument is weighted more toward the impact of citizen-militias versus trained professionals.

The impact of the citizen-army on political institutions has antecedents in the views of Niccoló Machiavelli and Thomas Hobbes.[44] To be sure, there is a certain hesitation when employing Machiavelli and Hobbes to defend an argument about the potential positive or beneficial impact of military influence. The secularism of both caused them to be denounced in their lifetimes as evil and godless. The current widespread and notorious perception of Machiavelli may derive from Elizabethan era interpretations, however.[45] Today he is often minimally described as immoral, more radically denounced as a devil and a teacher of evil.[46] Hobbes is more benignly described as "something of a bogeyman of political thought."[47]

Both believed the mass arming of the general population would lead to the dispersion of political authority. Machiavelli, a devout republican, advocated the practice. He found the classic Roman description of the citizen-soldier superior in every way to renaissance Italy's reliance on professional mercenaries. Hobbes, believing the passions of citizen-armies provoked the demise of ordered English society, preferred the institution of mercenaries for all but the direst national circumstances. Whereas the establishment of a citizen-militia was for Machiavelli the primary social engineering tool in structuring the republican state, sovereign reliance on mercenaries was for Hobbes a matter of right reason. It would keep the population politically inert.

Machiavelli advocated that greatness was achieved in the building of great states.[48] Patriots could use any means to ensure the survival of the state, including injustice and cruelty. When the nation is not threatened, however, cruelty and injustice are never appropriate. The epigraphic encapsulation of Machiavelli's philosophy—the ends justify the means—is therefore not accurate. Machiavelli writes that amoral means are justified only when employed for the imperative of survival of the state.[49] Personal ambition for individual glory is unacceptable, personal sacrifice for national glory is, however, tantamount to public immortality.[50] These beliefs lead necessarily to the denunciation of the mercenary, who fights only for personal booty, and to the glorification of the citizen-soldier, who fights for home and country.

Hobbes rejected the idea of instilling political passions in individuals through misplaced notions of patriotism.[51] Proper social behavior should be determined through right reason. The calculated and professional efficiency of the mercenary could be tapped by the sovereign to prosecute wars and guarantee state authority, without involving the bulk of the citizenry, thus avoiding the widespread destruction of general and civil war. Citizen levies, in this paradigm, should be reserved only for circumstances of national survival—never for limited, routine warfare. Only with the institution of a political sovereign powerful enough to mitigate violence, through monopolization of it, can humanity ever be free of violence. Only when free of the persistent threat of violence, is society free to prosper. The price, of course, is political subservience to a central authority. Participation in war only breaks down sociopolitical institutions, decentralizing power and accelerating the likelihood of widespread violence and war.

To the contrary, Machiavelli insisted it might be necessary to *instill* the threat of violence when it does not occur naturally. The state may find it expedient to cultivate an environment of constant readiness for war in order to keep the population poor (but not destitute), so it will remain industrious and not succumb to wickedness through idleness.[52] Perhaps more disastrous, in a peaceful state, society's most talented individuals will prefer to occupy themselves with the accumulation of wealth through the management of estates and business. Only in an environment of ever-present threat of war would those same talented individuals come forward to lead the state politically and militarily.

Machiavelli and Hobbes wrote prescriptively for the establishment of the good state. Both included assessments of military organization as aids or impediments to the achievement of political ends, though Machiavelli's position is much more important to his overall work (his military tenets form the core of his political treatises). In all things, Machiavelli despised the mercenary. On the opening page of his *Art of War*, Machiavelli describes the professional soldier as a lout and a boor.[53] What was rotten in modernity was equally rotten in antiquity, but Machiavelli believed the ancients had found the salvation of the state, and sixteenth-century Italy could be redeemed through a return to the politico-military institutions of Greece and Rome. Specifically, this meant the abolition of the reliance on professional arms and a return to citizen-militias.

Later political observers, many in general disagreement with Machiavelli's abrupt style of ethics, would nonetheless vent similar ideas. Typical was Rousseau, who insisted that all citizens must be soldiers by duty and none by profession.[54] These later theorists were laying the groundwork for democracy (an expansion of Machiavelli's insistence that the citizen-militia was the lifeblood of the republic) through an understanding and manipulation of military organization. It was in fact Rousseau's general sentiment that translated into the French Revolution's *levee en masse*, when the people rose to defend their *patrie* and establish the second modern democratic state. In this view, the citizen-militia is recognized and acknowledged as the military manifestation of democracy. Immanuel Kant, in a decidedly Machiavellian point, argued for an armed civilian populace because it would make war less likely than for the state that relied on smaller, professionalized mercenary forces.[55] Alexander Hamilton assumed "a well-regulated militia [is] the most natural defense of a free country" and "standing armies are dangerous to liberty."[56] Citizen-militias were considered of such vital importance to Hamilton that "if circumstances should at any time oblige the government to form an army of any magnitude that army can never be formidable to the liberty of the people while there is a large body of citizens, little if at all inferior to them in discipline and the use of arms, who stand ready to defend their own rights and those of their fellow-citizens."[57] William Bluhm has gone so far as to assert "the eighteenth-century theories of Alexander Hamilton and James Madison [represent] yet another version of Machiavellianism."[58]

William McNeill's position is typical of the strictly antitechnical Machiavellian view. He argues the Venetian system of hired soldiers was far more *militarily* effective than the militia of Florence, due to an inherent inability of the militia to adjust to the modern requirements of battle.[59] This was, at least partly, "because humanistically educated magistrates like Machiavelli were dazzled by Roman republican institutions."[60] True enough, "the perfection of firearms, and the subsequent domination of the machine on the battlefield" led many observers to eulogize the institution of citizen-soldiers.[61] Karl von Clausewitz wrote: "No matter how carefully we seek to combine the citizen and the soldier in the same individual, no matter how much we may regard wars as affairs of the whole nation, no matter how far our ideas may depart from the mercenary armies of former days, it will never be possible to dispense with the special nature of the professional routine."[62] In an age of increasing technologic complexity, only professional soldiers could master the intricate tasks of modern warfare. Earnst Breisach believes Machiavelli's generally perceived failure as a military strategist was that for him, "war was essentially applied politics."[63] Without doubt, Machiavelli agreed—the relationship between citizen and soldier is "not only compatible and consistent . . . but necessarily connected and interrelated."[64]

Hobbes recognized Machiavelli's argument, but feared the social ramifications of a mass army. He abhorred impassioned and superstitious thought, believing it to be the root cause of war, and instead viewed military service not as an expression of public virtue but as a logical derivation of the natural law of contracting.[65] In Hobbes's commonwealth, citizens "are to be completely immersed in private pursuits, and so not just politically passive, but inert."[66] This politically inert mass shall have no passion for foreign adventure and war, and so armies should routinely be levied through taxation and hire, and be professional or mercenary, rather than conscript.

Offensive versus Defensive Strategy

States with military forces organized for offensive operations will tend to develop a less centralized, more democratic political structure than states whose military forces are organized for defensive operations. A defensive military posture requires the capacity for internal occupation and is therefore conducive to the concentration of power that promotes authoritarian institutions. Conversely, an offensive military structure will have an outward bias, and will be less involved with issues of civil/internal stability. Of course, militaries have had a remarkable capacity to absorb both offensive duties and internal repression chores—the two are not mutually exclusive—but the general interest herein is the impact of one versus the other.

On this point of strategic doctrine, I am in at least semantic disagreement with Andreski's characterization of the "attack versus defence." He argues that: "other things being equal, the predominance of attack over defence promotes the territorial concentration of political power (centralization), while if defence becomes the stronger form of warfare, a trend toward the territorial dispersion of political power (decentralization) is likely to ensue."[67] Andreski is quite correct for *inter*state system relations, but the tendency does not hold for *intra*-state dynamics. When defensive fortifications and tactics are dominant, the system tends to evince pockets of authority in an *inter*state system. In other words, when defensive technologies are dominant over offensive ones, a state *system* can be expected to have a larger number of autonomous units. But *within* those sovereign units, at the *intra*-state level, the opposite effect is noted. The marshalling of power to hold smaller tracts of territory allows for more direct and coercive control of the individuals within those units.

When offense is dominant, dynamic states will swallow up their vulnerable neighbors, producing an interstate system with fewer (larger) autonomous state-level units. Internally, however, military power is pushed to the periphery of an expanding state, diminishing direct control of internal subjects. Command of the military from the center becomes inefficient, and authority to act disperses to forward units and an opportunity for internal liberalization and democratization. A reliance on defense will, within that state (not on the level of the system), cause a centralization of power, a heightening of control as the advantages of interior lines and static point defense allows far stricter adherence to command authority.

The abstract cognitive capacity required for offensive operations, as was discussed earlier, is much greater than that for defensive ones. When threatened, it is easy to make a mental connection between banding or grouping and military defense. Offensive operations are more likely to result in the establishment of prearranged or negotiated relationships. The individual soldier has greater leverage in offensive operations, where the threat must be sought out and engaged, than in defensive ones, where the threat is unavoidable. In the defensive mode, the combatant is likely protecting family, property, or comrades. In offensive mode, the combatant must either be coerced to engage in battle, moved through patriotism, ideology, culture, or religion to do so, or paid in some fashion. In the latter cases, the combatant must *choose* to go to war. In choosing, there is room for maximizing.

A military that is organized for offensive operations has in addition an internal decentralization of authority requisite in the need for independent judgment by operational commands. The fluidity and projection of military components beyond preset lines of communications and into a dynamically changing environment requires capacity for independent thought and adaptation. Defensive operations, on the other hand, allow for strict centralized control, predetermined lines of communication, and detailed options or plans for contingencies. Stratification of internal capacities through a strong organizational hierarchy is more likely in defense, where strict attention to defined functions and maintenance of position is demanded. Offensive operations must be prepared for a greater number of surprises, and individuals must be capable of a greater variety of combat functions.

In a related argument about offensive and defensive orientation, Alfred Stepan magnifies a change in the emphasis on professionalism that Huntington and Janowitz detailed.[68] The old professionalism was outward in its focus, concerned with the requirements of international conflict. The new professionalism, especially in South America and developing states, is defensive and internally focused. Huntington argued that the professional soldier, engaged in issues of external threat, manifests no interest in politics, as it takes time away from war preparation. Stepan countered that the new military's professionalism was focused on careerism and state development. In other words, the state, as supplier and supporter of the military, must develop at a rate sufficient to meet the perceived needs of the military, or the military will feel compelled to intervene. Stepan's point fails to persuade that an outwardly focused military would not recognize the same need for national development to support its own perceived requirements, even more so if the military is losing a war and begins to blame domestic policy-makers for lack of support. Nonetheless, the point that an outwardly or offensively focused military will be *less* inclined to interfere in domestic politics in normal or nonwar conditions parallels the argument that organization for the offense is more conducive to establishing and maintaining democratic political institutions than that required for the defense.

This separation of intra- from interstate analyses poses a theoretical problem for the state system. An offensively organized military will be perceived as a threat by neighboring states, and will be destabilizing to the interstate environment by promoting spiraling arms races, as each side perceives itself in a relatively weaker position vis-à-vis its potential adversaries. At least this seems to be the conventional wisdom. John Mearsheimer notes, "war is most likely to occur when offense has the advantage over defense" (though he agrees this is not a very useful distinction).[69] His characterization seems rather simplistic. The analysis here stresses the notion that an offensively organized military does not mean the state must *be* offensive. The offensively organized military relies on the ability to attack and punish a transgressor *on the offender's territory*, rather than to repulse an attack *on the defending state's territory*. It is a reliance on the doctrine of deterrence over that of defense that is important. This argument is tightly linked with the following one.

Capacity for Territorial Control
States with military forces organized for territorial occupation will be less likely to develop democratic institutions than states whose military forces are poorly organized for territorial occupation.

A military organized for territorial control or expansion must of necessity have occupational capacities or functions. This means the military must have a *police* capacity, an ability to pacify the newly acquired subject population and to defend territory. For military organization to have a positive effect on liberalization and democracy, its police or noncombat functions must be kept to an absolute minimum. This argument most clearly supports the notion that navies (and by extension air and space forces) tend to be more conducive to liberal democratic reform than infantry or land-based forces, but it differs critically with Hintze's and Vagts's descriptions of the political impact of navy-dominant and army-dominant military structures.

Both Hintze and Vagts argued that a geographic position allowing for the ascendancy of naval power would foster a more liberal, democratic regime.[70] For them, military force structure is dependent on geopolitical factors. Force structure then becomes the critical intervening variable determining the general character of government. While Hintze and Vagts use a different causal explanation, here I argue that the determinist characteristics of navies are their potential for strong force projection (equated here to offensive capacity and an extremely limited aptitude for internal policing). Despite some well-known examples of naval power forcing international political concessions, and spearheading successful democratic revolutions, their ability to coerce citizenry is remarkably poor.

The purpose of navies is to challenge or command the sea. They are extremely feeble tools of internal repression. The purpose of armies is to traverse, take, pacify, and hold territory. This function readily transforms to police control functions, limiting through capacity for direct coercion the public exploration of enhanced liberal democratic development. My argument is the liberalizing influence historically associated with navies should focus on its traditional organization for offensive operations, while armies are more often (than navies) organized for defense. When infantries are employed primarily on foreign campaigns, their democratizing influence may be maximized. It is this doctrinal focus on offense over defense, combined with a limited or weak structural capacity for territorial occupation that determines the trajectory toward or away from democracy, not some property inherent to boots or boats.

If the navy-dominant or army-dominant forces can have such an important and acknowledged role in political development, what is the effect of a state that relies on air forces, or perhaps on space power? Air forces, like navies, are generally organized for offensive military capability, emphasizing punitive, long-distance strikes and external coercion of enemies, and have a similar innate difficulty occupying territory. In this analogy, air forces should be inherently democratizing, but perhaps not as much as navies. Whereas the navy can project force into coastal areas—deeper inland with naval airpower—and must occupy territory, in ports or in beach invasions using attached army-like forces (marines), air forces can project power globally (today) and must occupy enough territory for airbases and logistics needs. In these locations, at least, navies and air forces have security units for territorial control. Where the navy is limited to coastal and island control (and occasionally major river systems), air forces are not so constrained. Paratroops can be placed in a wide variety of locations, subject only to their ability to be resupplied. While the arguments fit naval operations quite nicely, one should argue that the ability to cover more territory with aircraft (than with ships) could make an air force–dominant military slightly less democratizing than a naval-dominant one.

Space forces have not yet developed to the level of starship troopers, nor has the pace of weaponization in space allowed for direct ground attacks. Both these capacities are probably just a matter of time—not if, but when. In the interim, a force structure that is heavily supported by space power may have an inherently authoritarian vector. This is because the current use of space capacity is primarily intelligence gathering (reconnaissance and surveillance) and command and control communications—the first line of modern police power. The ability to see potential threats, to monitor them via electronic and imaging techniques, and to control forward units through global positioning and communication, all bode an authoritarian influence.

The defensively organized military *must* establish itself as an occupier of territory. The offensively organized force *can* have that function, but it is not necessary. An offensively organized force that is a poor occupier of territory is in fact the most suitable for participatory or democratic governments, and is less threatening to the interstate environment than one organized for both offensive actions and occupation. A state employing offensive deterrence can punish a transgressor state, but is in a poor position to challenge its sovereignty. The transgressor state is less likely to succumb to the security dilemma if it perceives its national survival to be less at risk. States employing this offensive/nonoccupational doctrinal structure need to maintain a military defensive capacity just sufficient to ensure its offensive capability is secure—not its entire territory. If competing states have adequate punitive deterrent offensive capacity, but neither can efficiently occupy the territory of the other, the interstate environment should be more stable.

Training, Discipline, and Combined Operations
Military organizations that incorporate combined arms, coordinated planning, extensive training, and rigid discipline, will be more likely to foster democratic values and institutions than militaries that rely on the superiority of individual combatants, ad hoc planning, and independent training.

This initially counterintuitive hypothesis is highly susceptible to misinterpretation. The rugged individualism associated with American-style democracy appears to be at odds with rigorous training and strict obedience to higher-ranking authority. Such a view instead argues that military training creates political automatons willing to subordinate themselves to a hierarchical, authoritarian political control structure that parallels the military chain of command. Bruce Porter passionately observed: "It turned out to be but a short step from the discipline of the military to the discipline of the Gestapo, the discipline of the commisars, the discipline of the concentration camp. One man's civil order was another man's *gulag*."[71] While such an outcome is possible in military training, it is not typical. The Gestapo, like the commissars, had their training in gang settings, their discipline instilled in political thuggery. Because the paramilitary police state's repressive organizations often *emulate* military ones, assuming their uniforms, insignia, and hierarchical titles (in an attempt to project a type of historical or institutional legitimacy), does not mean military-type training was the source of their perverted discipline. Indeed, these organizations and their leaders are for the most part the models of chaotic, undisciplined, and uncontrolled behavior.

The model of military training and its impact on society should not be taken from the pseudo-military goonery described above. Military-style discipline is important in democracies because it not only instills patience and subordination to authority; it instills respect for and acceptance of authority. With subordination to authority comes responsibility to subordinates. The soldier who subjects her or himself to a chain of command realizes a responsibility *from* that chain in addition to an obligation to obey. In properly organized, liberalizing militaries, certain minimum conditions must be met or the soldier has an organizational right of appeal (fully institutionalized even if a rudimentary code of military justice is evident).

In liberal definitions of democracy, some provision must be made to limit the capacity of the majority to do what it will with the minority. Basic individual rights must be recognized and established beyond the purview of the majority—through the instrument of government—to diminish. Roy Macredis and Bernard Brown provide perhaps the best explanation of how this transforms democracy from mob rule to enlightened authority in their description of the Lockean or *consensual model* of Government.[72] The formation of the body politic is an *act of will*, symbolizing the "cardinal rule that the majority of the people, through their representative institutions, govern."[73] But the majority is neither arbitrary nor omnipotent. It is bound and restrained by law. *Property rights* and *individual freedoms* are inviolable. Regular, fair elections must be held to guarantee these rights. A minority may be coerced only to the extent necessary to implement the basic constitutive agreement, but coercion cannot be used to silence or destroy the minority. Thus, the majority has the right to act while the minority has the right to protest, and—most critically—the *right to become the majority* if it can persuade defections to its point of view (hence the critical importance of free speech and assembly). This model is so powerful because it incorporates both the obligation to obey and the rights to criticize, protest, and oppose:

> It allows the *force* of the state to be transformed into authority, deriving its legitimacy from the basic agreement. Individual dissent is expressed not in disobedience, but through organized opposition seeking to present alternative policies. Thus, opposition in the democratic scheme is harnessed to the total political system, which is strengthened, not weakened, by political dissent.[74]

Within this brief appraisal of the character of liberal democracy are the values that *proper* military training and discipline is intended to instill. Ideally, for the democratic state, they are subordination of the needs of the few to those of the many, participation regardless of class, promotion, or assignment due to merit, a duty to obey the commands or laws of legal authority and custom, and service with honor. Discipline and respect for the law are thus vital to the efficient functioning of the liberal democratic state. Citizens register their opinions on matters of policy through franchise, but consent to the will of the majority. Such *subordination to the will of others* is integral to the democratic state, and can be learned in military service. Proper military discipline and training can in this way enhance the democratic citizen's ability to function correctly. Gang or unauthorized private militia training by definition provides the opposite of these values.

Perhaps more importantly for political participation, individuals learn self-worth as *component* parts of a larger group. Citizens participating in military service envision themselves as having a vital, functioning place in the state-as-whole. They become imbued with a sense of sacrifice for the state, a service that has certain benefits as well as responsibilities. The more rigorous and difficult the training, the greater the sense of sacrifice and, ultimately, of accomplishment. The more intricate and involved the drill, the greater the depth of cohesion and the more important each member becomes to the success of the group. Individuals learn to trust in the function of their peers, superiors, and subordinates. This helps inculcate respect and tolerance of other groups in society, minorities if you will, and strengthens the version of modern democracy called pluralism. The analogy to voting and electoral behavior is straight and true.

The critical capacity in stable democratic society is not for all to have a voice, but for all to recognize and accept the validity of all *other's* voices. Democracy is not strong when every *citizen* stands up to demand his or her own personal rights. This leads to bitterness, enmity, and mistrust of others, as politics of this type appears as a zero–sum game. Any rights or privileges one gains are by definition taken from others. Stable, lawful democracy can occur only when every citizen stands up to defend the rights of all *others*. The old saw, "I despise what you say but defend to the death your right to say it," is the essence of this view. The teamwork of military training can in this way be enormously conducive to social construction. Again, Weber is instructive: "democratization [lies] in the rise of disciplined infantry, the *hoplites* of antiquity, the guild army in the Middle Ages. The decisive fact was that military discipline proved its superiority over the battle between heroes."[75]

Heroes are in fact the conceptual anathema of democracy, where in legal and political theory all are supposed to be equal. Though all societies should have heroes as models for proper behavior, hero *worship* is the seed of dictatorship. The hero is the *indispensable* unit in the military machine, and the hero becomes revered. Soldiers may become afraid to fight if their hero is not among them, their relative worth is diminished. In society, heroes that leave the battlefield for politics are often unprepared to accept decentralized authority. They are accustomed to individual decision-making and personal adulation. This is not to say that initiative should be discouraged. Within the bounds set by political (civilian) authorities, individuals should be allowed to take charge, innovate, and lead. When individuals begin to fancy themselves greater or more important than the whole, however, democratic principles are challenged. It is one thing for the whole, or society, to place the good of the individual above all else; it is another for individuals to place their own good above that of all others. Samuel Finer notes that in the French Revolution: "Equality' of rights in the common association went hand in hand with 'fraternity'—brotherhood in the sense that all were equal parts of the same (and distinctive) human family."[76] This association was plain to the military theorists of the age. Common drill and liability for service were always considered the great levelers of the Revolution.

Militarism versus Military Science
States with militaries that emphasize military science or combat proficiency will be more likely to develop liberal democratic institutions than states with militaries that emphasize self-aggrandizement or militarism. While its absence does little to promote democracy, the presence of institutionalized militarism is one of the most powerful of the pro-authoritarian characteristics of military organization. Wherever it is entrenched, democratic institutions will be hard-pressed to maintain themselves, much less emerge.

In trying to come to grips with what militarism is, several writers have offered indices or scales to judge the relative level of militaristic tendencies in a given state or society. Martin Edmonds claims common and useful indices of militarism include "percentage of annual GDP devoted to defense, a frequent incidence of service intervention or interference in politics, the participation of service personnel in decision-making bodies, a high content of military subjects in the artistic, literary and recreational life of the people, a coincidence of military values and priorities in the everyday life of the nation and, perhaps the most relevant of all, the extent of aggressive, service-backed, foreign policies."[77] In these formulations, however, militar*ism* and militar*ization* are not distinguished.[78] This is an extraordinary disservice to the military, and an inherently dangerous one for democracy.

Alfred Vagts provides the most appealing differentiation between military science and militarism. The "military way," as he called it, is in essence the art of battle, "winning specific objectives of power with the utmost efficiency."[79] It is limited to the functions of war. Militarism, on the other hand, is unlimited in scope and transcends strictly military purposes. It has a tendency to permeate and become dominant over society. In so doing, it takes on the characteristics of "caste and cult, authority, and belief."[80] In order to clarify his definition, Vagts lists several characteristics that distinguish militarism. The first three are crucial.

The first is domination of civilians by the military. This refers to political dominance, official supremacy in which military leaders conduct the affairs of state. Vagts lists this characteristic first, and assigns it priority importance. Civilian control over the military is paramount in ensuring the state can retain or build democratic institutions. David Ralston sides with Samuel Finer in arguing that military respect for the principle of civilian supremacy over the military is moreover the key factor in inhibiting interventionism.[81] Soldiers rightly determine the strategies and tactics of battle, and should be given free reign in this regard, but they should never determine the propriety of the fight, nor how far to prosecute that fight once committed. The military informs the civilian authority, it never should be in the position of steering it.

Vagts's second characteristic is an emphasis on "military considerations, spirits, ideals, and scales of value in the life of states."[82] A state or society that places undue adulation on the trappings of war and on military virtues is on shaky democratic ground. A morbid fascination with war is a symptom of this characteristic, and it is often at its apex in a period of prolonged relative peace. The military enthusiasm of Britain's armchair generals was never as obvious as in the late nineteenth and early twentieth centuries, at a time when a generation had passed since a major continental engagement, and the British soldier was being deified literally as invincible. The glories of victories past were fondly misremembered. Much of the power of this characteristic may be a natural human response to horror. War is a vicious and terrible thing. Men and women who participate in it are changed forever. A natural psychological defense mechanism is to overlook the horrifying and dwell on the noble. Evils are not reminisced, though laurels often are. For the generation that grows up without its own war experience to harden it, the clamor for things military in appearance grows louder.

Militarism, Vagts claimed, is concerned with "all the activities, institutions, and qualities not actually needed for war."[83] As such, it is more likely to hamper than to hearten the principles of the military way, for it undermines proper military efficiency. It is a rise in militarism, not in military art and science, which paves the road toward authoritarianism. If a military force is deemed necessary for the survival of the contract state or society, a concentration on the skills of war within the military structure is key to preventing the military from engaging in interventionist militaristic activities and becoming the contract state's greatest threat. Charles Tilly identified "a paradox which many observers of contemporary state-making have noticed: armies of new states which are unlikely ever to fight an international war adopt the latest armaments, absorb the largest part of the public revenues, employ their might in putting down dissidents and guerillas, play the parts of arbiters, king makers and, on occasion, kings, yet fail repeatedly in their efforts to reform the social structure."[84] Times of war and preparation for war tend to breed patriotism and *esprit*. Times of peace, when the horror of war is forgotten and the glory of battle is misremembered, incubate militarism. The solution is to understand the importance of the peacetime military in shaping values, and to organize it to do so efficiently, and to never forget that training and evaluation are for military proficiency, and not military pageantry.

Discrimination in Placement and Promotion

As military organizations decrease cultural, social, or economic distinctions among their members, democratic values are strengthened and democratic political reform within the state tends to increase. Conversely, as distinctions are highlighted and class or caste associations related to rank or specialty, authoritarian values and government are fortified. As a corollary, *the fewer restrictions placed on military entry and upward (rank) mobility, the greater the tendency for development of democratic values.*

The military can be a powerful tool for both positive and negative social indoctrination. So long as military organization parallels inequitable social distributions (as in the aristocracy's monopoly on officer ranks), positive democratic change is hindered. The relationship is so powerful that many states have consciously used military service to train the aristocracy or to give the ruling class martial experience in administering and controlling the lower classes. Much less common until recently, liberalizing states have manipulated military organization to break down social barriers and promote egalitarianism. If military discipline is tapped for the purpose of social education, political allegiances can be influenced. In the case of fostering democratic values, among other things, the military can be a powerful bonding agent for society. Disparate social and economic groups that otherwise would not associate can in military service be compelled to interact, thereby increasing familiarity and weakening prejudice. In the latter case, it is in fact the rigid disciplinarian and hierarchical structure of the military that is directly tapped to transform the armed forces into a vanguard of social progress.

The United States in the twentieth century has been a particularly effective manipulator of the military's leveling effect. Lessons learned in military service are transferred to civilian life when the soldier returns home. Prejudices that may have formed through ignorance in civilian society are swept away through the familiarity of close military proximity. The soldier who has worked with and relied upon someone with a different cultural or ethnic background will readily substitute firsthand knowledge of others for hearsay characterization.

David Ralston further points out that modernizing non-Western states have (in many cases unwittingly) incorporated European ideals of liberal democratic participation in their societies while in the process of structuring their military forces along dominant Western models: "European-Style armed forces could thus bring people from what were the less eminent, less prestigious elements of society into positions of potential power."[85] In this way, Ralston claims the military acts as an "agent [of] social mobility' within previously stratified and 'fundamentally ascriptive' societies."[86] Consciously or not, creating large, Western-style military forces have had the unintended effect of increasing political participation in states that do so. The temporal correlation of military then civilian change adds weight to the basic assumption of the ontological priority of military organization, and opens promising avenues for foreign policy.

In order to function, liberal democracy in all its manifestations requires individuals to value both differences *and* similarities among others in their political group. This is so a sense of belonging, sharing, and trust can be fostered while at the same time allowing for the widest diversity of opinions and political options to be put forward for public scrutiny. Without this appreciation for the value of others, in all their unique manifestations, conflict cannot end at the ballot box, but must extend to violent opposition within the state. In other words, if one cannot accept or tolerate that others can and *should* have different values and opinions when making political decisions, liberal democracy becomes mobocracy. The minority must also accept the legitimacy of the majority's rule—so long as the majority does not proscribe for them the opportunity to become the majority. Silencing the minority, making it subordinate to the whim of the majority, is the core of Rousseau's impassioned argument that the man who disagrees with the free will of the majority must be *forced to be free*, he must be made to agree. Since the majority will is the perfect manifestation of national culture and value, he argued, the minority must be in error to oppose it. Only when the minority opinion is purged and the individual accepts the mob's will as his own does the state rule effectively. Such Rousseauian arguments are often cited as the basis of European totalitarian fascism.

It is critically important that cultural and religious differences are not denied in the road to social equality. Ethnic, racial, or gender traits must not be ruthlessly swept away. But at the same time, while truly participative society can celebrate the diversity of its various members, it cannot build a stable democratic political structure on that basis alone. Emphasis on diversity as the sole value of society fosters separatism, cultural competition, and ultimately racism. Emphasis on similarities, within a framework of tolerance for diversity, brings egalitarianism, cultural understanding, cooperation, and tolerance. If the military, in whose service the individual is expressing community altruism, is subjected to cultural, ethnic, racial, gender, or religious separatism, those values will be reinforced in social and political settings. To the contrary, if individuals are required to conduct themselves equally, regardless of social, cultural, gender, or political differences, and are equally eligible for service in all branches, equally subject to punishment, and equally posted for duty, then these values will be instilled and transported to society and to political institutions. As always, Weber is enlightening: "The *populani* know that they [have] fought and won the great wars of the [state] along with the nobility; they are armed, and hence feel themselves discriminated against and are no longer content with the subordinate class position which they have previously accepted."[87]

Loyalty to the State
The more military organization stresses loyalty to the state, the greater the tendency to promote democratic values and reform, and to discourage internal political interventionism (praetorianism). Conversely, the more military organizations stress loyalty to individuals, the greater the tendency to discourage democratic values and to promote internal political intervention.

Samuel Huntington's intent in *The Soldier and the State* was to empirically test the extent to which the democratic principles of America's Founding Fathers had been undermined and compromised by the maintenance of a large, professional standing continental army both within country and serving overseas.[88] In the process, he effectively presented the first definitive treatise on civil–military relations.[89] He high-lighted the importance of civil control over the military, and insisted it could be maintained through strict obedience to a constitutionally entrenched democracy, and through open and stable civil–military relationships. Subordination to civil authority required the recognition and cultivation of a distinct status of profession-alism for the military by the civil authorities. Professionalism, Huntington believed, was the key to preventing military interventionism, or *praetorianism*, and the most critical military organizational factor requisite in a democracy or democratizing state.

Professionalism has been repeatedly cited as a factor in the prevention of military interventionism, perhaps the greatest internal threat to emerging democracy. Gaetano Mosca went so far as to argue that the professional army was not only immune to interventionist impulse; it was an indispensable enhancer of internal state security. "The great modern fact is that the huge standing army is a severe custodian of the law, is obedient to the orders of a civil authority and has very little political influence," and, "[in] our opinion, the standing army as at present organized prevents the element in society which would naturally monopolize military power from enforcing its will by violence upon other social forces."[90]

But military professionalism is not a panacea. Bengt Abrahamsson, for example, suggested that the nature of professionalism included the professional duty to expand the authority and influence of the professional organization.[91] The military, he argued, should naturally try to persuade the government it supports of its view of world affairs, in order to obtain a larger piece of the government budget. Such activity may not in the best interests of the state, but the professional military no doubt recognizes itself as just one of several competing organizations for a limited budgetary pie, and that with-out such advocacy it will be edged out. In such a reality, for the military not to advo-cate its views and needs as strongly as possible would be a disservice to the state. In the end, fair and balanced competition will most efficiently determine the budget.

Charles Moskos severely criticized this occupational approach, in which the military is perceived as a job and individual's self-interest is paramount. He believed it was contributing to a deterioration of traditional military values and legitimacy.[92] Moskos insisted an "institution is legitimized in terms of values and norms, i.e. a purpose transcending individual self-interest in favor of a presumed higher good."[93] An occupation, on the other hand, "is legitimized in terms of the marketplace, i.e. prevailing monetary rewards for equivalent competencies."[94]

This jaundiced view of professionalism can lead the professional soldier to question the capacities of the civilians who run government. Samuel Finer wrote most emphat-ically about the problem of interventionism, and attributed its source to a natural desire for the military to seek increasing power. The military, claims Finer, "[h]aving cast off its political neutrality," will be unable or unwilling to extricate itself from dabbling in the affairs of "its civilian opponents."[95] In premodern or developing mili-taries, where allegiance was to a captain (or whoever was the immediate paymaster for services), an understanding of the abstractness of accepting allegiance for a government is not culled. In the modern army, where an emphasis on drill and a chain of command that allows for an individual not only to move up in rank but to ensure a leader will be available at any level, discourages personal allegiances, and enhances democratic values. The problem of military interventionism, the *coup d'etat*, is curtailed if the modern armed force is indoctrinated for loyalty to the continuing public power of the state, and not to the current head of that state or superior military officer. In this case the armed forces *can* act as a bulwark for democratic stability by allowing the social components to carry on their debates without fear of military intervention. This role, of course, requires strict obedience to an independent civil authority.

Ideal Military Structuring for Political Outcomes

It would be marvelous if the arguments presented could be perfectly quantified and correlated, placed in a calculating hopper, and results spewed out as incontrovertible proofs. As with all social variables, such accuracy is elusive. Reliance upon a measuring scale for determinist influences is highly susceptible to the GIGO principle: garbage in, garbage out. Nonetheless, if one is looking for general trends or affirming relationships, it is worth the attempt to quantify the variables, even if admittedly simplified. In this manner, basic validities can be affirmed and new research variables proposed.

The driving goal of this analysis has been to discern an organizational blueprint that maximizes the military's democratizing influence without encumbering its ability to fight. To be sure, the predominant goal of any reorganization of the military should be efficiency and effectiveness in combat. So long as that requirement is not forgotten, the military can be structured to provide state support through civic education and social engineering. In fact, should compatible democratic political structure be a concern of the military organizer, the paired goals of social progress and military competencies are for the most part complementary. What serves the military in its role as efficient protector of the state from *external* threat generally equates to a pro-democratic influence. It combines the realist need for strong defense in a world of anarchy while at the same time sowing the seeds of change for global peace in a world of liberal democratic states. Such an armed force would be: continuously prepared for war as an external deterrent; large enough to encompass a significant percentage of the population; open to all citizens; reliant on citizen-militias; offensively organized; a poor occupier of territory; rigorously trained and drilled in combined arms and unit combat; antimilitaristic, primarily through mission awareness and training; culturally undifferentiated internally and unrestricted in upward mobility; and loyal to the state.

On the other hand, should a despot intent on maximizing the military's organizational influence to promote authoritarianism wish to design a supportive military structure, she or he should ensure the military be: maximized for internal repression and prepared for external war only under imminent threat; small enough to exclude most of the population; open to one class or a limited segment of the population; a good occupier of territory with training in police functions; organized for defense; reliant on mercenaries; trained with an emphasis on individual combat skills; highly militaristic, in part through rigorous training for ceremony; stratified internally and limited by birthright and seniority for officer and NCO positions; and loyal to the person of the commander/ruler.

CHAPTER THREE

ANCIENT REPUBLICS AND RADICAL DEMOCRACY: ATHENS AND SPARTA

Such is the city for whose sake these men nobly fought and died; they could not bear the thought that she might be taken from them.

From the Funeral Oration of Pericles

Perhaps the most eloquent praise of democracy ever made, Pericles's Funeral Oration as set down by Thucydides some 2,500 years ago still evokes intense passion.[1] Pericles described the character, values, and activities of his people and his beloved city. He contended that the most cherished possession of Athenian citizens was not their wealth or happiness, as might be the case in other states, but rather their political and economic freedoms. He fully understood the inextricable link between citizens, soldiers, and government. And he insisted that Athenian laws, which established the world's first civilized democracy, were worth the many deaths his city had come together to mourn.

The occasion of the oration was the end of the first year of the Second Peloponnesian War (432–404 BCE). Pericles, as leading demagogue, was called upon to eulogize those who gave their lives so that the city might endure. All of them were volunteers. All of them were prosperous by the standards of the day, or had, because of their unique society, the hope of becoming affluent. They were not a specially trained subset of the population, not drilled from an early age in the martial arts, as were the armed forces of many of their enemies. They were ordinary citizens. Such men as these, whose lives were occupied by mundane daily business, socializing, and family responsibilities came bravely and wholeheartedly forward, forsaking comfort and wealth to do so, in defense of their most precious belonging:

> And when the moment came they were of a mind to resist and suffer, rather than to fly and save their lives; . . . on the battlefield their feet stood fast, and in an instant, at the height of their fortune, they passed away from the scene, not of their fear, but of their glory . . . . fix your eyes upon the greatness of Athens, until you become filled with the love of her [then reflect on those] who in the hour of conflict . . . freely gave their lives to her as the fairest offering which they could present . . . Make them your examples.[2]

Pericles's powerful and emotive words stand the test of time. We accept and recognize that brave men and (today) women must come forward to protect the liberal democratic state in its time of military distress, or freedom and liberty might perish. But do we properly regard that military requirement as an essential component of the free state, or as a necessary evil? This text began with precisely that question, and persists in an argument that military forces, conceived throughout as a complex organizational unit, not only protect the democratic state, but found, nurture, and sustain it.

The rise of classical Greek democracy, especially as it developed in the city-state of Athens, produced the only known durable and civilized state-level democracies until the American and French Revolutions more than 2,000 years later. The radical citizen-based democracy of Athens was one of a myriad of politically decentralized governing arrangements in geographically fragmented Hellas, representing the furthest end of a political spectrum clearly influenced by military organization and participation. Although military factors alone cannot account for the extent of the region's decentralization, significant differences in military organization do help explain variations within city-state governing arrangements. Athens, with its extraordinarily inclusive military structure, developed the most radical citizen democracy ever enacted in a society of scale. Athens' grand rival, Sparta, had an ingeniously distinct military organization, and developed a singular form of republican government with remarkable inclusivity for a narrowly defined citizenship group of warriors. Analysis of the differences in military organization between the two city-states highlights the power of the stated hypotheses, and provides initial evidence as to their strength and pervasiveness.

Greek Military and Political Institutions Before 800 BCE

The Age of Mycenaean Warlords (1600-1100 BCE) undoubtedly incorporated the same strategy, tactics, and organizing principles as contemporary Bronze Age civilizations of the ancient Near East and the Egyptian New Kingdom.[3] Homer's magnificent *Iliad* notwithstanding, the great poet's description of Trojan warfare was more likely a reflection of the methods and means applied in his own day than an accurate description of the ancient Mycenaean art of war. "Whatever the wise old Nestor might say of the ranging of armies, by tribes and brotherhoods, the battle of the Epic is, above all, of hero against hero . . . In their own day war had become something far different: it meant the uniting of armed men of the community to fight shoulder to shoulder, with an orderly, integrated valor."[4] The introduction and widespread distribution of bronze, then iron, weapons technology created successive and consistent military and political revolutions throughout the Mediterranean and Middle Eastern regions. Complementary tactical and strategic innovations impacting on military and political institutions were the introduction (and quick decline) of the chariot, followed by the rapid ascendance of the cavalry. Both horse-dependent tactics provided speed and shock unmatched on the battlefield. They were also quite expensive, and thus limited to the individuals who could afford to purchase and maintain them, creating a privileged class of knights who used military service as a path toward political power.[5]

In this early age, *war* was the prerogative of kings and princes, fought by and for the ruling elite. Most disputes between petty aristocracies were settled in skirmishes of nobility and their retinues, supplemented where needed by roving mercenaries. In larger conflicts, campaigns for significant territorial expansion and in defense of the same, where state survival might well be at stake, mass armies could be deployed. But arming the masses was widely recognized as a dangerous gambit of last resort. While heavily armed aristocrats were individually the most formidable element on the battlefield, they could succumb to sheer weight of numbers if the mass army's morale was high. For this reason, and usually only when desperation necessitated it, the poorer classes of society could be pressed into light, unarmored, pike and shield-type infantry service, arranged in tight though undisciplined mob formations. The trick of this mob tactic was to keep morale as high as possible while keeping training as low as necessary. The job of officers in this situation was more akin to that of shepherds prodding their flock to the slaughterhouse than to that of the modern tactician. If the mass was divided, the force would quickly flee and victory would become a rout, and this knowledge dictated the tactics of opposition forces.

War training for the mobs was limited, usually *ad hoc*, and specific to the battle at hand. Peasants, serfs, and slaves would of necessity be armed by the state, not having the economic wherewithal to arm themselves. They would, naturally, be lightly armed as possible, the most and best weapons reserved for the nobility. Armories were established *not* for the purpose of supplying and arming the population in time of threat, but for systematically *disarming* it in time of peace. In this way, mass armies would be useful on the battlefield, but would not pose a new *internal* threat to the state once the battle was finished.

Middle-class farmers, tradesmen, and artisans were also occasionally pressed into service, but they generally equipped themselves with the highest level of armaments they could afford. This was a common and practical custom for the ancient soldier, regardless of his social or economic rank. In an age of swarming every-man-for-himself combat, each individual would be highly motivated to arm himself to the best of his ability. The alternative was to accept the state's inferior basic issue of weaponry and huddle with the rest of the ill-trained mass as battle fodder, an unappealing option to any who could afford better. The better armed would have a greater chance of survival on the battlefield, and each survivor could expect to share in the available and allowable booty. Indeed, this latter factor must have weighed on the minds of soldiers who contemplated arming large masses of the poor—it diluted the potential loot to unacceptable levels! Hence the decision to purchase one's own arms was not only practical, it could be cost-effective.

Thus, mercenaries were the preferred supplement to the state's aristocratic forces. These included foot and horsed archers, seasoned warriors on horseback, heavily armed and armored infantry, and the most elite fighters, knights, and charioteers. Although the state could supply or supplement the mercenary's armaments, these professional soldiers were combat veterans who, like other master craftsmen of their day, were expected to maintain their own specialized gear. To be sure, part of their appeal was that they brought their own weapons, often of superior quality. More important, after the battle they were expected to take their pay and go home, effectively ridding the ruler or rulers of a potential armed internal threat. For reasons of battlefield prowess and efficiency, and not least of internal stability, when they could be afforded mercenaries were always preferable to armed throngs.

Mass armies of knights, mercenaries, and conscripts fought in grand melee. The prime concern of early military strategists was simply to get this hodge-podge army to the battlefield intact, well fed and supplied. Once fighting began, little if any battlefield organization could be discerned. The leader of each side maneuvered his force into striking distance of the enemy; all the while ballistae and archers harried the joining forces. Battle was initiated when the leader of one side or the other recognized a tactical advantage, and gave the order to charge—or until the masses of infantry and cavalry, working themselves into a seething (often drunken) bloodlust, could no longer be held back. Upon release of an opponent's force, the counter-options for the receiving side were to stand fast, break and retreat, or—preferably—charge in response. In the latter event, both sides attacked the other in a sudden crash, intent on overwhelming the opposing force and sending it into flight. This style of combat was undoubtedly terrifying, and some sort of discipline-instilling training must have occurred to get enough individuals simply to arrive at the battle site and participate. The bulk of this training, for the masses, was probably little more than political or moral indoctrination.

The participating individuals would have to be convinced that it was in their best interests to wage war. This could have been done with an economic incentive, the promise of loot or booty perhaps, but could also have come from a political source—increased freedom to choose or better living conditions. Depending on circumstances, either one might be cheaper than the other. But even more inexpensive and occasionally effective means existed. Indoctrination may simply have been the negative example of a hostile victor laying waste to the combatant's hearth and family. Fear of the outcome of *not* fighting could be employed to great effect. No matter how tyrannical the current ruling elite, the barbarians at the gate could be worse. Religious or moral idealism, too, could prevail upon the individual and carry him into battle. In this case, one fights because it is the god's will, or because to flee battle is the mark of a coward. Lacking a moral justification or an evil enemy as specter of doom, the mass army may simply have been coerced to fight. In other words, the soldier would be convinced that he would be killed if he fled. Fighting the enemy was a recourse that gave (at least slightly) better hope for survival. This last type of army, however, not only required an enormous commitment of resources to guard and monitor the mass, it was notoriously ineffective. Once battle commenced, taking one's chances in flight became increasingly attractive. Thus the breaking of one side's morale was the primary tactic of the day. The enemy's subsequent flight from the battlefield was the sure sign that victory had occurred.

Just such a description undoubtedly characterizes civilized Greek warfare in the age of the Trojan War. A defense-dominant strategy, heroic tactics, and a cultivated lack of mass training tempered what little emphasis toward political expansion the military might have provided in this era. With the demise of the Mycenaean and Minoan civilizations, possibly from a series of barbarian invasions by northern tribes, the Greek region entered into a profound Dark Age (1000–800 BCE). Links to the Near Eastern military tradition were severed. Greece, finding itself in a political, cultural, and military backwater, reverted to a primitive if unique style of heroic warfare. Impressing the poorer classes into mass infantries stopped. Battles were exclusively characterized by groups of high-born champions facing each other in single combat, and were "fluid, free-for-all encounters in which the great aristocrats of one state dueled with those of another."[6]

The principal change in strategy during this period was a decrease in the already poor ability to wage war offensively, or at any distance afield from the politico-military center.[7] Defensive capacity reigned supreme as the once extensive communication and transportation nets were degraded or destroyed. Dark Age Greece, in terms of military organization and strategy, closely resembled Dark Age Europe (some 1,500 years later). In this era of state-power deflation and retrenchment, anyone with the might of arms could carve a principality from the rugged terrain of Greece. A dispersion of political authority from king to warrior-lords fragmented the ancient monarchies, and the aristocracy grew in relative numbers. The lot of the Greek farmer, too poor to arm himself and now tied directly to the land in a feudal relationship, degenerated miserably. Aristotle would later claim that in this dark era the distribution of *political* power was easily discerned; it was simply held by those having their own equipment for war, and a predisposition to use it.[8] Indeed, the very notions of Greek warrior and nobleman became in this way synonymous: "The 'nobles' of 800 BCE were simply those who had weapons and horses, with experience of how to use these. With these things they were able to make lesser people obey and to insure possession (and ultimately legal ownership) of lands and other forms of wealth in their own families."[9]

Pre-Classical Greece provides a near-perfect demonstration of the organizational influences described in chapter two. Under the tutelage of the warrior-patrician class, where the bulk of economic wealth became concentrated and access to privilege was constricted, military preparation and readiness was kept at a level necessary to subjugate the countryside, but not sufficient to ward of an (unexpected) concerted external attack.[10] Dynastic and trade conflicts still occurred, and piracy and banditry were major concerns, but compared to earlier and later periods, pre-800 BCE aristocratic Greece was relatively free from major interstate conflict, and especially free of extra-Hellenic hostilities. The percentage of population engaged in war was limited to the ruling elite, but that group was relatively large compared to contemporary civilized regions of similar sophistication. The fragmentation and decentralization of the aristocracy in Greece was much greater than that of contemporary Asian regions, for example. Still, the total population under arms never went above Delbrück's democratizing requisite of 5 percent. In comparison, at the height of the Peloponnesian War, direct participation in combat was probably well in excess of Delbrück's 20 percent–threshold for the population to free itself from tyranny.

Only the nobility, of course, were routinely eligible for military service in aristocratic Greece. Anyone who could acquire arms could aspire to nobility. Mercenaries were common enough, though their influence on political development was equivocal, less than in contemporary Asian civilized states—due almost entirely to the nobilities' unwillingness to pay for standing mercenary armies. Nonetheless, the use of mercenaries in aristocratic Greece was an accepted practice. It allowed the warrior-elite to increase the size of its military force without arming the peasantry. It also was an acceptable method for limited social advancement.

At this time, warfare at any distance from the noble's center of power (his city and or fortress) was impossible. Supply and communications capacities were simply incapable of supporting even a minor offensive campaign. Moreover, and this fact held throughout the period, limiting the pro-democratic influence of the offense even during Athens' Golden Age, siege warfare techniques were underdeveloped. Even the most rudimentarily garrisoned walls could be effectively defended. Walled cities and fortresses could hold as long as their supplies of food and water lasted. Direct assaults were possible only if the besieging force was vastly superior in numbers and could field excess levels of manpower, as losses for the attackers could be expected to be much greater than those for defenders. The potential loss was so great, for example, that the numerically limited Spartans almost never assaulted a walled city.[11]

The capacity for territorial occupation however, was quite strong and so provides a strong impetus away from democratization. Having virtually no offensive capacity (in strategic terms), the aristocratic Greek state was by definition an occupying government. When the new ruler conquered his territory, he immediately established personal control over its lands and other properties, and established members of his family to oversee his domain. Inability to increase the size of his domain beyond the force of his own immediate attention is a key factor here. As the method of warfare was highly individualized, combined drill is nonexistent. Heroes fought heroes in mass individual combat. No coordination was required between allied combatants except the personal loyalty that might keep friends protecting each other's backs. Individual exploits were recounted at length at the drinking table, and reliance on others for survival in battle was probably seen as an insult. Clearly then, military arts and exploits were glorified beyond battlefield necessity, and militarism was rife.

Moreover, stratification in the military was socially determined. Combatants were of the nobility, or of the mercenary classes. Non-nobles were pressed into service on occasion, but quickly returned to civilian duty as soon as the crisis that forced their induction abated—precisely for maintaining that stratification. Some social and political movement based on merit was possible. Military rank was bestowed as a birthright, and promotion was based on noble association, but an individual well skilled and armed could carve out a kingdom based on force of arms alone. This kind of political entrepreneur did indeed exist, and was occasionally romanticized. Moreover, a skilled battle veteran could through loot and booty acquire the wherewithal to form a company of pirates or brigands, and offer the services of this company to the nobility as mercenaries. His military and hence social rank depended entirely on the number and capabilities of these soldiers and sailors. All of which highlights the place of loyalties in politics and in battle—entirely to the person of the ruler. It was not until sometime after 800 BCE that citizenship became associated with military service and economic station, over kinship.

The aggregate Greek military structure was clearly aligned to favor authoritarian political government. "The net result [was] that about 900 BCE the individual had almost no rights, being absorbed in a totalitarian kinship group, in a system of such groups with no state and no real idea of public authority."[12] Yet from this violent period of totalitarian dominance, the world's firsts known postprimitive democracies would emerge. By 450 BCE, the poorest residents of the most powerful of the city-states would reach a zenith in personal rights, liberties, and responsibilities.

The historical record shows that profound military structural reorganization preceded and directly contributed to the astounding political reversal.

Hoplon, Hoplite, and Phalanx: Foundations of Greek Social Equality

Waves of northern barbarian invasions forced changes in Greek military strategy from the offense of marauding heroes to the defense of walled manors, dispersed centers of authority as mobility and communications lines were disrupted, and shattered existing political and economic structures. This is the transformational capacity of war, repeated throughout history. It does not build so much as it indiscriminately destroys. Yet in its wake, it leaves open the possibility of new political structures to fill the ruined void. Following the period of retrenchment, a new warlord nobility, whose power was based in mastery of the dominant military techniques, emerged and then prevailed.

With time, the invaders slowly established sociopolitical routines, and life became more stable. Political stability allowed populations and tribute bases to increase. After 800 BCE, however, interrelated economic, demographic, and technological developments prompted new changes in the prevailing strategies and tactics of war. Governing structures slowly changed to accommodate them. Most critically, iron became readily obtainable for farm implements and craftsmen's tools as well as for weapons, and productivity increased with its availability. Greater productivity spurred trade, and trade increased the wealth of cities. Horses and state-of-the-art armaments became cheaper and in some areas abundant.

As personal incomes rose, the number of individuals who could conceivably seize political power on the basis of military strength increased proportionately, and the post-invasion aristocracy was uncomfortably threatened. They responded predictably. The rate of structural change one might have expected with the new economy was blunted by the aristocracy's deliberate practice of siphoning off the growing wealth of its population through coercive taxation, and directing it instead to its own extended kinship groups. These actions temporarily undercut and prolonged the natural rise of a powerful new underclass. Of note, in a decidedly Machiavellian observation, as the nobility's wealth increased, the previously endemic warfare decreased. The rulers became less interested in the fickle vagaries of battle and more concerned with acquiring great wealth, and began unavoidably dispersing it to the artisans and craftsmen who could satisfy their avarice. The *ozio* of Machiavelli's cyclical view of history inevitably set in, leaving the warlord regimes ripe for destruction.

As extended families with ties to the new nobility naturally grew, the soft life of the courts combined with ever more limited battles to increase the numbers of those with kinship ties, and the Greek notion of aristocratic citizenship began to take form.[13] All magistrates, military officers, and priests were members of ruling families. All land belonged to them and they held all wealth beyond subsistence. Service to the state became the basis for citizenship, but it remained exclusive to kinship in the best families. Accordingly, military service to counter external and internal threats was expected of them.[14]

It is interesting to speculate how long an aristocracy might maintain itself before giving way to popular government. Machiavelli attempted it, and developed a cyclical model based on historical rhythms modified by the actions of great lawgiver princes. All governments, he believed, were doomed to fail. But strong states could be forged that would last centuries, if established by good laws and ruled by great men. In a more precise conjecture, Carroll Quigley estimated that so long as the portion of the population that could equip itself for war is 5 percent or less, the legal powers the extant nobility had acquired and routinized could be maintained.[15] This is an astonishing formula, and is undoubtedly a rough estimation, but it is based in sound deliberation. Below that rate, new warrior-lords could either be defeated as they rose up and challenged for dominance, or could simply be bought off—incorporated into the existing aristocracy. The process could continue indefinitely, thought Quigley. But, if the population were armed at a rate of 20 percent or more, the edge given the aristocratic minority by the organizational and institutional strength of the extant social order would be overcome.

While the numerical formula cannot be proven here, the logic is sound and describes precisely the impetus and format for the rise of Greek republican and democratic forms of government. The military factor common to all Greek states was the adoption of a new fighting method, based on a specific type of armor that rapidly dominated the ancient battlefield. This form of tightly massed infantry increased the armed percentage of the population to high enough numbers that the aristocracies could not maintain their privileged positions, and every state that adopted the new methods became at least a modified republic. Military innovations in naval warfare increased the combat eligible population of Athens's citizenry to the highest in the known world, and prompted the most radical governing democracy ever seen.

Phalanx

The heavily armored *hoplite* infantryman, operating in a closely coordinated mass formation called a *phalanx*, is the military innovation most identifiable with classical Greek warfare. Precise dating is difficult, but the phalanx formation probably developed between 750 and 650 BCE.[16] The hoplite style of armor and armament preceded the phalanx formation, and may have originated in the Greek settlements on the Aegean coast of Asia Minor, what is today Turkey. The dramatic success of the innovative Greek style of armaments and battle against the traditional aristocratic methods of the mainland Persian armies ensured its spread to peninsular Greece. The critical point is that *following* introduction of the hoplite phalanx, and within a remarkably short period, Greek political institutions underwent radical political alterations.

By 700 BCE, the Greek world had progressed commercially and industrially so that a significant percentage of the population outside the established aristocratic kinship groups could afford to equip themselves with the best available iron weapons and bronze armor. These turned out to be the helmet, shield, leggings, and pike of the hoplite. As increasing numbers of individuals acquired not only the panoply of equipment that marked a warrior, but the retinue that carried his provisions and sustained him on marches, these new warriors began to assert themselves politically. The difference in their approach was that the hoplites asserted their claims *as a group*, not as individuals.

Bands of well-trained foot soldiers working in concert were able to defeat the mounted knight who so clearly represented the old aristocracies, but only if they relied upon and worked closely with each other.[17] This fusion of individuals into a coherent whole represented the kernel of the democratic ideal. "The cohesion of the whole mass of men counted more than individual heroics. The Homeric Kings, who went out before their people to challenge their equals in single combat, had no place in the phalanx; pre-eminent strength, beauty, and swiftness of foot were no longer the first qualities demanded of a leader."[18] A dominant leader was, in the age of the phalanx, not a heroic warrior, but a master tactician and organizer. Here we see that the catalyst that ushered the downfall of the traditional nobility was a drastic change in warfare tactics, based in a very minor change in weapons technology.

Combat from the Mycenaean Age consisted of individualistic sparring. Warriors rode onto the battlefield, dismounted (the stirrup had not yet been invented, making horseback combat precarious and a blow from a rider considerably less forceful than one from a well-based infantryman), threw some javelins or other projectiles to harass and disrupt the enemy, moved quickly to engage an opposing warrior, and fought until one side capitulated or fled. The shield of the warrior had a strap at the center for battle, and a sling for carrying the protective instrument over his back, decidedly valuable in the event of a retreat.

The phalanx style of combat was entirely different. Soldiers making up the phalanx were named after their particular shield, the round *hoplon*. An innovation in holding the shield allowed it to be heavier and integrated into the mass of the formation. The shield was smaller than previous ones, but instead of one handle, it had two—one at the center for the hand and one on the side, where the arm was inserted up to the elbow. The hoplon was smaller but heavier than its predecessors were because it was covered entirely with metal. Previous shields, normally made of wood and covered with leather, were ringed with metal edges and usually incorporated a small metal disk mounted at its front-center. What allowed for the heavier weight, and the critical innovation that revolutionized warfare, was the second short strap at the edge of the shield. Instead of holding it at the awkward end of the hand, the arm was inserted into the latter strap to the elbow. This minimal change allowed a warrior to absorb a blow with the full strength of the arm, and to push with it, making it an auxiliary weapon. Conspicuously absent was a sling for which to throw the hoplon over one's back for protection in retreat. This was an intended modification to strengthen unit cohesion. The only option the hoplite had to facilitate a panicked retreat was to drop his shield and run, unfettered but with his back unprotected from enemy slings and arrows.[19] Shield forward, remaining in solidarity with the mass, maximized his chances of survival.

Now that the warrior could maintain position while absorbing an enemy pike or sword strike, a new tactic quickly evolved. Soldiers could stand together in formation and were harder to dislodge from their relative positions. Initially, two or three hoplites could cluster in battle, protecting each other's backs and sides, and presenting a less penetrable and more formidable force. The larger the linked group, the more powerful it became, and the more coordination it required. Accordingly, an inevitable military change due directly to the hoplon was the facilitation of coordinated formations of infantry and attendant requirements for prebattle drill and training.

The hoplon shield was still small enough that it only protected the left two-thirds of the body, leaving the pike or right side somewhat vulnerable. The tactic employed was to march in formation with each hoplite's right side protected by the overlap of the next hoplite's shield. This led to an instinctive and powerful sense of reliance upon one's associates for protection, and must have added immeasurably to the hoplite's sense of group loyalty. This new and perhaps artificial type of kinship, based on battlefield association instead of blood ties, was a powerful bond found only in the war experience—and fully transferable to civilian relationships after the fact.

Of course, if everyone is protecting the person to his left, the rightmost file had no protection but its own sword or pike, and so the entire formation had a tendency to drift to the right as it engaged in battle. This tendency required a new and sophisticated system of maneuver to help maintain control, and a set of tactics to overcome the problem. Practice as a group with the formation in peacetime, drill in other words, was vital to the success of the phalanx. The Spartans proved particularly adept at the phalanx maneuver, limited though it was. Based on the tendency of the phalanx to outflank the left side of the enemy formation, the Spartans added the technique of performing a "wheel round to roll up the enemy line."[20] The ability of the Spartans to outmaneuver other forces was due primarily to the inordinate amount of time they spent in training, but a quirk of history tells an additional tale. Men marching in formation do better if a noticeable musical rhythm is present. The flute, with its high-pitched sound, can be heard over the din of battle, and so the Spartans employed flute players to carry an appropriate tempo tune. By changing melodies, the formation could be instructed which formation and maneuver to effect, and precisely when to do it. Spartan cohesion and precise team actions led as much to their legendary battle victories as their extraordinary individual skills. And military science arguably began with the needs of the phalanx, as doctrines for group weapons employment and movements were developed, tested, and employed.

Groups of infantryman thus trained and equipped could use the force of combined mass to their advantage, countering the strength of any individual warrior no matter how strong or skilled. All they required was cohesion and morale; both increased with experience. While battlefield tactics advanced considerably, the acme of Greek warfare would not occur until the heroes of nobility were defeated and opposing phalanxes met head on. The standard phalanx engagement still consisted of two sides moving toward a great collision of arms. The degree of difference from mob clashes was of an order of magnitude. The standard phalanx was eight or more rows deep, and at least a dozen men wide. The unit would march into position and begin trotting in unison, arms locked and picking up speed as the sides came near. With a torrent of shouts and the weight of both formations approaching at full run, the two would ram each other in an attempt to shock and knock down the front rows of the other. With the enemy on its back and in confusion, one's own first two rows would engage any opposing hoplites standing, while back rows could dispatch the fallen and scrambling. Such a thundering collision would be swift and merciless. Between matched foes, however, the initial clash could prove indecisive, and armies would be face-to-face in an almost choreographed grisly ballet. While the front rows were too occupied with spear combat to lock arms and push, back rows were not so constrained. Lines behind the front assisted not only physically by pushing their mates forward, adding their own strength to the arms of their forward comrades, but morally as well by shouting encouragement. The resulting image is more like that of a rugby scrum than a Napoleonic era combined arms engagement, but still much more disciplined than the old style of mob or heroic combat. It also highlights the value that each member of the formation contributed to the combined success. So important was the role of morale and encouragement from the latter rows, that period tacticians always recommended putting the best hoplites in both the first *and* *last* rows. The side that was more disciplined and cohesive could put more force into its charge and sustain its attack, and would generally prevail.

The phalanx owed its dominance in battle in part to oddities of the Greek experience, including a tendency not to employ cavalry in the mountainous terrain, and a common history and culture that inclined to make warfare between Greeks a relatively civilized (if somewhat irrational and gruesome) institution. Battles were fought in open and flat terrain. Ambushes were unheard of. Rules of engagement were for the most part observed and maintained. But the reasons for developing the hoplite formation are far less important than the subsequent political development that was influenced by it. The key point in the rise and routinized employment of a coordinated infantry formation tactic was that group victory, not to mention *individual* safety, now no longer depended on individual prowess or courage or other heroic capacity. It depended entirely on tight discipline and *group* cohesion. The battle experience and training of the nobility was wasted against a determined formation of egalitarian hoplites.[21]

Although the phalanx was original to the Greeks, not so was the notion of a coordinated mass of pike infantry, though they may have been completely unaware of its predecessors. Yigael Yadin observes that a phalanx-type formation, complete with shields and coordinated pikes, had its antecedents in Sumerian warfare.[22] The Stele of Vultures (ca. 2500 BCE) shows a formation of soldiers marching in step behind locked rectangular shields and presenting a formidable array of joined spears.[23] That this formation was used is not surprising; it is a straightforward tactical innovation that any intelligent general should have been able to design. What is surprising, given its probable battlefield superiority over unorganized groups of individuals, is that in Sumeria, as in every other place it may have been tried before it was institutionalized by the Greeks, it was quickly abandoned.

The only explanation that makes sense is that the great despotisms of the Ancient Near East could not allow the political and social upheavals that followed wherever the phalanx-type military innovation was employed. In discussing the Stele of Vultures, Robert O'Connell observes: "They are clearly people with a stake in society, the very types necessary for a style of warfare which demands that the participants fight at close range and face danger in a cooperative fashion."[24] In Greece, there was no imperial authority that could perceive the danger the phalanx-type formation posed to concentrated authority and effectively halt its deployment. If just one of the many city-states adopted it, others must follow. As a direct result, emerging Greek notions of *polis* citizenship vice kinship citizenry emerged, and then increased as the size of the military group increased. In this way, the phalanx helped solidify the relationship between military service and political rights.

With widespread incorporation of the phalanx, military organization had taken a decidedly democratic turn. Between 800 and 700 BCE the presence of war was endemic, if predominantly internal war and popular rebellion. Preparation for war became pervasive and innovative. The hoplite phalanx allowed for military participation at a rate probably unprecedented since the break from tribalism into civilized urbanization. Accordingly, scope of eligibility for service soared. In Athens, especially, the change in eligibility requirements was profound. Upon entering manhood, all citizens would *voluntarily* spend a year in garrison at the port of Piraeus, during which they would eat at a common mess and be trained by elected officials in the art of hoplite warfare (at public expense).[25] Following successful training, they would receive (again at public expense if needed) a sword and shield. This was the route to participatory citizenship

Reliance on mercenaries as supplementary forces dropped dramatically. With the development of the hoplite and the glorification of the citizen-army, Athens quit hiring hoplite mercenaries altogether. Nonresident *metics* could serve as mercenaries in the fleet, when needed, and there came a hotly debated contemporary concern over the propriety of paying the *thetes* for their service as rowers; but not for the fiduciary reasons of old. Contemporaries were worried that doing so would turn them into citizen-mercenaries vice citizen-soldiers.

Siege warfare techniques remained underdeveloped, but with the introduction of hoplite warfare and the rise in economic capacities of the city-states, extended offensive campaigns became possible. For the most part, these actions consisted of trampling an opponent's croplands and orchards. The enemy would be thus goaded from his fortifications, and pitched battle on the relatively level and open farmland ensued. If engaged, campaigns could be short and decisive. Despite a renewed capacity for offensive warfare, the development of the hoplite further constricted the capacity of rulers to occupy territory, however. The phalanx was designed for battle only, and was useless in traditional policing functions. The main reason this factor is not emphasized more in the Greek political experience is due to the Greek propensity for colonization, a (then) relatively benign method of territorial occupation.

With the rise of the hoplite phalanx to counter the individual superiority of the knight, coordinated training became the determinant of victory. The amount and complexity of training to participate in the phalanx was not particularly protracted, however. Aside from some limited drill in maintaining formation on the move, the tactics were simple. What distinguished the successful phalanx was the integrity of the formation, which was based on both discipline (unmatched in Sparta) and civic morale (an Athenian attribute).

More than just the ability to move in step, the phalanx required a firm discipline and group devotion, as subsequent ranks maintained formation integrity by immediately filling holes created during combat as the dead and wounded fell out. Perhaps more importantly, follow-on ranks would "exercise principally a physical and moral pressure," encouraging the front-line combatants and pressing them forward.[26] Even though the rearmost ranks were less likely to come to the front of the line and actually use their weapons before battle was concluded, they were afforded the same armor and weaponry as those in the front line. In this way, every soldier was fully and equally liable and ready for combat. Distinctions were minimized and unity of movement and deed intensified.

Equality within the ranks was paramount as those in the rear had to provide encouragement and esprit to those in the front. "Least of all, then, would it have been desirable to put possibly unreliable men, slaves, in the rearmost ranks of the phalanx."[27] Unequal members of society, it was presumed, would be subject to panic and flight, destroying the moral strength of the phalanx. Combat veterans were placed in the last ranks to mitigate these concerns, and the number of citizens that could claim personal valor in the direct face of an enemy increased. Not only was a greater percentage of the citizenry able to claim a boastful place at the victor's table, the distribution of heroic effort served to prevent elevation of the heroic to a narrow aristocracy.

The Spartan's accidental discovery that the use of pipes assisted the individual hoplite's advance in an orderly manner, thus maintaining the enhanced strength of the disciplined formation in battle, prompts a philosophical interpretation of democratic values. Delbrück remarks: "In this context the piper is nothing other than the [embodiment of the] tactical formation; a group of heroes engaging in individual combat does not march in step and would, by the irregular noise of their advance, even drown out the pipers."[28] Regular, rhythmic melody characterized the movement of the mass, and epitomized the philosophical and political changes wrought by the formation of many individuals acting in concert to defend the state. And it was to the state they pledged their loyalty. After the expansion of citizenship subsequent to the hoplite reforms, writers began to speak of love of polis, and loyalty to one's city. The Athenian citizenship oath, for example, expressed no loyalty to individuals, with the exception of a comrade still fighting in battle for the polis.[29]

The mass infantry formation required manpower, leading to the lessening of internal military stratification. In Athens, the standard was to divide the population into four classes. The richest class served on horseback, and the next two classes (small farmers and merchants) as hoplites. "Before Athens had a fleet, the very significant lowest portion of the citizenry, the Thetes, therefore, were completely free of any obligation for military service."[30] They were also free of much political power. This is not to say thetes or slaves suffered no liability. Each hoplite had a servant accompany him into battle—to assist in carrying equipment and foraging for supplies—and they may have had auxiliary combat duties such as transporting friendly (and killing enemy) wounded. When Athens acquired a significant naval capacity, thetes served on board ship as rowers and a trustworthy slave accompanied hoplites into battle. Hans Delbrück asserts the class divisions were not political, for all citizens had equal rights, they were only for the expedient purpose of assessing military equipment contributions, including the outfitting of ships.[31] The critical argument in the equality of the military role of poorer classes is that in time of crisis or need, thetes would be outfitted by the state for hoplite service.[32] It is at this point in his description that Delbrück insists military reform must precede democratic reform: ". . . universal suffrage without universal military obligation is not conceivable."[33]

Golden Age and the Peloponnesian War

The innovation of the hoplite phalanx revolutionized all of Hellas. It tore down the old kinship nobility and established independent states ruled by brothers in arms—loyalties formed in battle and not at the hearth. Kinship citizenship was rapidly replaced by service citizenship. To freely take arms in defense of the city was the only evidence needed to vouch for one's worthiness.

The Greek military–political system is perhaps the classic example for studies of the relationship between arms and state. It is a complete system, complex enough for sophisticated analysis yet small enough to incorporate in its entirety. Its utility is enhanced by the many socioeconomic and cultural similarities between units of analysis, allowing for uncluttered comparisons of its extremely varied political milieu. In other words, its geographic compactness and relatively small homogenous population lends itself to a microanalysis of a macro-phenomenon. It is, especially with its example of the Peloponnesian Wars, descriptive of a complete system engaged in the most complicated social activity, systemic or hegemonic war, but at a level small enough and with a commonality broad enough to isolate fully its complex interactions.

Despite its geographically small size, Hellas (as the Greeks called it) was far from unified politically. Its mountainous terrain, pocketed with inlets and useful harbors, and surrounding the island-studded Aegean Sea, geographically isolated its settlements into fertile valleys and trade choke points. What is Greece today can properly be described as a peninsula of peninsulas, but Hellas extended from the Italian and Sicilian colonies of the Western Mediterranean to the grain-producing settlements of the Black Sea. Outposts stretched from Southern France and Northern Africa, but the center of the Greek culture was the Aegean basin and its adjacent lands. There were large population centers clinging to the Turkish coast, and small villages of little more than mud-thatched huts. With all this diversity, however, Hellas shared important characteristics. A common language, further cemented by a shared religion and literary (poetic) history, bound them. Differences were apparent. Dialects in language were pronounced, but all Greeks could understand and communicate with one another. Various cities revered specific gods over others, but all recognized the importance of the Oracle at Delphi. And all cities respected and participated in the Olympic Games, an annual test of skills and opportunity for interaction.

So obviously Greek were all citizens of the many city-states that dotted the landscape that they referred to themselves in all things as Hellenes. All who did not share their language and culture were called *barbarians*. Solidifying their profound sense of unity was an ability to join together when necessary to defend their culture against powerful enemies. The most notable of these were the spectacular defeats of the Persian Empire's twin attempts to bring the nettlesome Greeks under their formal control at the beginning of the fifth century BCE. Under the leadership of Sparta on land and Athens on the sea, the vastly outnumbered Greeks dismantled the armies and fleets of Darius and Xerxes. Typical of these warrior peoples, when the external threats were extinguished, they fell to squabbling amongst themselves.

So far, the region has been treated at the macro level. An attempt has been made to chart characteristics common to all of the Greek military. The structural implications of military reform and subsequent change in governing institutions is bolstered by the evidence, but while all states increased political participation to some degree during the period, results were not uniform. From vestigial (now constitutional) monarchies to radical mob democracy, the changes affected states in different ways. If the differences in governments within Greece can be correlated to differences in military structure within the phalanx and other armed forces, the theory can be deemed more robust. Thus, the greatest of the city-states, Athens and Sparta—epitomes of the military-organizational variables that so clearly defined political institutions in their day—are separated out for analysis.

Military Reform and Athenian Democracy

In the sixth century BCE, following the rise of the hoplite phalanx and the military and commercial importance of the fleet, the lower classes that had been impressed into service to protect the various city-states became agitated and unruly throughout Hellas. They began to demand political rights from the old aristocracy. Since the masses were now armed and trained for combat, the aristocracy had to bend, or it risked losing all to the armed throngs. In every case but one, Sparta, it appears the aristocracy either did not bend, or did not bend enough. From among the people sprang champions who agitated for popular support, and with renegade armies destroyed the old aristocracy polis by polis. In neoclassical economic terms, they were political entrepreneurs. They offered an option. These new champions had no models of popular rule to guide them, and might not have heeded them were they available, for they had no desire to share political power once having seized it by force. Upon driving out the older aristocracies, they established themselves as extralegal dictators, the so-called tyrants.[34] The masses, thus betrayed by the ambitions of the tyrants, found they had simply traded one ruling despot for another.

And so it turns out that democracy was an uninvited idea. The rulers did not want it and the masses, who knew they wanted more political power but had no archetype to guide them, were ignorant of it. Nonetheless, emboldened by the military power endowed by the phalanx, they continued their demands for political change, and the new tyrants were successively deposed and replaced. In many cases, a surviving remnant of the old aristocracy could regain a ruling position, due to its legacy and vestigial internal organization, but usually at the cost of some lessening or dispersion of political power. In this manner, despite the cyclical reign of despots, broader dispersions of rights could happen accretively. In Athens, class struggles followed the basic script. Tyrants had usurped the old aristocracy by at least 630 BCE, but by the beginning of the sixth century, the old if politically diminished aristocracy had returned.[35]

In 594 BCE, one of these restored aristocrats, a man named Solon, was selected as Athens' chief magistrate, or first archon. His rise to power is not clearly understood, as he apparently held widely known populist ideals. Once in preeminent office, he quickly outmaneuvered the rest of the aristocratic council and, using the time tested model of his predecessors, ensconced himself as the new tyrant. With absolute power, he forced his will onto the state. Uniquely, rather than aggrandize his own wealth and power, as tyrants before him had done, Solon used his authority to become the great reformer of Athenian society. The middle classes, the once-independent farmers that now made up the vital core of the new phalanx army, had managed to become impoverished by calamitous debt. The old aristocracy, as holders of wealth, made injurious loans at exorbitant interest. When the farmer became irreparably in arrears, his collateral was seized, and his land rented back to him in a ruinous tenant farmer arrangement. The terms were so inequitable that the farmers became the economic slaves of the aristocracy, getting deeper into debt every year with no hope of climbing atop their mountainous burden. Failure to repay loans or attempts to leave the tenant farms were punishable by the severe criminal code set up by the aristocracy for just this purpose, known as Draco's laws. In this manner, the old aristocracy slowly seized by legal and economic means what force of arms had recently denied them—almost all of the land surrounding Athens. As a form of correction, at the end of his first year in office Solon ordered the liquidation of all public and private debts, effectively emancipating the center of his middle-class military support. He also repealed Draco's criminal code, and replaced it with a much more lenient one.[36]

Like Lykourgos of Sparta before him, Solon first addressed military reform before attempting the sweeping economic or political ones just mentioned. His most enduring contribution was the effective reorganization of sociopolitical society into four classes, based not on family or birthplace, but solely on military needs and wealth. All classes were expected to serve the state directly, and as called upon, with no substitutions allowed. The highest and least numerous class—effectively the old aristocracy—was required to maintain the means necessary to participate in war as cavalrymen. The next two classes were incorporated into the phalanx as hoplites. The second class was defined as those farmers and tradesmen able to provide or afford their own weaponry. The third class, wealthy enough to remove themselves from economic pursuits for the time necessary to train and campaign, but not so wealthy as to afford the panoply of hoplite equipment, had their weapons issued to them by the state. Despite this purely economic distinction, made simply to lower the burden on the state's coffers, no preference was given to the second class in training or in battle. The fourth class consisted of those residents too poor to extricate themselves from the day-to-day maintenance of their families, and no military service was expected of them. They could, however, hire themselves out as porters and servants for the hoplites, and so could serve in this voluntary manner. Solon then decreed that all males of Athenian birth would now be allowed a single vote in the political assembly, though only members of the top three classes would have access to public administrative offices. The lowest class, the *thetes* (who could not afford to outfit themselves as hoplites), could furthermore not serve as magistrates, but they were given the right to sit on juries. This concession became an unintended practical power of veto for the thetes, as virtually all decisions of top three class magistrates were subject to review by the court system. The critical observation here is that society was politically reorganized to resemble the practical demarcations of the radical new military structure, and not vice versa. All of Solon's democratizing reforms can be seen to have a basis in, or been a response to, prevailing military needs and practices.

Moreover, thetes were no longer permanently relegated to lowest-class citizenship (nor were the highest classes permanently established). Thetes had access to means for increasing their wealth, including trade and business, and once they crossed the income threshold of the next class, they could move up politically as well, simply by maintaining the training and/or armaments of the higher class. Ultimately, as we shall see, thetes who did not march as servants on campaign were expected to serve in the Athenian navy, and in lieu of weapons issue, they were paid for their service by the state. When the fleet later became the most powerful in the known world, and the recognized guarantor of Athenian sovereignty, restrictions on thete's political participation would be eliminated.

Following his term as archon, Solon remarkably stepped down and left the city in exile for ten years. He claimed his motives were to ensure that the reforms he had instituted received a fair incubation, uninfluenced by his presence. Solon was no doubt honest in this assessment (though detractors argued that he was simply avoiding retribution), but his absence had the unfortunate effect of ensuring that none of his reforms had a chance for survival.[37] They were too radical to become accepted in mere months without the equally radical reform in military structure that would occur later. And so Solon's reforms were incomplete, and without question presumptive. At any rate, they did not long survive, and cycles of tyrannical and aristocratic coups continued for the next 100 years. Still, most observers then and now credit Solon's reforms as the foundation and guide for the unique structure of Athenian democracy.

The tyrannies had always proved a thorn in traditionalist Sparta's political side, as the viability of extralegal or nonconstitutional government was seen as a threat to the political stability of its republican institutions. The specter of tyrants flouting the law so long as they had the power to do so was anathema to the Spartan's deep respect for institutions. So, in 510 BCE Sparta intervened in Athenian politics directly and put down the then-existing tyrant. The external destruction of the tyranny allowed for a period of political exploration in Athens, and the Athenian democracy as we know it from classical descriptions was established sometime around 461 BCE. Openness to new ideas combined with a growing commercial capacity had vastly expanded Athens's population, popularity, and power, and in short order Athens became Sparta's primary political, ideological, and military rival.

Meanwhile, Greek city-states along what is now the coast of Turkey had been brought under the domination of Persia, by Cyrus the Great. In 499 BCE, a number of these city-states joined in rebellion against the Persians, and despite mainland Greek support, were brutally defeated. The Persians recognized that the Greeks would be a constant thorn in the side of their empire if the whole of Aegean Hellas could not be brought under their power. Thus in 490 BCE, King Darius launched an expedition against the Greek mainland. The Persian naval transport supporting its army was met en route by the Athenian navy, and routed in the famous battle of Salamis. This action propelled the Athenians to leadership stature within the Hellene world.

Ten years later, King Xerxes of Persia tried to conquer peninsular Greece with a much larger force than the one of his father. Legends describe more than a million men marching along the coast of Greece, supported by the largest navy ever assembled. The true size of the force was undoubtedly less than 50,000 men, it was still an extraordinary logistical feat for its day. Athens alone could not stop the Persian two-pronged advance, but in concert with the other maritime Greek powers (and after a brilliant evacuation of Athens—women and children were taken to safety so the men of the city could prosecute the war where the Persians were weakest, and not have to worry about their families under siege), the combined Greek navy defeated the Persians at the battle of Marathon. The Spartan-led combined Greek forces soundly defeated the Persian land army, which entered Greece from the north, at Plataea in 479 BCE. How is still a matter of great perplexity, and Thucydides suggests, probably correctly, that it was due to a series of hideous mistakes on the part of the Persians. The legends of those two battles ensured that Hellas now had two military leaders—Sparta on land and Athens on the sea.

After the war with Persia, Sparta turned inward and concentrated on domestic matters. Athens, absent the Persian navy, ruled the seas, and expanded its trading ties enormously. Two years after the Persian defeat, Athens was approached by most of the maritime Greek city-states to manage a league formed to ensure against the resurgence of Persian power, and to rid the Aegean of commerce-raiding pirates. The league was chartered on the tiny but religiously significant island of Delos, hence the name Delian League.

While Athens was charged with leading the league, members were assigned quotas of military ships to support the combined navy. Athens had by far the largest contingent, but many other states made sizeable contributions. Still, Athenian ships were superior to those of any other state, and the cost for maintaining them no greater than for that of one's own war ships. Within a few years, most of these states simply began paying Athens to supply and crew their requisite number of ships. Payments were made to the treasury at Delos, and Athens took withdrawals as needed. Eventually, allied members voluntarily agreed to let Athens carry the burden of military defense in exchange for financial contributions. The Athenians fulfilled their part of the bargain, maintaining a fleet of more than 300 war ships, not only deterring a return of Persian naval power, but also clearing the trade lanes of pirates and brigands. In 454 BCE, however, the league treasury was moved from Delos to Athens, and payments in kind were made mandatory, with quotas established not by agreement but by Athenian decree. Having given up their fleets for commercial growth, the League members were in no position to object. The illusion of an alliance was gone. Payments were enforced, participation was mandatory, and Athens was the master of the League, or more correctly, its empire.

Athenian seapower brought commercial dominance and Athens ruled an ever-richer trading empire of coastal and island-based cities. Although Athens continued to refer to these city-states as allies, if an ally attempted to quit the League, or suspend payments, Athens quickly and brutally squelched any resistance. In its defense, Athens did create a public good in the form of a vibrant, mutually beneficial trade economy by suppressing piracy in the region, and kept most of the maritime Greek city-states free from Persian control. It also frequently supported democratic elements of allied city-states against oligarchic or tyrannical attempts to assert control.

From 460 to 446 BCE, Athens and its empire fought the Peloponnesian League in the First Peloponnesian War. Note that it was not until nine years into this war that the reforms creating the radical democracy described below were instituted. For most of this preliminary conflict, Corinth, not Sparta, was the primary opponent of Athens. Formal peace with Persia in 449 BCE allowed Athens to turn its full attention on the Peloponnesus, swinging the war in its favor. In 446 BCE, Sparta increased its support to Corinth and invaded Attica, prompting the Athenians to accept a negotiated peace.

The Thirty Year Peace signed by the combatants recognized the legitimacy of the Delian League with Athens at its head, and could be construed as a minor Athenian victory, even though Athens was forced to renounce claims on all mainland territory captured in the war. Athens used the interlude to expand its influence in northern and eastern Hellas, and, most unacceptably to the Peloponnesian League, in the area around Megara (the vital strip of land between Corinth and Athens). Just 14 years after the 30-year treaty was signed, fearing the rise in power of Athens, Sparta initiated the Second Peloponnesian War.

The most remarkable feature of interregnum and classical Athens was its radical democracy, the fact that *any citizen* could participate equally in its assembly. Because the assembly was open to all, the Athenians were particularly susceptible to effective orators. Such men were called *demagogues*, because they could rise to power not on the basis of arms, but on their dramatic persuasiveness. So critical was this skill that books of rhetoric were best-sellers. Even Aristotle believed that his own work on the subject was his most important academic contribution, and in his day it no doubt was.

The assembly could make political decisions without limits. Despite Pericles's profound and impassioned defense of respect for the law, the assembly was unbounded. The vagaries of such governing capacity led most students of politics to condemn and despise this form of rule as no more than tyranny of the majority. Decisions of momentous importance could be made and reversed in a span of days or hours. Whereas the unwritten Athenian constitution was for the most part revered and followed, it was open to interpretation of the most dangerous kind. Lives were at stake, as well as livelihoods, and no better example of the evils of such a governing form is evident than that of the case of Mytilene.

Before the victory at Pylos, when it appeared that Athens might lose the war, one of its imperial possessions, the colony of Mytilene on the Turkish coast, successfully rebelled. Mytilene refused to pay the tribute that kept Athens and its empire solvent, and so the Athenians sent a force to lay siege to the city and bring it back into the fold. It is interesting to note that in this age of inefficient siege craft, direct assault against manned parapets and walls was the least desirable option when attempting to capture a city. The first endeavor was usually to goad the besieged forces to come out from behind their protective cover and fight with honor, on the battlefield. Volleys of insults and desecration of family lands and gravesites outside the city were the general means employed. Failing that, the most common way to take a city was to gain access to its interior through guile. Guards or others with access to the city gates would be offered bribes of money and safety. In the case of Mytilene, events led to a different outcome.[38] The city had not expected the strong Athenian response, and so had not prepared well for a siege. It became apparent to Mytilene's rebellious king, Salaethus, that relief from his Spartan allies was not forthcoming. Salaethus decided his only hope lay in attacking the besieging Athenian force on the plain outside his walls. He broke open the armory and issued heavy hoplite-style equipment to the common people of the city, who had previously only been lightly armed or had served in support roles. Hoplite status gave the people new power, and they refused to obey the king's orders. They demanded that the king abandon his alliance with Sparta and instead seek a new alliance with Athens. Salaethus, with the prospect of losing control of the city forever, was forced to accede to the people's wishes and come to terms with the Athenians.

The passionate assembly of Athens was not willing to forgive the Mytilene its transgression so easily. They brought the rebellious city back into its Delian Empire, but determined that a punishment must be meted out as an example to all other allies, so as to strengthen their control. There were two major blocs, those who believed in a devastating punishment to dissuade all future consideration of rebellion, and those who felt a more lenient—perhaps economic only—punishment would be more appropriate. After all, most Mytileneans did go against their ruling king and return the city without a fight. Perhaps just enough tribute to recoup the cost of the expedition, and a little more for good measure, would suffice.

The former faction carried the day. A ship was set out to tell the expeditionary force to execute all the adult males and sell all the women and children into slavery. The city would then be repopulated with 500 Athenians and made over into a loyal colony. On the next day, perhaps due to fervid discussions the night before, the issue was reopened. The leader of the faction supporting maximum punishment, Cleon, began by cursing the inefficiencies of democratic governance. Vacillations could serve only to weaken the empire, he said, for though Athens was a democracy at home, it was surely a tyrant abroad.[39] The maximum punishment was due to Mytilene, since it had revolted not because it could no longer bear the harshness of Athenian rule, but because it had seized on a moment of Athenian weakness. In this way, it was the worst possible example. If Athens did not deal with Mytilene severely, then any other state seeing a window of opportunity would do the same.

Diodotus spoke on behalf of the leniency faction. He began with a lesson on the dangers of impassioned rhetoric, and admired the capacity for a democracy to revisit decisions when cooler heads prevail. The brilliance of Diodotus's response is that he refused to rely on issues of justice or compassion, but solely on the merits of state interest. Would a strong punishment or a more lenient one be in the best interests of Athens? He made an analogy to the value of capital punishment in criminal cases. The murderer always thinks he will not be caught, or tries to keep from being caught once having murdered. In these cases, capital punishment (the equivalent of which was being meted out to Mytilene) is not a deterrent. The only one deterred from future murders is the murderer himself. Thus, Cleon's argument that severe punishment will deter other states is incorrect. What it will do instead, Diodotus insisted, would make cities that had rebelled be unwilling to negotiate or rejoin the empire. They would fight to the end, forcing Athens into costly sieges, and leaving nothing for them to recoup financially if successful. The city would be destroyed and of no future use to the empire. With a lenient punishment, states will know that surrender is a bearable option, and this will weaken their resolve. Once returned to the empire, they can be impelled to accelerate their financial contributions to the defense of Athens.

Diodotus's argument carried the second day, barely, and a new punishment was negotiated. A ship of volunteer rowers was dispatched to Mytilene, and they rowed valiantly night and day to reach the city before it was too late. Just as the executioners were about to put sword to the population, a lookout spotted the incoming ship's signal, and waited to hear the news. The reduced punishment was still harsh. The thousand Mytileneans thought most responsible for the rebellion were executed, and the remainder stripped off their land and forced to work it as sharecroppers—paying directly to newly assigned Athenian landowners.

The Mytilenian example shows that the assembly was the source of all political power in Athens. But such a body is too cumbersome to carry out all administrative functions. So, a Council of 500 citizens was selected annually to organize the daily meetings and establish a speaking agenda. With a typical assembly holding in excess of 20,000 citizens, the council was vital, and its role critical. The Council of 500 would also be routinely appointed to execute decisions of the assembly. While the assembly highlights the power of the people, the council highlights its commitment to equality. One of the most incredible institutions in the democracy of Athens was the selection of council membership—by lottery! Imagine a belief in the political and legal equality of every person so strong that it could tolerate such a method. Every citizen, no matter how well endowed with intellect, oratory, or charisma, was equally liable to serve. Council members were selected for one-year terms, after which they could never again be re-appointed.

To prevent abuses while in office (beyond the structural institutions of severe term limits and random appointment), a Council of 501 was similarly selected to act as a judicial review board. Every officeholder, upon completion of service, was required to come before the board and refute all claims of corruption. If they could not, typical punishment was banishment. For many Athenians, who loved the city more than their own lives, banishment was a sentence worse than death.

Military affairs were somewhat less open to such radical egalitarian principles, though not much less. It was generally recognized that strategic and tactical prowess was a capacity both innate and honed through experience. Therefore generals, or *strategoi,* were elected to office. The public, in its aggregate wisdom, was thought to make the best selection here. Generals, like all other officials, had to be reviewed at the expiration of their term, usually one-year, and were subject to as many reelections as their competence allowed.

Citizenship in Greece was therefore extreme (the most radical until at least 1863–64 in the United States), and arguably, citizen participation has never been approximated. Of course, women and slaves were excluded from citizenship, as were the large population of foreign-born residents called *metics.* Through particularly meritorious military or personal service slaves could earn their freedom (slave generals were not unheard of) and metics could gain citizenship, but this was not as revolutionary as the notion that economic class should have no effect on citizenship. Rich or poor, one citizen had one vote.

How is it that Athens developed so radical a democracy if its essential military experience was so similar to other states of the day? Clearly, its economic and trade interests played a large part, as did the fortunate introduction of the great reformer Solon, but these factors do not account for the *radical* differences we observe. Other pro-democratic states, with similar trade interests, did not go as far politically as did Athens. Another variable is needed, and for a theory that assigns predominance to military organization, a military one should be readily evident.

The Fleet and Athenian Democracy
The reforms of Lycourgus and Solon were not unique in Hellas. Cypselos of Corinth, faced with similar problems, took the radical step of redistributing land to a large portion of his military serving population. The resulting growth of a middle class of

small landowners provided the basis for the respected hoplite citizen-army of Corinth. Wherever the phalanx was dominant, political inclusion was greater. But Athens developed *radically* democratic institutions. Hence the phalanx may be a *necessary* precondition for the emergence of Athenian-style radical democracy, but it clearly is not *sufficient*. Where Athens differed so obviously from Sparta and its less liberalized neighbors was in the unique organization and powerful influence of its navy.

Before the Classical Age, military ships and fleets were used exclusively as an appendage of the supply and reinforcement requirements of warfare; they moved troops and victuals. Fleets consisted of primarily trade vessels pressed into military service. It was actually the Phoenicians who developed the first war galleys, ships devoted solely to naval operations. They had no dual-commerce role, and so were of a significantly different design than the slower, large capacity trade vessels, but they were still primarily used for transport and occasionally for maneuvering to the side of another ship for boarding. Sometime quite shortly after the development of the phalanx the Greeks perfected the *trireme*, a long and narrow three-tiered multi-oared craft designed for high speed, maneuverability, and ramming.[40] This ship would have been extremely inefficient for commerce, but in war it was unmatched. The trireme quickly became the Greek's naval fighting vessel of choice.

Speed and maneuverability were the decisive factors in naval combat. In their search for faster and nimbler ships, Greek engineers found that in battle, the number of oars (relative to the weight of the ship) that could be brought to bear was the decisive element. To maximize the oar-to-mass ratio of their fleet, the Greeks developed a three-tiered system of interlocking oars. The result was an amazingly complex propulsion system that required tremendous coordination and practice to make it work. Massed manpower became the critical edge in naval combat just as it had recently become on land with the phalanx. The same impetus for dispersed political power that animated veterans of the phalanx became evident for sailors of the trireme.

Two techniques for naval combat then predominated: boarding, in which ships would negotiate near enough to an opponent that planks could be slung from deck to deck and hoplite auxiliaries could engage directly in land-style hand-to-hand combat; and ramming, in which one ship would propel itself toward another, employing its heavily armored prow to crash through the opponent's hull. Both techniques required a tremendous amount of maneuvering skill, coordinated rowing, discipline, stamina, and morale to be done effectively. Unlike trading or transport vessels, which required quality officers but unmotivated, even disinterested labor for propulsion, the trireme required highly skilled and inspired rowers to achieve a combat advantage. As in land combat, rabble and slaves as oarsmen were not generally as effective in naval battle as trained and highly motivated freemen. The technique for inspiring slaves to row with all possible effort was to chain them to the ship. If it sank, they went with it. No doubt this was motivating in battle, but probably not so in practice. Thus, free rowers that had worked and trained together generally proved superior to slave galleys. The psychological underpinning of morale and teamwork that influenced hoplites to seek democratic political institutions acted on the trireme rower. Each was an integral part of the whole.

Of interest, Quigley notes that in the debate over which tactics were preferable in naval engagements, democratic states tended to favor ramming while oligarchies went for boarding.[41] This is in part because oligarchs believed in the superiority of the individual hoplite warrior, and boarding fit well with their view of the navy as merely a conveyance to and from battle. Despite the fact that the individual hoplite was the combatant in boarding operations, the phalanx formation could *not* be employed in ship-to-ship battles. Hoplites fought alone at sea, an advantage for the style of heroic warfare in pro-authoritarian military organizations. Democrats preferred ramming because it required more sophisticated rowing and maneuver. It thus elevated the importance of the rowers, effectively making them integral combatants and not merely workers. Further, democracies were unhindered in using their abundant supply of free citizens as rowers, while oligarchies had to impress servants and serfs, or hired mercenaries, to do their rowing for them. On the sea, advantage went to those states that could accept their poorest members, who could serve the state militarily in no other manner, as full citizens.

Like Spartan warriors, who man-for-man were unmatched, Athenian ships, unit-for-unit, were unsurpassed in fighting prowess. This is partially explained by the fact that Athens was one of the first city-states to recognize the value of combat seapower, and aggressively pursued it, but mostly it is due to its capacity to crew the new warships with free citizens rather than mercenaries or slaves. By the time of the Persian War, Athens had already developed the world's largest and most powerful combat navy. Probably some four thousand oarsmen were needed to operate its ships. At the height of Athens' naval capacity during the Peloponnesian Wars, up to 10,000 rowers may have been trained and employed. In Athens, unlike anywhere else in Hellas, the oarsmen were recognized as vital on water as the hoplite on land, and were thus accorded equal privilege and political status in the community.

The most far-reaching Athenian political innovation, full citizenship to any male born of Athenian parents, regardless of social or economic class, is directly tied to this requirement of naval warfare. Most citizens of Athens agreed that the poorer elements of society were being called to shoulder a full share of the burden for the states' military and political autonomy, but were forced to provide a vastly disproportionate share of their personal resources in order to do so. The time required for training on the triremes, and the brutal effort involved, was extremely difficult for those on the edge of poverty to provide, regardless of their patriotism. Athens remedied the disparity by providing *all* citizens with a pike and hoplon (beyond the reinstituted reforms of Solon), and *paying wages* for combat sailors. This was a remarkable innovation for its day, coming at a time when Athens refused to pay for supplemental hoplite mercenaries (relying entirely on un-reimbursed citizen volunteers until the ill-fated Sicilian expedition). Nor did Athens ever institute any form of *compulsory* military service. To be sure, military participation was expected—it was a sign of vibrant political participation—but it was not mandatory. A poor citizen living at subsistence may have the highest loyalty and desire to serve his polis, but simply might not have the means to do so. All of his productive time would be spent in the pursuit of sustenance for his family. With the introduction of pay for naval service, even the poorest citizen could now fully participate in the defense, and hence the politics, of the city-state. Indeed, pay for service became an attractive option to civilian pursuits. Many citizens were able to make more in military service than in private life, presaging the modern argument that military service culls its recruits from the dregs of society. The result was that a vastly greater number of poor citizens were taking up arms and fighting for the polis than rich ones, and bit by bit gaining a proportionately greater share of political power.

Not only was the fleet and its unique manning requirements a spur to democracy, it became a bulwark for it. In 413 BCE, Syracuse with the help of Spartan leadership defeated a huge Athenian expeditionary force sent to conquer the island of Sicily (thought necessary to ensure the city's food supply should the Persians succeed in cutting off Black Sea grain). With at least a third of its military power destroyed, many of its allies seized upon this moment of Athenian weakness and declared their independence from the Delian League. In desperation, Athenians turned over their government to an oligarchy of 400, hoping it would be more efficient in war than democracy had been. It was not. The Athenian fleet remained stubbornly democratic and refused to comply with the commands of the new government, and forced the restoration of democracy to Athens.

At this point Thucydides's *History* ends. He died before completing the work. Fortunately, Xenophon picks up the tale in his history, *Hellenica*.[42] Not all of Athens erstwhile empire rebelled. Fearing a resurgence of Persian power in the political vacuum that would be left over in the event of Athenian collapse, a surprising number remained in the league. No doubt this was because Athens remained their best hope for retaining at least a semblance of autonomy, and the Greek cities preferred Athenian hegemony to Persian domination. Besides, if the enemy of my enemy is my friend, then the option of joining the Persian-financed Spartan side was suspect.

Ultimately, Persian support of Spartan naval operations turned the tide of war. Sparta could never have constructed a fleet with its own resources; hence, the Persian support was critical. But it came at a stiff price. Persia wanted Athens destroyed so it could regain control of the Asian coast, and possibly some of northern Greece. Sparta had built its reputation among former Athenian vassal states as a liberator, but its complicity with the Persians made the liberator claim incredible. Persia, for its part, began to play a delicate game of giving the Spartans just enough to threaten the Athenian navy, but not enough to create a significant counter to their own plans for later conquest.

After the restoration of democracy in Athens, the city tried to regain enough of its empire to remain indefinitely solvent. A Spartan-led, Persian-financed naval force defeated the Athenian fleet in 405 BCE at the battle of Aegospotami, and Spartan land forces were finally able to lay effective siege to the city. In 404 BCE, Athens unconditionally surrendered.

Sparta was remarkably lenient, considering the precedent set by the Athenians at Melos. It demanded all but 12 triremes of the Athenian navy be transferred to Sparta, and that the long wall between Athens and its port at Piraea be dismantled. In this way, Athens was militarily disabled but not destroyed. An oligarchic form of government, the Thirty Tyrants (whom Socrates refused to serve) was instituted by the Spartans, but was quickly overthrown and democracy was restored in 403 BCE. Ten years later, the long wall was rebuilt. Plato's *Academy* was established in 385 BCE. Still, Athens never recovered from war and plague, and by the end of the fourth century had half the population it had at the beginning of the war. Sparta fared even worse.

Its allies turned against it and the *helots* rebelled again and again. By the end of the fourth century, Spartan military prowess was legendary, but no longer a factor in Greek affairs.

Democracy in Athens would ultimately be crushed by outside invaders, first by the Spartans, then the Macedonians and Romans. After the Spartans departed to tend to bigger troubles at home, the democracy of Athens was revived and a Golden Age of art and literature ensued. Even under the control of Macedon, the Athenian citizen enjoyed greater individual freedom than virtually any contemporary city. As the phalanx was proven inferior to the legion, and the navy was utterly defeated precedent to Roman occupation, military service became the exception for Athenians. Gradually, democratic influences fell away, and the military was reorganized to promote an authoritarian form of government.

Military Reform and Spartan Republicanism
Athens was the most radically democratic of the Greek city-states, due to its incorporation of the masses into its navy. But there were other forms of democracy and republicanism in Hellas. Each was unique and based on a particular form of military service. Sparta, Athens' longtime nemesis, is a classic case.

Sparta was founded by invading Dorians in the tenth century, and by 800 BCE was a conglomerate of four unwalled villages ruled by two hereditary kings with separate and distinct lineages. Situated at the center of the largest and most fertile valley in mainland Greece, for much of its early history Sparta went about the business of subjugating its nearby neighbors. In time, Sparta came into control of a rather smallish empire, and in the process created a distinct set of social and political institutions. Individuals were classified by their status relative to Spartan citizens, and territories by their relative autonomy. The latter were defined essentially by distance from the core city, and had increasing autonomy the further they were from Sparta proper. Nearest the city were the conquered territories of indigenous peoples the Spartans called *helots*. This was the empire of Sparta. Several nearby city-states were forced into unequal alliances with the Spartans, and this was their ring of hegemonic dominance. These cities were useful to the Spartans because they supplied both tribute and conscripts to support the Spartan army. They could not decide foreign policy, but so long as they met their tax and conscript quotas they were allowed to rule themselves domestically. Finally there were the Spartan Allies proper. These were completely independent states that had forged a regional and durable alliance called the Peloponnesian League. The League was entirely voluntary but stable because of the mutual benefit the major states provided. As we shall see, the Spartan military was unmatched man for man, but was too small to conduct major campaigns. In return for mutual loyalty, Sparta could count on phalanxes from the Peloponnesian states, and the allies could request and receive Spartan trainers and officers to bolster their military units.

The individual subclasses of the Spartan system were *slaves*, individuals purchased by Spartan citizens to do domestic chores, carry and maintain equipment, and occasionally oversee financial interests; *helots*, the wretched former denizens of the fertile Spartan plain who were formally property of the state and attached to the land in a serf–feudal relationship; and the *perioikos*, relatively autonomous non-Spartan city dwellers who conducted the financial and trade operations forbidden to Spartan citizens, but necessary for the functioning of a city of any size. The worst off of these were the helots. At least the slave was subject to manumission, and could be freed by his master. And slaves were freed, quite typically for bravery in or in support of battle. A helot, as property of the state and tied to the land, could never be set free.[43]

The Spartan notion of citizenship was based in its practice of providing each Spartan-born warrior with a plot of land from which to receive supporting revenue. As its population grew, Sparta was pressed to conquer new lands to endow its combatants. But the benefits of ownership in the new lands were given only to those who fought in the campaigns to take them. After the Messenian Wars of the late eighth and early seventh centuries, a significant number of young warriors who grew up during the campaigns but were too young to fight came of age, and found themselves economically and politically disadvantaged relative to the older veterans. The Spartan leadership claimed that these young warriors were not fathered by Spartans (who had spent considerable time away from home in the Messenian campaigns), but probably by rapacious perioikoi (or even helots) in their absence, and therefore didn't deserve a plot of land. They were dubbed *Partheniai*, or offspring of unmarried mothers.[44] This younger generation claimed they were being systematically disenfranchised by an older and cowardly generation that feared going to war to secure new lands. Even their requests to go to war on their own, to carve out viable lands for themselves, were denied by the elders. These parthenai had been trained for war and were prepared to fight for their desired status, and rankled at their subordinated political positions. A rebellion was plotted but failed in execution. The young warriors involved were sent forth from the city to establish a colony in southern Italy, where it was hoped they would no longer pose an internal problem.

The rebellion was symptomatic of the central political problem in Sparta, brought on by the increasing number of now fully armed and trained warriors demanding an equal political and economic voice. The export of dissidence through colonization was a temporary measure at best, and had the added problem of sending the best and most dynamic of its citizenry abroad, never to return. In part due to this intentional draining of its manpower, combined with a decided *lack* of military discipline, Sparta began to lose control over its territory. Sometime after 675 BCE, possibly after the shattering Spartan defeat at the hands of the Argives in the Battle of Hysia (669 BCE), need for a radical change in the sociopolitical structure of Sparta was obvious. In the wake of ignominious defeat, and with its proud tradition in tatters, Sparta was ready to heed the call of reform.

The great lawgiver prince of the Spartans was Lykourgos. He established the Spartan Constitution known as the *rhetra* sometime after 665 BCE, and while it was therefore not the 400-year-old Constitution Thucydides wrote of in his *History*, it was the oldest and longest lasting constitution of the Greek World, admired throughout Hellas for its wisdom and stability. To be sure, in a world constantly wreaked by war and violence, stability was a highly prized trait. Recognizing that military factors were at the heart of Sparta's problems, Lykourgos's first actions were to lay down a system of rules for military education that emphasized discipline and loyalty to the state. Only then, after dictating changes to the military that society as a whole might have been unable to accept, did Lykourgos reform the Spartan social structure and construct its constitution. *All* citizens, roughly defined as those born of Spartans who had survived their military training, *and* who had received land in conquered territory with assigned helot laborers, were granted rights in the assembly. These citizens called themselves *homoioi* ("equals"), because their citizenship provided them with a recognized *minimum* of established political and legal rights. Spartan citizens were not considered equal before the law, but a floor of basic rights and privileges were nonetheless assured.

It was only in the wake of Lykourgos's harsh military reforms that Sparta gained its notorious reputation for stoicism and its mind-boggling martial tradition. The process of becoming a warrior, and from there a citizen, was rigorous to a point of disbelief. Spartan mothers raised all male children until they were weaned, between the ages of three and four. At this point they would be placed outside the home with no clothing or resources, expected to survive on their own. If they managed to reach the age of six, through hunting and thievery, they were apprenticed to a young adult warrior, who would oversee their military education and physical training. Sparta was essentially a homosexual society, and the boy was not only the squire of the older warrior, but his lover as well. The practice was intended to build even closer bonds than just those shared by men who fought with each other in combat. All warriors resided in the barracks and ate in a common mess. Their typical meal was a mash of barley and honey, supplemented by whatever meats were retrieved by the younger boys. After a life in which all activities but the martial arts were forbidden to him, and presumably after several glorious campaigns, at the age of 30 he would receive a plot of land, complete with helots to work it, as his means of personal support. At this time his old trainer and erstwhile lover would arrange to find him a wife, so that the procreation of future generations could commence. The warrior continued to reside in the barracks and eat at the common mess until the age of 60, when he could retire to his home if he so desired.

So rigorous was this training that no warrior from any other state could match the Spartans in one-on-one combat. So powerful had the myth of Spartan invulnerability become that contemporaries believed no Spartan soldier had ever surrendered in combat. Their lot was to fight until victory, or until death. It was said that to fight the Spartans one needed ten times the force, so as only to be equal. Fortunately for most opponents, such a force was not difficult to gather. The process of becoming a true Spartan warrior-citizen was so grueling that only a small number made it to adulthood. By the beginning of the Second Peloponnesian War, it is likely that there were less than 4,000 Spartan warrior-citizens all told; by the end, there were fewer than 2,000. When the Roman conquests finally came, there may have been fewer than 400 Spartan warriors alive, and their brilliant if ruthless culture came to a discomfiting end. Spartans were sold as slaves to carnivals and freak shows, where they were kept in cages. For a few coppers one could poke through the bars at the Spartan with a stick, making him bleed but verifying that he would not cry out in pain, no matter how agonizing the torture.

Although Lykourgos's reforms were in response to civil strife engendered by younger warriors against older, the pervasive continuing problem for the Spartans was their brutal occupation of the Peloponnesus and the indigenous helots. Outnumbered perhaps twenty to one by their feudal serfs, the helots were constantly disposed to rebel, and did so at the merest sign of Spartan weakness. Though the origin of the dual monarchy (two equal kings) system is obscure, there is little doubt that it was retained because of the contingent requirements of fielding both externally oriented and home-based suppression armies. One king would lead no more than half the Spartans on campaign while the other would stay home with the remaining forces to quell domestic disturbances. While military leadership was imparted to these warrior-kings, real political (decision-making) power was not theirs. It was placed instead in the citizen assembly and two higher ruling councils.

The Spartan assembly was open to all citizens—a distinct minority to be sure, but essentially all adult males (warriors) of Spartan lineage. All citizens could speak there, but voting privileges and office holding within the assembly were stratified. The assembly existed primarily to pass information, up and down the military–political hierarchy, and select representatives to the Council of Elders. For political decisions such as when to go to war, with whom to ally, tax rates, and the like, the Council of Elders functioned as the executive authority. There were 30 members of this council; the 2 hereditary kings and 28 aristocrats elected for life from the ranks of Spartan citizens who had achieved the venerated age of 60. Both the size of the council and the presumed wisdom of the aged warriors enhanced the reputation of the Spartans as slow to act, and very conservative.

The Council of Elders elected from its own members five officials called *ephors*. The official duties of the ephors were primarily in judicial review, but their unofficial status as the most respected of the warrior-elite allowed them to make a broad array of decisions that were abided by all members of the state. It was the ephors who, in 426 BCE, made a series of momentous decisions that led to the interim Peace of Nicias, and changed Hellenic politics forever. In that year, a party of Athenians en route to Sicily noticed that the ancient fort of Pylos on the west coast of the Peloponnesus had been abandoned. They correctly reasoned that if fortified and manned, the site would be an excellent staging base for arming and supplying the ever-rebellious helots. Sparta, recognizing the strategic value of Pylos, decided to lay siege. Because of the location of Pylos at the end of a narrow peninsula, the adjacent island of Sphacteria had to be taken before any kind of successful assault could be launched. A force of more than 400 Spartan veterans landed on Sphacteria to prepare the attack. By virtue of some extraordinary good fortune, an Athenian fleet happened by that was able to cut the Spartans off from the mainland and strand them on the small island. The Athenians next burned the island's heavily forested vegetation to the ground. From their ships and from Pylos, the Athenians were able to harass the Spartans—now without cover and mired in choking ashes—with stones and arrows. The ephors assembled on a mountain overlooking the scene and quickly realized it would be impossible to reinforce their fellows through traditional means. They decreed that any helot who could swim to the island with bladders of fresh water and food would be freed from the land that had bound them for so long, an unprecedented manumission. Befitting a process described earlier, direct *military* service—if not direct combat—was worthy evidence of expanded political rights. The effects of that decree were mixed. A number of helots took up the challenge and performed the required functions, allowing the Spartans to hold out. But that was merely the short-term affect. The notion that helots now *could* be freed through valorous service intensified their innate desires for liberty. For the rest of its existence, Sparta would need the majority of its troops to remain home to quell helot ambitions.

Amazingly, the Spartans held out for 72 days, though by the end their number had dwindled to just 120 hoplites left alive. Exhausted, starved, and gravely wounded as these few Spartans were, the Athenians still found it prudent to land 2,400 slingers, archers, and hoplites on the island to mount a final attack. So impotant were the lives of these 120 warriors, now perhaps 5 percent of the remaining citizenry, that the ephors demanded the besieged surrender. They then offered to accept virtually any terms for an equitable peace as ransom in order to recover them.

Athens wanted to wring maximum concessions from the Spartans, and refused to negotiate realistically. They paraded the Spartans to cheering throngs at home, and kept them prisoners for four years. The entire Greek world was in shock at the spectacle. That Spartans might surrender rather than die fighting was astounding. The prestige accorded Athens was immense, particularly in view of the fact that before the victory at Sphacteria, the Athenians had been getting the worst of the war. In time, Athens realized the war had stalemated and accepted the Spartan offer to negotiate terms. The subsequent Peace of Nicias was uneasy to say the least, and before long Athenian adventurism undermined the treaty. Yet the power of the ephors was clear. No other person or group could have made such momentous decisions, contrary to the very culture of the Spartan state, than this group of old warriors.

Thus the proper political view of Sparta is not as a militaristic oligarchy, without rules or law or respect for individual rights, but as a unique military republic the like of which we shall never see again. Whereas the specifics of the Spartan constitution could not have been projected from the correlations discussed in chapter two, the inevitable and inexorable move to a more power-dispersed form of government is easily discerned. A breakdown of military characteristics for the Spartan armed forces would show a similar overall path toward decentralization as that of Athens, Argos, or Corinth, but with specific differences. The subtle contrasts in Spartan and Athenian military organization suggests that while both states had significant liberalizing influences, Athenian political structures would be expected to be more democratic than those of Sparta, and indeed this is the case.

Conclusions

Greek rediscovery of the coordinated military formation laid the foundation for the establishment of citizenship-based city-states. The phalanx represented the increase in wealth and rise of upward mobility coincident with the emergence of Hellas from its Dark Age. Increasing numbers of individuals could afford the panoply of equipment that marked a warrior, and the new warriors began to assert themselves politically. Bands of foot soldiers working in concert were able to defeat the mounted knight who so clearly represented the old monarchies, but only if they relied upon and worked closely with each other. This fusion of individuals into a coherent whole represented the kernel of democratic government.

After 500 BCE, preparation for external war was constant, and required a predominant share of city-state resources. Athens, for example, was at war 2 out of every 3 of the 150 years separating the beginning of the Persian Wars (490 BCE) and the Battle of Chaeronea (338 BCE).[45] Moreover, war in this age was often total war. A city-state that succumbed was at the mercy of its conqueror. Total destruction could be expected. In wars of aristocrats, when only the well born were armed and fought, the peasant's liability in war was tangential. Starving was a distinct possibility if fields were destroyed or soldiers were quartered for an extensive period, but the political fortunes of the disenfranchised were rarely changed in battles of this nature. It was simply not to the aristocrat's advantage to destroy those peasants he might acquire in battle. But in the Classical Age, when all had a duty to participate in war, all could be held equally liable for its outcomes.

Offensive operations steadily rose in the period, from virtual nonexistence before 800 BCE to a relatively common occurrence four centuries later. By the Peloponnesian Wars, Athens had developed an offensive guerrilla strategy that included amphibious landings at weak Spartan positions. The tactic was to sail out of protected ports and, after disabling enemy fleets, land here and there on the enemies' coastal areas and lay waste to cities and fields in their homelands. Attica, the area around Athens, was voluntarily abandoned in recognition of the Spartan League's land superiority. Had the Athenians not maintained naval superiority, they would have had to accept battle or capitulate (and in the end, when Persian finances supported a Spartan fleet that effectively countered the Athenian one, that is exactly what happened). Clearly this is a strategy that recognizes an inability to occupy territory. Nonetheless, there are authoritarian impulses at work. Despite its guerilla strategy versus the Spartans, Athens was able to maintain an extensive economic empire and did attempt to occupy Sicily. The empire was militarily subjugated by the capacity to control commercial sea lanes, however, meaning that Athens did not have to occupy its empire to maintain it, and that fact is significant. Athens' small population (the largest in Greece but still not over 250,000 at any time) made physical occupation and policing of its empire impossible.

Reliance on combined drill grows during the period, but for the Athenians is even more influential than in the other Greek city-states, due to its incredibly well-trained navy. Rowers needed to train together on a regular basis, as did the phalanx if it was to be effective. There were some exceptions even to this general rule. Beyond common drill in hoplite warfare, a few combatants would be trained (or would train themselves) in the more sophisticated battle arts, such as archery and fencing.[46] These skilled arms-bearers were more likely culled from the richer families, as the schools were not publicly funded. And they were barely integrated into strategy. Acting as adjuncts, they were tactically useful but not honored in the same manner as the hoplites or rowers.

Militarism had reached a democratic nadir in aristocratic Greece, but in the more democratic states had begun wane by the Classical Age. With the end of the Second Peloponnesian War, and the clear demise of Athenian military power, military glorification faded significantly. Although Athenians admired their military—especially naval—prowess, and felt all had a military duty to the state, by the Golden Age of Athens philosophers and artisans were the most venerated citizens. Yet, even before this, Thucydides tells us that Athens was the first city in which citizens walked about unarmed.[47] The antithesis of militarism is the development of a military science, the art of battle, and a shift in military concerns from individual glory to functional service for the state. In this area, Athenians probably led the way in Classical Greece. Naval battle tactics were the most developed in the world. By the fifth century BCE, building on its scholastic tradition, military arts were being taught by professional drillmasters in permanent military schools.[48]

All of this led to a remarkable lack of internal stratification, perhaps the profoundest change from three centuries earlier. This democratizing factor was maximized in Classical Athens after salaried service in the fleet was instituted, but falls short of modern conceptions. The criterion of providing *equal quality* arms (necessary in the phalanx formation) for citizens who could not afford them was unprecedented, and in Athens may have led to the revolution that provided its superior navy. The contention that navies have an inherent democratizing capacity that land forces do not has already been described and refuted in this study. The Athenian example is affirmed by the expedient fact that Athens was a functioning republic (if not a radical democracy) before it possessed a large military fleet. In the Athenian context, however, the fleet had a marked influence in *reinforcing* the commitment to universal franchise in an already democratized state. There is a common assumption among historians that slave labor figured heavily in the fleets of antiquity, at the very least in time of extraordinary levy (emergency in war), but quite commonly in routine commerce. There is little reason to believe that the Athenians would not have continued the practice were enough slaves available to crew the war fleet. Having made every Athenian-born male a full citizen after the hoplite reforms, Athens was forced to use its citizens in the labor-intensive, punishing role of oarsmen. That a full citizen could be used effectively in a role generally reserved for slaves was remarkable. Hoplite service brought commoners into roles traditionally reserved for nobility. Naval service brought them into roles normally associated with the lowest classes. Both were accorded equality of status under the law, and it may have gone a long way in tearing down extant social barriers.

Loyalty to the state reaches its premodern zenith here as well. After the expansion of citizenship following the hoplite reforms, poets began to write of love of polis, and loyalty to one's city, as the highest moral value. By the time of Pericles, service to the state was the highest Athenian ideal. Unfortunately, the sway of demagogues made it possible for Athenian loyalties to quickly turn. Perhaps it was because the democracy rose so quickly, and fell too soon, that the idea of the state never took firm enough roots to justify Pericles's magnificent speech.

So we see that changes in strategy and tactics, combined with revolutions in weapons technology, significantly influenced the development of political institutions in ancient and classical Greece. While it would have been impossible to predict the specifics of Spartan republicanism and Athenian democracy from the vantage of 800 or even 700 BCE, an understanding of the impact of military organization on the future of political institutions should have led an outside observer to conclude that both states would become distinctly less centralized and authoritarian. Of the two, military innovation and change in Athens was more radical, and greater movement toward democratic political institutions should have been expected.

CHAPTER FOUR
EARLY REPUBLICS: SWITZERLAND, THE DUTCH, AND FRANCE

War is an ugly thing, but not the ugliest of things. The decayed and degraded state of moral and patriotic feeling which thinks that nothing is worth war is much worse. The person who has nothing for which he is willing to fight, nothing which is more important than his own personal safety, is a miserable creature and has no chance of being free unless made and kept so by the exertions of better men than himself.

John Stuart Mill (1873)

Profound social change is often preceded by technological innovation. The stirrup, for example, has been credited with transforming post-Roman Europe into a feudal society locally dominated by petty overlords.[1] With the ability to stand solidly on stirrups attached to a saddle, instead of clinging precariously with the pressure of one's knees, a mounted warrior could bring to bear the full impact of his arm and beast, and a devastating charge on the battlefield could sweep away any unorganized resistance. Those who could afford the expense of full body and horse armor, plus maintenance for himself, his horse, and his retinue, could presume to assert political dominance over a relatively compact area. Appropriately, with the demise of the Western Roman Empire, the sociopolitical system that emerged in the Medieval Europe was characterized by a large number of dispersed and relatively independent fiefdoms.

The post-Renaissance gunpowder revolution changed all that.[2] With relatively little training, a musketeer could defeat a knight in combat, whose lifetime of preparation in the martial arts would end in a flash. Guns changed not only the face of battle, but also the fabric of society. Few were surprised. A similar antiaristocratic innovation, the crossbow, had caused a furor with its introduction a few centuries before. In 1139, Pope Innocent II organized an international conference to outlaw this horrible new weapon, in full knowledge that its widespread use would threaten the extant social order. Combat would become plebianized, proponents of the nobility argued, without chivalric honor. The deleterious effects of such a weapon on political stability were obvious, and terrifying. Despite the laws, crossbows entered into common use, in castle defense particularly, but also at the side of many a nobleman who could afford it. But the sociopolitical revolution so many expected, to be spawned by legions of crossbowmen triumphant in battle, never occurred.

The reasons are simple, if not obvious. It did not threaten the fortified castle, and ammunition was expensive. Mostly, however, it lacked the vital organizational ingredient of the gunpowder revolution; no radical restructuring of the military was needed to deploy it. Unlike the gun, the crossbow was integrated into the extant organization as simply another type of muscle-powered projectile. Less useful than the English long bow on the extended battlefield, but highly accurate and deadly in close quarters, it was simply another choice in the panoply of weapons available to the professional warrior.

The handheld gun did not enter onto the scene fully formed. The first useful application of gunpowder in Western warfare was as a bombard—a siege weapon. The crossbow, even in its enormous manifestation called the trebuchet, could not break down the walls of the noble elite. The lords remained ensconced in their citadels with only an increased wariness in their ventures outward. The bombard and cannon ended that defensive advantage, the last bastion of noble independence. With castle walls falling around him, the knight was forced to come out and fight. Once on the battlefield, no mass of mounted warriors could withstand a concentrated volley of gunfire from an organized contingent of disciplined soldiers. Aristocrats who could afford large harquebusier and pike armies began to consolidate their territories. Advances in metallurgy, long-distance shipping, and bureaucratic innovations made gunpowder—in all its military manifestations—desirable and unstoppable. Armed forces grew. Military power could be mathematically determined by a simple count of who could field the most guns, and the democratization of Europe slowly but inexorably spread.

The revolution was not immediate, but evolved over two centuries. Early on, direct involvement of ordinary citizens in war was still widely considered undesirable. Burghers would rise to the defense of besieged cities, and militias would be formed for specific, and short, campaigns. But any long-term public mobilization was clearly dangerous to the social order. So the organizational innovation that emerged in response to the increased manpower needs of the nobility were the independent professional mercenary units, the military entrepreneurs of their age. These were the *compagnies d'ordonnance* of France and Burgundy, the *freischützen* of Germany, and the *condottieri* of Italy.[3] Mercenary armies provided their own weapons and training, and contracted for specific battles or campaigns. Naturally, they obtained the latest in technological development, especially firearms and cannon. Hence, they were cost-efficient for the usually cash-strapped nobility. Pay-as-you-go wars could be fought with cash reserves or on credit. And not just the aristocracy employed them. When a nobleman defaulted on a loan, the Italian bankers would just as readily employ the condottieri to aid in collection.

The transformation of combat from the heroic, and in many ways symbolic, chivalric code to the profit-seeking formations of professional mercenaries had some unanticipated side effects. As the usefulness of the traditional man-at-arms, whose "equipment and servitors was thus proving both inefficient on the battlefield, and expensive to sustain" diminished, "so their pretensions grew. Their armor became impossibly ornate, their tournaments more costly, their social status more jealously hedged around a heraldic lore."[4] A military force that is never used, nor has any reason to think it will be, in this way fosters true militarism. The larger and more militarily useless the nobility became, the more entrenched was its opposition to liberal reform.

The direct effect of the transformation from fealty to paid professional service was in its impact on the organization of the state system. The hire of "free lances" initially "enhanced the power of the princes—so long as they had the money to pay for them."[5] But as the size of forces grew in order to prevail, the size of the treasuries dwindled. Power became based on money, and the great banking houses began arbitrating the relative differences between states. The loyalty of the aristocracy quickly became less important than the health of the economy, and the ability to extract taxes and fees from the population. With the rise of the mercenary army, and then paid citizen-militias, came the reform of the state bureaucracy, and its direct involvement in the lives of every citizen for securing revenue. The apparatus of the state grew, and so did the organization of the citizenry. More and more the princes were required to call forth the parliaments, estates, and diets to exchange revenue information. The king or lord would gather the non-noble representatives of society to prevail upon them for more funds, essentially providing a justification for war in order to collect taxes more efficiently. In return, the representatives could tell the king how much they were able to pay without unduly disrupting the economy. Ultimately, the assemblies would tie appropriations discussions to approval and consent, and through the power of the purse, assert their independence.

Internal revenue was hardly the only source for expanding the state coffers. War had always been a means of amassing wealth, and conquest and consolidation of territory expanded greatly as the vicious cycle of war making and war funding spiraled. Originally drawn from surplus population under the aegis of feudal lords and kings, the most notorious mercenaries were those soldiers deployed in foreign lands. In support of homeland defense, mercenaries would often be restricted from plunder, and would require payment from the treasury. In support of foreign invasions, as was the case of the lengthy English campaign in France, their pay could be taken from the lands they ravaged. It was also in foreign service that the mercenaries would become perversely professionalized. It soon became the interest of these soldiers-for-hire to prolong the outcome of war to extend their period of paid service.[6] Some bands became entirely independent of the nobility and marched from estate to estate, city to city, demanding payment for the privilege of not being sacked. Such a system cannot be maintained, and the transfer from mercenary forces whose loyalty was dependent on a fickle treasury to civilian ones whose loyalty was to the state was perhaps inevitable. The story of that transformation is illustrated by the evolving roles of the Swiss, then Dutch and French contributions to military organization and change.

The Swiss Model

The Swiss developed a rudimentary federal-republican governing form before the introduction of gunpowder, a story that highlights the role of military organization in state building at the expense of mono-trajectory explanations drawn solely from technology. The Alpine Swiss provinces, or cantons, were relatively poor regions that had marginal economic returns from herding. Pastoral rights were the apex of law and politics, and to ensure them all able-bodied herders were encouraged to bear arms. For this reason, a strong aristocratic authoritarian government did not emerge. When invading military entrepreneurs entered with the notion of establishing fiefdoms, a call went out to defend the meager grazing lands. A rapid and unified response was required of the entire body politic. Invaders were ambushed as they passed through narrow mountain passageways by herders armed with *halberds*. These were enormous long-handled axes intended to penetrate the heavy armor of the knights as they were trapped in mountain defiles by smashing down on them from ledges high above. They also had a point and hook, for stabbing and pulling the horseman from his mount.[7] Alpine battles were brutal, and quick. Few lords with expansive goals found it worth the danger to subjugate the cantons given their low economic return. Not only was invasion difficult and deadly, the cost of maintaining a garrison would not likely be recovered. Military necessity and preference in response to geographic imperatives prevented the establishment of feudalism, and allowed a basic association of relatively independent yeomen to endure.

Despite its location in the middle of Europe, the Swiss cantons were treated as an obstacle to be gone round for most of its history, rather than as a strategic military location or high ground. But "the construction of a bridge over the gorge of Schoellenen opened the Gotthard Pass, transforming the medieval alpine [region] into a major route of passage, taking two-thirds of the traffic between the burgeoning economies of Italy and the Low Countries."[8] With the flow of trade came income, and with wealth came a burgeoning population that could not be supported by the local economy. It also finally made the cantons an enviable target for imperial expansion, as it sat astride the two halves of the Hapsburg and Holy Roman Empires. Unable to penetrate the cantons for conquest, the Empires attempted a strategic blockade. Several of the cantons formed a defensive alliance in response, and in 1393 formally united into a political confederation with a representative Diet.

All men from the age of 16 to 60 were now obligated by law to carry arms and participate in the defense of the community. In return, they were considered full citizens of the Republic. This action is the font of Swiss political liberty, modeled on the Germanic tribal form of general levy in return for general political participation. The defensive requirements of the realm, in which citizens of all cantons came to the aid of any that was attacked, meant that mobilization had to be extremely swift—and quite short. The incursion needed to be repulsed quickly so that the herder-citizen could return to his property and manage his household. Thus, the Swiss preferred to engage as soon as possible. As invading armed forces increased in size, and more and more the Swiss were confronted with invading units of foot soldiers, their weapon of choice changed from the halberd to the pike, or long spear.[9] Their formation changed with it, from the mass of hacking halberdiers to one of coordinated phalanx, drawn directly from the Greek model of Alexander. The halberd underwent transition, and the size of the axe decreased until it was little more than a decoration on the extremely long pikes of the phalanx. As with the ancients, from whom they drew inspiration, the effectiveness of the pike "depended absolutely on the men remaining in these formations, since individual pikemen with their eighteen-foot weapons were almost entirely helpless against more agile, more lightly armed opponents of every kind."[10] Delbrück provides an account of the Swiss method in his description of the

Battle of Laupen (1339).[11] The Swiss formed up (habitually) into three large squares, or phalanxes, with pikes bristling from the front. The first square was 30 by 30, formed of a thousand rugged woodsmen from the forest cantons. The main unit followed, comprising 3,000 men placed in a 50 by 50 square. The third square, a rear guard, was composed of 2,000 men, arranged in a 40 by 40 square. In front of each were a number of crossbowmen and other skirmishers to harass and confuse the enemy. Contemporary preference for pikemen (occasionally used in England and Holland) was to operate as static "hedgehogs," a battlefield deterrent to cavalry charges. At Laupen, the opposing forces spent most of the day encircling the Swiss squares. The first two squares maintained their positions, but the rear guard—thinking the probing encirclement had isolated them from the main force—panicked and fled. At that point, the mass of invading knights charged the front square. Perhaps because the light was fading, and the knights did not relish the thought of retiring without glory, their patience broke. The square rebuffed the charge, which was unable to penetrate the dense bristle of pikes. Then came an enormous surprise. The Swiss had been training in the ancient tactic of charging with the pike formation, using shock to dislodge the enemy. Once the knights had been weakened by the static defense, the main body began to run forward. The front square engaged the remaining knights and separated them from their accompanying foot soldiers before settling into an indecisive standstill. The main square charged and routed the unprotected infantry, and then moved to relieve the front square, completely overwhelming the knights and winning a stunning victory. As with the ancients, the only way this could work was if the troops were disciplined and held solidly together.

When Charles the Bold of Burgundy invaded the Bernese Canton in retaliation for an incursion into his territory, he had assembled some 14,000 men and the largest concentration of artillery ever fielded.[12] He was faced with 19,000 Swiss pikemen, but at least 9,000 of his professional soldiers were equipped with the latest firearms. Supremely confident in the capacities of his professional compagnies d'ordonnance, Charles marched out to engage the Swiss, who appeared hesitant to attack his fortified camp. The Swiss had become rightfully wary of artillery. Their close-packed squares were easy targets, and an accurate cannonade could completely disrupt their tactics. Whenever artillery was unavoidable, the Swiss would move quickly against it, limiting the volleys that could be dispatched, and securing propitious conditions for the rest of the battle. In this case, the Swiss marched quickly to meet the Burgundians while they were still on the move, so they would not have time to set up their cannon. The sudden appearance of Swiss forces surprised the Burgundians, but the relative strengths of the two sides meant that the battle was far from decided. For some reason, still unknown, the rear forces of the Burgundians panicked and fled. The main body thought it had been surrounded, and in its own panic was routed.[13] The stolid reputation of the Swiss warrior was confirmed.

Because contemporaries understood the relationship between citizen-armies and citizenship, the Swiss model was not copied until 1479, and then only by the desperate Burgundians who had experienced its power firsthand.[14] Maximillian, husband of Charles the Bold's daughter Mary, employed the system in the Battle of Guinegate in a rout of the French. The French were arrayed in the manner of the professionals of the day, in compagnies and with considerable knights and archers. Maximillian's force was smaller, but it was organized by a Swiss count in the manner of his country. Of note, the soldiers he used were from the Burgundian provinces in the Low Countries, who would take the military knowledge and skills to their homes and apply it in an eventually successful revolt.

More battles and more victories, not with the new technologies but with the ancient tactics, made the Swiss highly desirable mercenaries. And there were many available. Once again, the burgeoning economy had led to an unsustainable population, and the defensive political constitution of the Republic precluded territorial expansion. In time, the Swiss found they could extract a communal profit from the mercenary business, as its mobilization system was perfectly adapted for the transition to mercenary entrepreneurship. When a call for soldiers came, the canton would select the appropriate number of young men to go to battle, something often done by lot. The number would be limited by the amount of time the force was expected to be away (usually a function of distance) divided by available rations and pack animals, as the relatively poor cantons and towns were expected to victual their soldiers. Often, due to the expectation of booty, more men were ready to march than could be supported, and so some would go to battle on their own.[15] For mercenary wars, the canton or town would negotiate a price for a fixed number of warriors. The community would then provide token pay to its citizens (who were anxious to go for the possibility of riches in loot and booty, and not for their paltry portion of the negotiated fee), and pocket the rest. The cantons did provide a nominal service for their interdiction. They made strict limits on the use of the pikemen, including a requirement that they be subject to recall in time of emergency and that they remained under Swiss and not martial law.[16] For the good of the community, young Swiss were encouraged to seek their fortunes in the pay of foreign armies.

The Swiss apparently did not routinely drill or train in common. The rudimentary phalanx had two requirements; stay in step and stay together—functions that could be practiced on the march. They acquired expertise in pikesmanship on their own time, and were expected to come to battle with their weapons and ready to fight. They were, in addition, notoriously brutal. It was said the Swiss would not take prisoners, but kill all that they faced. More of an effective psychological advantage than truth in all cases, the hard lifestyle of the mountain herder enhanced the overall image of Swiss military effectiveness. Indeed, their code of military discipline was harsh. If they failed to show for a call to arms, their house was destroyed. If they ran from battle or called for others to do so, they could be struck dead on the spot. Delbrück asserts it was this *discipline*, combined with the repeated success of the squares, which made the army so egalitarian yet managed to leave a privileged civilian hierarchy in place. Passions of the peasantry for more influence in canton affairs were bought off by success against foreign armies, and by the mercenary wages and other loot they received from foreign adventures.[17]

The local governments also tended to use part of the skim from mercenary payments for public works. Most important to the stunted growth of liberal democracy in the cantons, despite its republican foundation, there was no invasion threat to generate any kind of democratic bargain between the soldiers and the aristocracy. Wealth was the payout for military service. Military organization that included a high percentage of the population in arms, emphasized discipline, and provided an outlet for upward social mobility helped move the Swiss cantons to a more dispersed form of governing power. But a lack of coordinated training, focus on defensive strategy, and a glorification of the mercenary soldier prevented a full transition to liberal democracy.

The Swiss model ushered in the first real military–social revolution of the modern era. Geoffrey Parker asserts, "The first important break from the conventions which dominated medieval warfare was the triumph of Swiss pike squares over the mounted knights of Burgundy in a series of pitched battles (1475–77) [that] removed a crucial restriction on the scale of warfare in Europe."[18] The warhorse and retinue was expensive, and in addition legally restricted to social rank. "There was no such bar to the number of men who could be recruited and issued with a helmet and sixteen-foot pike."[19] In the past, armies had been small and highly socialized. Combatants knew each other, and combat was often symbolic, usually limited. The new order meant that success would be determined by the size of the forces involved, and in the face of fire and steel, on their discipline.

The Rise of the Dutch Republic, 1477–1621

One of the common denominators of the early republics was a fortuitous geographic position. The Swiss were protected by the Alps, the Venetians, and the Dutch by estuaries and swamps. All occupied less desirable terrain in terms of wealth or potential agrarian revenue, providing them respite from wandering brigands and conquering armies. Perhaps because of it, they sought alternate routes to wealth. As they sought efficient means to protect their growing resources, all became innovators in warfare.

The Dutch position at the edge of Europe was fortuitous in many ways. The region had long been perceived a "seedbed of theological, intellectual, and social promiscuity."[20] Hendrik Van Loon attributes a location near the sea to its liberal character: "the country was not favorable for the development of petty tyrants. Liberty has always followed the shores of the ocean. [In a country] open on all sides and surrounded by water, the disgruntled subject could sail away and begin a new life within the walls of some near-by city."[21] Where a government is based on force and coercion, it must continually apply force to prevent its people from seeking a more benevolent alternative. Where territory can be consolidated easily, as in the great empires of the Middle East, there may be nowhere for the downtrodden to go. In the Netherlands, there was an opportunity cost advantage in good government, and a tradition of debate as to what precisely constituted the best state.

But its liberal character and economic prowess were not the only sources of contemporary wonder. "Military men took a keen interest, especially in the period down to 1648, in the military revolution carried through in the United Provinces . . . characterized not only by innovations in artillery, tactics, fortification, siege techniques, and military transportation, but by a vast improvement in the discipline and orderliness of the military."[22] Discipline became the real basis of the relationship between the soldier-citizen and the modern state, not gunpowder or any technical innovation. Although a significant portion of the population served in the army and navy, it is these innovations, carried on without exposing a majority of the population to direct service and liability, that prompted the rise of the Dutch Republic.

The Scheldt estuary, a marshy and waterlogged region, was in the late Middle Age a backward, thinly populated and dangerous area, tangential to the northern region and unknown to most of the world. Agricultural activity was limited to the high ground and to sporadic locations where ad hoc drainage and irrigation systems had been crudely fashioned. Around 1200, however, systematic and increasingly large-scale construction of dikes was implemented, and the land reclaimed from the salty bogs was intensively farmed. This activity increased both the population and relative wealth of these hardy people willing to battle back the sea, and in the process brought the attention of its neighbors. It also allowed for a sophisticated, if rudi-mentary form of bureaucratic government to be installed. The great dikes and polders required constant maintenance and coordinated construction to be profitable, and local polder boards were established to organize and mobilize the population for a common good. The Dutch people organized militarily against a natural enemy, maximizing their production with individual subordination to government.

Swamps and marshes, and now dikes and canals, were not the only lines of defense for the Dutch. The great rivers of the estuary, especially the Meuse and the Waal, afforded tremendous protection from Southern invasion. The northern provinces, led by Holland, found themselves increasingly united by common interests and geography. Still, by the mid-fifteenth century, the so-called Low Countries— including the ten southern provinces dominated by Brabant and Flanders—were under the nominal control of the duke of Burgundy. In 1477, under Flemish leadership, the provinces rebelled and forced Mary, the Duchess of Burgundy, to concede the *Grand Privilége*. This charter gave the parliamentary States General of the 17 provinces the right to convene on its own initiative, and severely limited the power of Burgundy to levy taxes and raise troops.[23] The States General, like most parliamentary institutions of the time, had been established to expedite the process of levying taxes. The crown could explain to representatives of the people the need for taxes, in order to collect them with less coercion. It was also a conduit for fiscal information up the chain, as the people could explain to the crown how much they were *able* to pay in taxes. It was a system designed to facilitate governing through information sharing, but in time all such bodies began to take on not only advising responsibilities, but also consent powers. The seven northern provinces had joined in the rebellion, but had apparently been seeking a separate charter for themselves. The duchess complied and granted a separate Grand Privilege to the provinces of Holland and Zeeland.

The solidarity of formation tactics was transferred to the Low Countries following the Battle of Guinegate, when Maximillian and a force of Netherlander conscripts employing the Swiss model defeated a traditionally organized French force. The conscripts returned to a region already in sporadic revolt, and integrated their experi-ence into a full-scale military rebellion against Burgundy then Hapsburg Spain. The concessions of the Grand Privilege were an outrage to the Hapsburgs, related by marriage through Maximillian to the Burgundian duchess. Upon Mary's death in 1482, Maximillian ascended to Burgundian regency on behalf of his son, Philip, a move supported in Burgundy but opposed throughout the Netherlands. His plan to ultimately pacify the Low Countries and extract revenge was put on hold with an incursion by the French king, Charles VIII. Maximillian was forced to weaken his occupation, and was unable to supplement his Burgundian troops with the fickle Flemish and Dutch troops. The combination of fewer occupying Burgundians and a coterie of battle-hardened veterans left behind encouraged the provinces to rebel again. The reconquest took ten years, but by 1492 Maximillian had recovered the provinces, revoked the Privileges, and regained Low Countries conscripts as the backbone of his military power.

The revolt against Maximillian was led by the influential guilds, and was unsupported by the traditional nobility. The land-holding magnates and *jonkers* preferred traditional Hapsburg rule to that of the rebellious burghers, and generally stayed loyal to Maximillian. The rebellion was also unorganized, and its suppression underscored the problems of a lack of central leadership. The Hapsburg return was neither particularly harsh nor ubiquitous. Maximillian (and Philip after him) had more urgent concerns, allowing the rebels to properly organize, particularly in the north. By 1504, the *Grote Raad* (Great Council) was reestablished to be the supreme judicial authority of most of the Netherlands.[24] The swelling middle class in prosperous Holland began to assert itself politically, as well, garnering most local nonmilitary (still reserved for the nobility) administrative positions.

It probably cannot be overemphasized that from the 1477–92 rebellion to the inauguration of the Dutch Republic in 1579, the provinces were racked with the conflicts of the Reformation. The introduction of radical Protestantism, and its acceptance in the northern provinces, is likely the most significant liberalizing influence for this case. But I assert it was not enough by itself to affect a full transformation. I cannot delve deeply into the religious foundations of democratic government, except to acknowledge that Protestantism, with its emphasis on a direct relationship with God, is more conducive to democracy than Catholicism, with its priestly intermediary reminiscent of a bureaucratic aristocracy. Calvinism and its "democratic church organization appealed to the Dutch; church authority emanating from the congregation, which exercised it through its chosen representatives, the elders; the minister a spiritual ruler not by any magical influence transmitted from the apostles but by virtue of his election."[25] Such an independent spirit was a clear threat to the authoritarian and religious leader of the Catholic Hapsburg Empire, and exacerbated geographic and linguistic divisions. In response, the persecution of the inquisitors was uncompromising, and conflict was perhaps inevitable: "King Philip would not relent, the Calvinists would not repent."[26] Nonetheless, military innovations and restructuring contributed significantly to the Dutch sense of liberal government, and may have been the critical intervening variable in its transformation to a republic.

The Hapsburgs drew on the resources of the provinces to pay for their own subjugation (or protection, from the Hapsburg view). Flanders and Brabant were the primary sources of revenue for the south, Holland for the north. This allowed the Hollanders to develop the tax extraction and recruitment bureaucracy necessary to fill military ranks. Most of the Burgundian occupiers were mercenaries, and many of them Germans. Very few soldiers were culled from the local populations to prosecute internal repression, but the direct link between the labor of the Dutch and the role of the soldiers was patent, and so the contribution of large parts of the population in support of military requirements was clear.

Although the guilds dominated the urban centers, a key organization was the local militia, or *schuterijen* (military guild).[27] These militias were as much social organizations as military ones, and were more likely to be called out to quench a fire or repair a dike than repel an invasion. Their military duties did tend to exempt the poorer elements of society, as arms and provisions (especially food and drink) were at the expense of the members. Still, the military defense of the town or city was a solemn duty, and a great deal of prestige was accorded membership. Proud people, finding themselves dominated by another, will often develop a mythos to sustain their dignity. In the early sixteenth century, "mirrored in the humanist controversies" of the day, a founding myth emerged.[28] Tacitus had described the people of Batavia, presumed by the Dutch to be located in the seven northern provinces, as heroic warriors, the only people who had successfully resisted the imperial desires of Rome. Tacitus's account was taken as evidence of a martial and freedom-loving spirit in the Batavians modern ancestors. What parts of the myth were true is impossible to verify, but it had an extraordinary influence on the emergence of a Dutch proto-nationalism. It cemented a sense of unity. It instilled a patriotism and group-identity necessary to the function of democratic government. As Pericles described in his magnificent funeral oration, no democracy can stand that ignores either the law or the common good, and for the latter a sense of community is essential.

The processes of consolidation and bureaucratization of the increasingly wealthy Netherlands were causing significant stresses on the antiquated social and political class system. The jonkers were becoming marginalized by the Hapsburg innovations, which included placing non-noble guildsmen and southern provinces nobility in positions of authority. The practice increased after 1540, when the Hapsburg Empire engaged in an expensive and prolonged war with France. The Low Countries were becoming the Hapsburg's most lucrative source of income, and it was perhaps natural that Charles V would rely on them not only for financial support in the war against France, but due to its proximity, also for the recruiting, provisioning, and billeting of foreign troops.[29] In 1552, Charles raised 109,000 troops in Germany and the Netherlands.[30] With the massing of troops in Holland, Charles began to recognize that its strategic importance relative to all Europe had eclipsed that of Italy. The Emperor began "routinely using the Netherlands as his chief strategic bulwark and resource, in pursuit of goals which were vital to him but had little to do with the Netherlands."[31] The scale of military operations escalated. Philip's thirst for men, money, and supplies to prosecute his foreign wars appeared unquenchable.

From 1559, the States General of the northern provinces met almost continuously to debate what were seen as unreasonable and unfair demands. William the Silent, Prince of Orange, a magnate whose eloquence belied his title, had gained considerable reputation for his military prowess. "At eighteen he had been given his first army command, a troop of horse, at nineteen an additional colonelcy of foot, and at twenty he became, over the heads of older men and by imperial favour, lieutenant-general of the troops in the Netherlands."[32] After Phillip II's accession, William became the primary organizer of the Hapsburg war with France.[33] He was also an astute politician, and began manipulating the situation for his own personal ambitions. To do so, he had to negotiate the labyrinthine Dutch government. "The Netherlands [that William knew were] neither a state nor a nation, but a tangle of countries, duchies, and seignories, which had been amassed over generations into the hands of a single ruler, confusingly styled the duke of Burgundy. Each of the seventeen provinces had its separate privileges, its greater and less nobility, its Courts of Justice, while in their midst the cities exercised independent rights of their own, with their law courts, guilds, trade-boards, municipal councils and time-honoured constitutional charters."[34] The leading officer of each province was called Stadholder, the chief magistrates of the cities were Grand Pensionaries. The Stadholder was commander in chief of provincial military forces, chair of the local state general (parliament), inspector of dikes and social services, and chief justice—invariably a nobleman.[35]

Discontent came to a head in a religious crisis in 1566. Philip was relentless in his repression of Calvinism, to the point that a delegation of 300 jonkers, mostly Catholics, journeyed to Brussels to ask the regent, Philip's sister Margaret, to abolish the inquisition. The request was denied, but one royal official was said to disdainfully describe the jonkers as "nothing but a crowd of beggars."[36] William quickly turned the tables on the discourteous aristocrat by adopting the name of beggar for himself, and urging all of his supporters to do the same. They used the rebuke as a source of pride, and began pinning beggar's purses to their coats. Overnight, William became the symbol of resistance to Hapsburg domination.

The Rebellion of 1566–67 was short-lived. Although the militias refused to act against the iconoclastic mobs, government troops recruited by Margaret and led by friendly jonkers in the north effectively ended the rebellion long before Spanish troops under the cruel duke of Alva, dispatched to pacify the provinces, arrived.[37] Alva's 10,000 veteran troops entered the northern provinces without resistance, but Alva was determined to punish the Dutch for their actions. He immediately sentenced all the people of the Netherlands to death, subject only to his personal acquittal: "Alva would have utter submission or genocide."[38] He established the so-called Council of Troubles to investigate the rebellion and punish the guilty. Ultimately, the Council of Blood, as it was called by the Dutch, condemned 9,000 persons to death for treason or heresy. Although most fled the country, more than a thousand were rounded up and executed.[39] A significant number of those executed were of the nobility, and when William the Silent called for a new rebellion in 1568, many of the jonkers who had sided with Margaret a year earlier now rallied to the Prince of Orange and against Alva.

William was able to liberate the provinces of Holland and Zeeland, and establish the Free Dutch navy called the sea-beggars. Those Calvinists who had taken to the sea, "which offered them freedom and a means of subsistence by means of piracy," rallied to William, and fought and routed the Spaniards wherever they encountered them on the water.[40] Their numbers were initially small, but the sea-beggars proved more than a military annoyance. The Spanish navy, it turned out, was doubly threatened. Many of its crewmen were Hollanders and Zeelanders, and no comparably qualified replacements could be found when the old hands refused to serve on imperial ships.[41] With some trepidation, William provided "letters of marque from the Prince of Orange," allowing the sea-beggars to claim legal status as a recognized navy, and not as pirates, when they preyed on the Spanish fleet.[42] The activity fit perfectly with the tendencies of this nation of seamen, who had already begun outfitting their trading vessels with cannon, and saw in the battle with the Spanish an opportunity for riches through the aptly named privateering.

The sea-beggars proved a significant fighting force. Their daring gained the admiration of all the Dutch, made it impossible for Alva to retake the coastal areas, and completely disrupted resupply from Spain. In 1569, Alva made the mistake of convening the States General (for the first time in ten years) to make his case for more revenue in response to the threat.[43] He wanted several new taxes, the most infamous of which was the "tenth penny," a 10-percent sales tax. The States General was coerced into accepting the measure, but the provincial States refused. Eventually, the ten southern provinces formed a union that came to favorable terms while managing to eliminate the tenth-penny requirement. But the seven northern provinces refused to join in the accommodation. With this event, the Netherlands was permanently split into two political identities. In the north, the town militias were directed to forcibly collect the Tenth Penny. Almost all of them had refused, putting themselves in open contempt of the occupying forces.

Hated as the tax was, more grievances were needed to trigger an independence revolt.[44] They were amply supplied. As the Council of Troubles expanded its mandate from punishing rebels to persecuting Protestants, it rightly became viewed as a return of the insufferable Inquisition. In response, the sea-beggars deliberately joined their cause to Calvinism, a stance irreconcilable with Spanish Catholicism. They willfully put themselves in a position with no viable retreat. For anything less than political freedom, the alternative was death. The Revolt of the Netherlands, the attempt to carve out a new nation and not just a rebellion against oppressive policies and taxes, dates to the actions of the free fleet; specifically, the occupation of the small port of Brill.

The sea-beggars had routinely used ports in England to refit and hide from the Spanish. Queen Elizabeth, wary of antagonizing Phillip II, expelled them in 1572. Alva had moved a great number of his forces south to counter the French, and so the South Holland port of Brill was left without a garrison. Roaming sea-beggars seized the town, hoping to make of it a permanent base of operations. When news of the occupation reached the port of Flushing, the citizen-militia drove out the garrison there and beseeched the sea-beggars for assistance. More than 800 moved from the swelling force in Brill to do so.[45] The rebellion was now officially a revolt, and the militias in a majority of Holland, Zeeland, and Friesland cities claimed them for William.

William mustered a force of mostly German mercenaries to invade the Southern provinces. He was convinced a successful revolt would be possible only with all 17 provinces united, but he found little support there and was quickly driven out by Alva, who then turned his attention to pacifying the rebellious cities, mostly in Holland. At Delft, Haarlem, Leiden, and Utrecht, citizen-militias bravely fended off the professional Spanish troops. Thus, "It was the seamen, fishermen, and the middling sort who formed the backbone of the Revolt."[46] By the winter of 1572,

William had managed to organize a national citizen defense force of some 15,000 valiant but inexperienced soldiers. To oppose him, Alva mobilized some 38,000 Netherlands troops (almost all southern Walloons), to augment his 10,000 Spanish and—eventually—29,000 Germans.[47]

The city of Amsterdam was the last bastion of the Hapsburg Empire in Holland. The Catholic regents, emplaced by Alva, had managed to retain effective control in the early years of the Revolt, but thousands of expatriates returned, including formerly prominent Protestants. Demonstrations against Catholicism began to weaken the authority of the regents, and the ambitions of the returning Protestants turned the general demonstrations into specific rebellions against the government. In 1578, a militia-based coup brought down the regents and sent 30 of them into exile.[48] The militia was then formally purged of all Catholic influences and all Catholic churches in the city were closed.

For the most part, the northern provinces were in sympathy with the sea-beggars and independence from Spain, though not necessarily from the South. Philip concentrated most of his efforts on recovering the important southern provinces, and finally succeeded in doing so, culminating in the Pacification of Ghent (1576). He was greatly assisted by a fiscal crisis due to the simultaneous campaigns against the Netherlands and Ottoman Turks, which caused the emperor to suspend all payments to the Army of Flanders. The Spanish and mercenary soldiers rebelled, abandoned their garrisons, and went on a looting rampage. The emperor had no choice but to allow the southern provinces to raise their own troops to protect Brussels and Antwerp. They did so, and the new levies promptly joined with William, though their solidarity was based less on respect for William of Orange than on a mutual hatred of the pillaging Spaniards. William had an army in the field, and was the best chance to stop the depredations. The States General convened on its own initiative, the first time it had done so without royal summons in almost a century, to recruit and to provide a defense force.[49]

This is an extremely compelling example of the *Warrior State* thesis in practice. The Empire had failed in its implicit bargain to defend the provinces from enemies foreign and domestic. Directly in response, the external crisis of marauding armies allowed the States General to extract political concessions in exchange for military support. The two leading provinces, Brabant in the south and Holland in the north, neither controlled by the Spanish due to the crisis and the rebellion, formed an alliance to subdue the mutineers. The Pacification of Ghent stated that all the provinces were loyal to the emperor, but that the States General would continue to meet in Brussels to deal with religious and local political issues. "In Holland, as at other decisive moments in the early stages of the Revolt, the town councils to ensure that they had the public support that they needed, consulted the civic militias on the terms of the Pacification before ratifying the agreement."[50]

The Pacification of Ghent was a loose federal treaty providing for all the provinces to unite in their efforts to expel the rampaging Spanish army. The States General would consider all matters of shared interest, "as soon as peace had been restored."[51] The emperor's new governor, Don Juan of Austria, had no troops and no funds, and no option but to agree to send the Spanish troops out of the region and to accept the terms of the Pacification regarding joint governance. Don Juan would not relent on the issue of religious tolerance, however, and William rallied the provinces on this issue. Don Juan was forced to flee Brussels, and to recall the imperial troops (what few he could recover). For six years, William resided in the south and fought to end Spanish domination throughout the provinces in what he thought was the decisive battleground. But Holland and Zeeland consistently refused to recognize the authority of the States General over their own States. Moreover, most of the leaders of the south wanted a swift and, most objectionable, a Catholic end to the Revolt. This Holland refused. In recognition of its radical rebellion, leading roles in the long fight against Spanish oppression, and because of the increasing Protestant–Catholic schism, the seven northern provinces gravitated to the leadership of Holland.[52]

The north was especially fearful of the return of any form of the inquisition, and the "Union of Holland and Zeeland" (1575), the first joint government below the level of the States General and precursor to an independent Dutch state, specifically forbade the investigation, persecution, or punishment of anyone for private beliefs and religious practices.[53] In 1578, several moderate provinces, worried about Catholic retribution in the wake of military successes by Don Juan, petitioned the Union to assist them with troops and the strengthening of their fortifications. A conference was called to draft a simple security alliance among the northern provinces, but the Hollanders managed to push through an expanded version of their Union with Zeeland.[54] The terms of the Union of Utrecht (1579) created the modern Dutch state, but had unanticipated consequences for the region. The southern states, desirous of a general union of all the Low Countries under the States General, preferred reconciliation with Spain to closer unity with the radical rebels of the north under the terms of Utrecht. With his authority unraveling, Phillip took the reactionary step of banning the States General, and dispatched the duke of Parma to retake the Netherlands. William urged the States General to transfer its fealty to King Henry III of France's younger brother, the duke of Anjou, arguing that the only way to depose one sovereign was to adopt another. Anjou agreed to accept the privileges of the States General, and so in 1581 the Act of Abjuration was passed. The Act officially repudiated Phillip and all official reference to him, based on a list of grievances that would prove to be a model for the later U.S. Declaration of Independence.[55] The Act enraged the Hapsburg emperor, who had already issued an edict proscribing the prince as "chief perturber and corruptor of entire Christianity and especially of the Netherlands," and calling on all and everyone to "free us from this pest and deliver him dead or alive." The reward for doing so was a sum of 25,000 crowns in gold or estates, full pardon for any crime committed, and a patent of nobility. The prince's answer to this ignoble document was a fiery *Apology*, in which he reviewed his life and the part he had played in the Dutch Revolt, refuting the charges against him.[56] The Act of Abjuration required all officeholders to swear allegiance to the duke, something the States of Holland and Zeeland refused to do. Allegiance was instead sworn to the Union, making Anjou's regency suspect.[57]

Parma was increasingly effective in his military campaign, and so Anjou attempted a coup to increase his authority and disband the States General. The citizens of Antwerp resisted and forced the duke to abdicate. As his supporter, William drew the ire of the southern provinces, and by 1583 had to abandon his southern pro-French strategy and moved his headquarters to Holland. William was dejected, though still committed to the Revolt. Discussions began in the Dutch States to elevate William to sovereign in a constitutional monarchy, but no decision was reached before Phillip's revenge would be realized. William the Silent was assassinated by a cabinet maker motivated by religion and the huge reward Philip had promised for the prince's death.[58]

The revolt had lost its personal symbol, and a shadow of pessimism lay heavy upon it. But the Revolt was only championed by William. The Hollanders had made sure it was never his personal crusade. Johan van Oldenbarnevelt, Lord Advocate of the province of Holland, took over nominal leadership in William's stead. He was the "legal adviser and spokesman of the delegation of nobility to the Assembly of the States of Holland. In that capacity he was the first to cast his vote, . . . drew up the agenda for each meeting, he opened, read, and answered the letters of envoys abroad [making him] leader of their foreign policy."[59] Not knowing of a viable alternative, and in dire need of protection, the States General authorized Oldenbarnevelt to appeal to French King Henry III to take over as sovereign, circumscribed by constitutional limits. He refused. With nowhere else to turn, Elizabeth I was similarly beseeched. She, too, initially refused; recognizing that to do so would make her the irreconcilable enemy of Spain. But by late 1585, Parma was enjoying considerable success in the south, and Elizabeth knew that if the Spanish controlled Holland they would have easy access for an invasion England. She negotiated the Treaty of Nonsuch (1585), in which she received the right to nominate the Dutch head of state and military, to be called the "governor-general," and to be guaranteed representation in the government, in return for military support.[60] The Treaty had enormous ramifications. The nascent Republic became an effective protectorate of the English, but as the first international treaty negotiated by the Dutch, it established them as an externally recognized independent state. Elizabeth then sent Robert Dudley, earl of Leicester and 7,000 troops to assist the Dutch. Inept, Leicester engendered bitter hatred, and returned to England after just two years.[61]

The States General began to sit continuously after Leicester's ignoble exit in 1587, permanently after 1593, at The Hague.[62] The nobility had sided with Leicester, but his disgraceful return to England stripped them of their influence and left Oldenbarnevelt in charge of the government.[63] By 1588, without English or noble support, the future of the Republic was in severe doubt. Parma's gains were many, and the United Province's position was precarious. But the erstwhile covenant with England had precipitated the enmity Elizabeth feared. Philip seized the moment of rebel weakness to send the great Spanish Armada against England.[64] The approaching menace of the "Invincible Armada" meant that Elizabeth needed the Dutch fleet if she would have a chance of surviving the pending invasion.[65] The fortuitous, if not miraculous, defeat of the Armada by both weather and a spirited channel defense opened the door for a dramatic rise in power for the Republic.

Though defeated at sea, the Spanish army was making significant gains throughout the Low Countries in 1589. The Republic turned to William's 17-year-old son Maurice to lead its military, but it needed more than just field generalship from the young heir. It needed a new kind of military, one that would serve the state's needs but that would not threaten it from domestically. The consecutive ravages of Burgundian, then Spanish, then English troops meant that the Dutch would never tolerate a military force that was undisciplined or loutish. From 1591 to 1604, Maurice, with his cousin William-Louis of Nassau, transformed the small Dutch army into the model of the modern military, and completely purged the Republic of its Spanish occupation.

The Military Revolution of the so-called long sixteenth century (to 1640) was finally to culminate. Gunpowder had been introduced almost 200 years before, but technology and economics limited their widespread effectiveness. It was not until Maurice's organizational and training reforms that firepower was considered more important on the battlefield than shock, "that the pike was there to protect the musket and not the other way round."[66] New gunpowder weapons required new tactics and strategies, larger and better-disciplined armies and fleets, new defensive fortifications, and a drastically increased sophistication in logistics. All this engendered a comprehensive social displacement that presaged political change throughout the Western world. The first political effects of the Military Revolution are evident in Italy, Switzerland, and Burgundy. The culmination occurs in France. But perhaps the most significant transformational adaptations occurred in Holland, under Maurice of Orange.

Maurice's tutor and confidante was Justus Lipsius, whose *Six Bookes of Politickes* applied a neo-stoic philosophy to both military and civilian life, the latter enhanced by training and discipline learned in the former.[67] Lipsius taught at the University of Leiden, established by William the Silent as a reward for its heroic defense in 1575, and which was attracting the brightest philosophers of the age.[68] Lipsius was a follower of Machiavelli, and understood the Florentine's passion for Republican government and its necessary base in a soldier-citizenry. Where Machiavelli erred, according to Lipsius, was in his belief that the citizen-militia should be drilled infrequently, and without punishment, to make them eager to participate. To the contrary, the citizen can only be as loyal and disciplined in political and religious life as he is in military service.

Maurice and William-Louis saw the decisive point as drill and discipline.[69] Battle in any age requires tremendous fortitude simply to appear on the field and not run away. In the age of firearms and close-order volleys, the experience must have been terrifying. The cohesiveness the soldiers in formation needed, required them not only to stand firm in battle, but also to conduct intricate maneuvers and firing sequences, could be instilled by continuous drill. With rigorous and unremitting practice, the soldier learns to act without thinking, to move without hesitation when ordered, and to continue in the face of carnage. In the phalanx, personal courage could be supplemented by the mass. The most timorous could be placed in the center of the square, where they would be safest. With the new strung out front line, and rotating fire, every soldier would stand in turn at the front rank and expose himself directly to the enemy's guns. This took extraordinary, and some might argue, mechanical self-control. In a word, discipline.

Drill was first needed for practical military necessity. Maurice and William-Louis began to systematically change the basic military formation from square to shallow rank in order to maximize firepower.[70] The square was a simple formation, and a good one for pike work, but it was extremely wasteful for firearm combat. It gave the front row force in a charge, but the wider the formation relative to its depth, in theory, the more weapons that could participate in the dispatch of a volley downfield. The rapidity of volley fire was also affected by the amount of time it took to reload the single-shot muskets of the day. Early attempts at massing gunfire had as many as ten ranks. Upon firing, the front rank would face about and go to the rear of the formation. Each rank would do so in turn, with back ranks slowly return-ing to the front. The musketeers would have to reload during this movement, complicating it greatly. As reloading procedures became easier and faster, through both drill and technological advance, the number of ranks could be reduced while retaining the same rate of fire. This increased the effective width of the formation while not increasing the number of soldiers in it. It was also possible to have the front rank kneel, allowing the rank just behind it to fire at the same time, doubling the intensity of the volley. These two ranks would then move to the back of the formation to be replaced by the two behind them. It is not difficult to imagine that extensive training was necessary to pull off these intricate maneuvers in combat. It is also clear that the army that could do so most efficiently would have a great battlefield advantage.

Maurice also apparently reintroduced the old Roman two-part command. In this form there is a preparatory command followed by a command of execution.[71] This enhanced the precision of the movements (e.g., right . . . face; to the rear . . . march) at least as much as the drum or fife had been found to enhance in-step marching. The Swiss are widely recognized as the first modern force to reintroduce music to help keep them in step as they marched, but a drumbeat is not enough to ensure the "well-choreographed ballet" of Maurice's intricate maneuvers.

A more important activity dredged from Roman history and reintroduced by Maurice and William was the art of the spade—the ubiquitous digging of the ancients. The Roman army always fortified its camps, even when staying over for a single night while on march. This limited the distance an army could travel on a given day, but it made the possibility of a surprise attack remote. The earthen works and other field fortifications the Romans invested in were a great part of their tactical success; "the Romans themselves knew and stated that it was not only *virtus* and *arma*, but also their *opus* (work) that gave them victory over their enemies."[72] The problem was that in the professionalization of the military over the previous three centuries, especially the case for military entrepreneurs, digging was seen as an affront to their status. Of course, it also took away from the noblesse of their profession; to fire at an opponent from behind cover was not considered manly or virtuous.[73] Maurice fixed the problem directly. He made it the first order of his army that it would be well paid, and always paid on time.

"Maurice's own estimate of his success was that he could get his soldiers to dig."[74] The fact was actually quite consequential, and tied in to the notion that not only would his troops be paid well and on time, but also they would be paid year-round. There was no sense that upon finishing a campaign the troops would be free to sign on with another bidder. That there were no higher bidders than the Dutch was no doubt important as well, but by keeping them in continuous service the drill and digging were not wasted if never used. They were prepared to war as needed, and could bring the battle to conclusion quickly and decisively without worry for another payday. And the mercenaries would always fight under the Dutch banner, would always defend the Dutch people, and in tremendous crisis would fight (and dig) along side them. A sense of belonging became instilled in the mercenaries. Combined with the traditional Dutch propensity to take in groups that had been forced to flee their homelands (Jews from Spain and Poland, Huguenots from France, Puritans from England), the mercenaries began to develop a type of ideological patriotism and loyalty above that of family, tribe, and ethnicity.

It was certainly not that the Dutch people were too timid to fight, and therefore took on a mercenary army. They had been the coveted mercenaries a century before. It was simply that maritime military and commerce requirements consumed all the available Dutch manpower.[75] But the mercenary army was not an entirely comfortable alternative to a citizen-militia, for good reason. The population had been besieged for too long by Spanish mercenaries and Leicester's English. "At the heart of Dutch reforms was the need to protect civil society through tighter discipline and regular payment of the troops at relatively short intervals."[76] So long as the payments came on time, and they always did, the soldiers had no impetus to mutiny. Orderliness and discipline were the assurances of Dutch military practice. So subservient to the civil authority did Maurice's troops become that by 1620 the Venetian ambassador to Holland could remark with astonishment that local towns actually applied to have garrisons quartered in them, as the economic benefit was good and the threat of debauchery and other typically soldierly disturbances was absent.[77]

With regular pay came a sense of permanent association with the state. For that pay, soldiers were expected to train vigorously, fight valiantly, and refrain from loutish behavior characteristically associated with men of arms. To clarify the soldier's obligations, the States General's [first] code of military conduct was published in 1590.[78] But this code did more than tell the soldier his obligations; it specified his rights. Discipline was continuous, and infractions were dealt with seriously—but fairly, and within the legal rights of the defendant. Courts martial were instituted to ensure due process of law.

More than discipline in the enlisted ranks was needed—so too for the officers. Maurice established the Dutch military academy at Siegen to produce capable officers for his new system. Though crowded with noblemen (especially foreign nobles, eager to learn the new methods), the Academy also incorporated the middle classes, and once a graduate entered service in the Dutch military, promotions could be expected on merit. And Maurice needed the output of the academy. The old mass squares had few commands to master and very few commanders. The smaller, faster Dutch formations had at least twice the officers of the much larger squares. More importantly, these were established uniformly and based on a strict hierarchy. Battalions were reduced to 550 men, these into companies, and from there into platoons. The unambiguous chain of command greatly assisted coordination and control, and "[in] this way the army became an articulated organism with a central nervous system that allowed sensitive and more or less intelligent response to unforeseen circumstances."[79] The reform was yet another inspired by the Roman legions, in this case the flexible maniples.

For all this, "[by] 1597, the Dutch standing army was the most proficient technically of any in Europe and the second largest after the Spanish."[80] Though most of the paid troops of the standing army (not inclusive of the militias) were foreign mercenaries, they were in the continuous service of the Dutch, and ultimately were incorporated into Dutch society. When combined with the sizeable all-Dutch crews of the navy, then the world's most formidable, we see a contextually very high military participation ratio.

Although the intent was to form a grand citizen-army, along the lines recommended by Machiavelli and Lipsius, the Dutch economy found a way to incorporate the citizenry into the defense of the state without subjecting them to direct offensive liability (they were always under the communal threat of siege): "For although Article 8 of the Union of Utrecht declared that a general census should be taken of all people between the ages of eighteen and sixty, in order that a regular militia might be established among them for the defense of the whole country, no such militia had ever been organized. Except in one single province the census had never been taken. It was found to be infinitely cheaper to hire troops to do the fighting than to drill a busy and commercial population for a work which they had neither aptitude nor liking."[81] Perhaps this reliance on mercenaries was the primary factor in the Dutch Republic approaching great individual liberties but not making the next step to liberal democracy. Indeed, the freedoms of the Dutch were profound, even "the servants," wrote a contemporary French nobleman, "have so many privileges that their masters dare not even beat them."[82]

There were other contributing factors limiting the Dutch transition to full political participation of all its citizens. Although the navy had a clear strategic focus outward, the survival of the state depended as much on its intricate fortifications and defensive emplacements along the rivers and canals. Thus, the Dutch army was an army of occupation, equally apparent in the rise of its colonial empire after 1590. Moreover, the commercial development of the Dutch, which included the takeover of the shameful Portuguese slave trade after 1621, may have hindered the moral impetus for democracy that seemed stronger among the contemporary Huguenots and later the English.[83] It was the lucrative trading networks the Dutch had built through fierce competition, especially in the Baltic, that laid the basis for the economy that could support Maurice's new military. Safe behind their river and dike fortifications, manned with a highly trained and well-paid army, buttressed by safe inflow of supplies and cash from their Navy-secured supply lines, the Dutch could watch, manipulate, and profit as the rest of Europe bled dry in the Thirty Years' War (1618–48).

Still, the tremendous preparation for war, the liability of all levels of society for its successful prosecution, relatively egalitarian entry and promotion requirements based on merit, loyalty organization based on the state and not the military commander, and mostly the extraordinary discipline and professionalism of the Dutch military worked to establish and then maintain the Free Republic for more than two centuries. Other countries would adapt the Dutch military model, most immediately and successfully Gustavus of Sweden. The similarities between the Dutch peoples and the Swedes made the transition facile, and it was Gustavus who truly led Maurice's new professional army into battle. The Dutch form would also be adopted by the parliamentary forces in England under Oliver Cromwell, emerging as the New Model Army and leading to extraordinary excesses but also the English notion of protestant military-citizenship. But it was in France, which began adapting the Dutch model in earnest—while at the same time reducing its reliance on foreign mercenaries—that would see the full transition to democracy.

France, 1660–1800

The era of modern liberal democracy began at the end of the eighteenth century with the emergence of two profoundly revolutionary nation-states in America and in France. Though the results were similar—by the middle of the twentieth century both were strong and stable liberal democracies—the paths taken diverged. The United States freed itself from British colonialism and maintained a steadily strengthening liberal democratic form of government. France freed itself from its own feudal past, but the first French Republic was ruthless, violent, corrupt, and decidedly short-lived. A series of revolutions were necessary before reforms stabilized. Both states had a legacy of economic, cultural, technological, philosophical, and political factors that contributed heavily to their processes of democratization, and the case that follows will not overturn the strong arguments that favor each of these as powerful intervening variables on the paths to democracy. What they should do in addition is strengthen the argument that military organization is an intervening variable *at least* at the level of influence of the aforementioned ones, and may be *the* critical or tipping point factor in spontaneous democratic revolutions.

The full story of the French military's contributing structural influences on the events of 1789 begins in the reign of Louis XIV (1643–1715). The "Sun King," so named because all of Europe was said to revolve around him, represented the apex of absolutist French monarchy, and without question at the beginning of his reign his military was organized to maximize authoritarian rule. His power was extraordinary. His notorious claim, "*l'etat c'est moi*," was no doubt exaggerated, but Louis and most of Europe probably believed it.[84] He ruled with an assurance of divine right that was unshakable, and his desire for greater glory led him to engage in virtually continuous war. A list of just the major wars of Louis XIV, in which all of Europe at one time or another opposed France, include the War of Devolution (1667–68), the Dutch War (1672–78), the War of the Grand Alliance (1688–97), and the War of the Spanish Succession (1701–14).

The France inherited by Louis XIV was the wealthiest and most populous state in Europe, but Louis was endlessly beset with the problem of effectively mobilizing the full power of his realm. His ambition simply outpaced his finances. His reign was thus characterized by ceaseless efforts to increase the efficiency of his military and to extract greater war-fighting capacity from the state. Although he did not radically transform the nature of French monarchy, his continual search for refinement of the existing tax-extraction system ultimately overcame feudal legacies and resulted in the practical and now classic model of the modern absolutist monarchy.[85]

The primary evidence of Louis's great power was his ability to raise and maintain the largest European armed force since the late Roman Empire. His accomplishment came despite ceaseless contention with an antiquated system of clerical and noble privilege, including significant tax exemptions that severely impinged upon efforts to field his armies and navies. Without these constraints, Louis XIV might have raised a military force that would have rolled over all of Europe. To be sure, Louis's Finance Minister Jean-Baptiste Colbert greatly enhanced state revenues, from 37 million livres in 1661 to 65 million in 1671—while at the same time reducing the royal debt from 30 to just 8 million livres—but he did so using conventional methods of ruthless coercion and vigorous oversight.[86] Although the fiscal efficiencies of his minister were greatly appreciated, it was not a vast and unlimited military budget wrested from a corresponding economic expansion that allowed Louis XIV to prosecute war at a level higher than any European monarch before him. Rather, it was a series of military, bureaucratic, tactical, and strategic reforms that changed the way Europe envisioned and conducted warfare.[87]

Under Louis's top field commander, Sebastien Vauban, offensive tactics began to overwhelm the defense. To Vauban, whose specialty was siegecraft, no fortress was invulnerable.[88] The privileged position of the nobility, once safely ensconced in their citadels and thereby able to defy the larger armies of the crown, became untenable. The rise of gunpowder and canon had already made the high stone and mortar walls of the medieval period obsolete, but under Louis's able tactician, the process was completed. To be sure, Vauban was as adept at designing and defending fortifications as he was at destroying them. His star-shaped earthen work designs could resist determined cannonade, and were copied for years. To counter his own constructs, Vauban devised intricate trench warfare models and sophisticated tunneling and demolitions (sapper) operations. This siege and anti-siege brilliance made it possible for Louis XIV to conduct most of his wars on foreign soil, a capacity that probably added to Louis's reputation for bellicosity.

Vauban's genius was not limited to the static siege. He also appears to have invented the bayonet socket, which allowed the musket to be fired while the bayonet is attached. This simple adaptation, greatly enhancing the deadly effectiveness of the strictly disciplined infantry charge, must have taken at least as much courage as self-control. Firing rates were cumbersome in this period. Superbly trained musketeers could discharge their weapons (inaccurately, at ranges over as little as 50 m.) only one to three times per minute. Infantry charges would attempt to stay just out of range until a volley had been loosed, and then rapidly close before the enemy could reload. As effective ranges increased, the window of vulnerability closed. With the Vauban bayonet modification, infantry could charge with a loaded weapon, waiting to fire until close range, then loosing a withering volley on the static defenders just before crashing into the (hopefully) disorganized defenders. The new tactic increased training requirements and returned to the musket formation an element of the Greek phalanx's disciplined charge.

Increases in the military population and a gradual reversal of the dominance of the defensive under Louis XIV did not destroy the independent power of the French nobility. That was a process begun in the gunpowder revolution of the previous century, one that would ultimately lead to the dismantling of aristocratic power throughout Europe. He only presided over its final demise. The enduring reforms that concern us here, and that would set the stage for the revolution 70 years after his death, were administrative. Unwilling to accept the consistent bumbling of some of his inept subordinates, Louis persistently infringed on the traditional prerogatives of his officer corps. He began by eliminating the custom of venality (purchasing commissions) in his elite *Guardes du Corps*. In a complementary reorganization, he standardized the entire national regimental system, providing regular orders of battle for all units and eliminating the practice of naming a regiment after the officer who mustered and commanded it. He further limited the discretion of officers in compensating their troops by establishing a uniform pay scale for all ranks.

It should be plain that Louis did not intend to democratize his realm in any fashion. While these reforms had the ultimate affect of eliminating the officer as a cognitively dampening layer between the state and soldier, a potent liberalizing influence, it was intended solely to enhance standardization and efficiency, and to combat fraud. Previously, officers received a lump-sum payment for delivering a regiment of specified size for a designated campaign. One of the more common methods for an officer to recoup his venal investment was to hire soldiers and subordinate officers at discount, siphoning off the difference for personal use.[89] Soldiers at a discount were often of dubious quality, and numerous recorded examples exist of recruiting over- and under-age limits, and impressing mentally and physically deficient persons to fill out the battalions. With standardized pay, the military-recruiting incentive switched to a competition for the best qualified rather than the cheapest, though the social margins remained the principal source of enrollees. But it could not eliminate fraud and graft; it merely changed the preferred methods of operation. Under Louis's new system, the most widespread abuse was for an officer to over-report the strength of his unit, effectively collecting pay for absent or phantom soldiers—a practice that persisted into the Seven Years' War. To combat problems of indirect profiteering, Louis XIV established a Quartermaster General to eliminate the "grosser swindles" in supply and provisioning of troops, integrated battalions into permanent regiments for greater peacetime control, and for the first time standardized uniforms, weapons, and training.[90]

Louis XIV also initiated a rudimentary military school system, especially important for the technical requirements of an increasingly complex artillery corps, but critical to the development of engineering and naval operations as well. Moreover, as the military school increased formalized drill and training (a basic element of a truly professional modern officer cadre), a necessary precedent to the establishment of full militarily influenced liberalizing conditions. A standardized promotion system for officers and noncommissioned officers (NCOs) was also founded, based on merit and education, that complemented the traditional commission and promotion system based on noble birth and seniority. Standardization is a further critical component of creating an egalitarian military influence within the social milieu, and upward mobility based on objective merit is a powerful start. To be sure, noble-born officers maintained significant privilege, especially in social activities and access to the crown, but the new French military needed experts at all levels. Increasingly, these were drawn from the non-noble middle class.

Not only recruitment and promotion, but also training became standardized at this time. Harsh and repetitive drill became a hallmark of the French army under Louis XIV's notorious Lieutenant-Colonel Jean Martinet. Himself a commoner of obscure origin who rose through the ranks on the new merit system, Martinet became commander of the king's own model infantry regiment. His reorganization of small unit infantry maneuver and instillation of by-the-numbers musket and bayonet drill were instrumental in the overall reorganizations of the French military. They were also widely adopted by other modern militaries, and the name Martinet became synonymous with the soldier who reacts like a puppet on a string to the orders of his commander. Jean Chaumejan and Claude de Metz carried out similar reorganizations for the Cavalry and artillery, and by the end of Louis XIV's reign, his forces were the best trained in Europe.[91]

Most important for the foundations of democratic revolution, Louis increased the size of the French army from no more than 100,000 under Richelieu to a maximum of 392,000 during the Wars of the Spanish Succession (1701–14). The rapid, four-fold expanse of Louis's army is more remarkable when one realizes that Richelieu's army was a fourfold increase over French forces that preceded him. The average French army at the beginning of the century comprised no more than 25,000 troops. Louis XIV's was 16 times that.[92] The navy was significantly increased as well, from a token force at the beginning of his reign to over 100,000 men by 1690.[93] Naval spending rose from 300,000 livres in 1660 to 13,400,000 livres by 1670.[94] Not only was the actively serving portion of the population dramatically increased under Louis XIV, a significant portion was also serving in the democratizing fleet.

The reforms of Louis XIV established the primacy of royal control over the entire state, and while initially causing the centralization and concentration of power to the monarchy; it began the crucial process of personalizing the relationship of the state to *all* its citizens. Loyalty was expressed not to the local commander, who previously had personally distributed wages, but to the crown itself—though still in the person of the king. Indeed, Louis XIV took great comfort in this change. He apparently believed that his personal position coincident with the state made his government immune to the well-known antiaristocratic effects of a large citizen-army. The people loved him (and his power), and the best way to ensure their loyalty was to make them his direct subjects. So unshakable was his faith in his popularity, Louis took the risky step of fully incorporating the previously semi-independent provincial militias into the armed forces structure of the nation. By standardizing the training and equipment of *all* military formations in France, this innovation had the additional affect of enhancing mobilization by providing quick turnaround recruit-ing pools for the regular army and navy.[95] It was also lauded by his advisors, who agreed that the independent militias were the only remaining source of meaningful potential opposition within his realm. By making them part of his own loyal army, it was believed that Louis had eliminated the possibility of rebellion.

With the massive growth of his military, the most far-reaching and consequential of Louis's reforms were undoubtedly those establishing a centralized bureaucracy to administer and control the expanded armed forces.[96] After 1700, "instead of congeries of independent, uncontrollable, inefficient units there had come into being a disciplined and articulate body with a single centralized administration capable of putting several hundreds of thousands of men into the field and keeping them there for years."[97] Louis XIV and his able assistants were consciously trying to centralize power in the state. They believed the ultimate end of their reforms would be an unassailable—and benevolent—absolute monarchy. Instead, they created an organi-zational dynamic in the military that would quickly go dormant in the hands of his less competent heir, but would have positive implications for the development and birth of a politically decentralized Republican France a century later.

Indeed, so revolutionary were Louis XIV's military modifications, they should have produced an almost palpable political effect. That they did not may actually be tribute to Louis's overall popularity. The simple fact is that the king appeared to be having success in his wars against all of Europe, and a budding nationalism may have acted to sustain his rule. There is little argument with success.

Although several of Louis XIV's modifications clearly impinged on the individual freedom of the typical Frenchman, the overall effect was to create a structurally liberalizing influence. Unprecedented mobilization and standardization reforms created a military that had crossed the threshold of influence from centralized to decentralized political structures. All ten factors from preparation for war, composition of forces, strategy and tactics, and professionalism moved from a strong authoritarian influence at the beginning of Louis's reign to a reasonably strong participative one at the end. Although Louis's reforms clearly strengthened the crown in relation to the aristocracy and clergy, as intended, the impact on the general population was at least equivocal. The average French citizen was now under vastly increased direct control from the state, but that loss of autonomy must be weighed against the extraordinary excision of control by the nobility. Ultimately then, we should expect to see increasing pressure toward political decentralization and, given the times, some form of constitutional monarchy. Indeed we do.

The crown was now responsible for the well-being of the average Frenchman in a way never before contemplated, and military reforms helped spur a new spirit of independence in the population. Their increasingly severe commitments to the state were widely recognized, and compelled even his most able commander—Sebastien Vauban—to plead with Louis for a lessening of the burden on his overtaxed subjects.[98] When near the end of his reign Louis demanded even more, to his astonishment, his newly armed subjects rebelled. Repeatedly they would do so thereafter, looking for redress of their grievances; but with no model of democracy to inspire them, their efforts were spasmodic and easily repulsed.

Louis XIV's legacy would be tarnished, both contemporaneously and in perspicacity. He left an empty treasury and a bewildering web of foreign entanglement to his successor, Louis XV (1715–74). The reputation and standing of France dwindled as the sickly and unresponsive grandson of the Sun King epitomized the decay of the *ancién regime*. French troops went routinely unpaid, desertions were common, and commanders were loath to test the loyalty of their subordinates in battle. The raw power and tremendous prestige of the Sun King's reign had tempered popular discontent, as international success itself became an internal political pacifier. But under his successor, the crown became a government abhorred by its people. The record of provincial estate and national *parlement* intransigence increased significantly after 1715, and continued throughout the first half of the century. The people wanted more autonomy and political independence, and the weak monarch was barely able to resist, but no galvanizing hero or event rose to trigger a statewide coordinated response. When Louis XV lost the Seven Years' War, however, the impetus was in place and a notable upswing in liberalizing pressure was evident.[99]

French Military Reforms in Response to War
The disastrous Seven Years' War (1756–63) was a key turning point for both the military and government. Lee Kennett describes France as a "nation [that] entered the conflict without enthusiasm, fought without distinction, and emerged from it without victory."[100] Fifty years of political lethargy had drained the once-splendid regime of its inspiration. By 1763, France had lost the lucrative fur and trade income

of its North American colonies and had run up a financial debt that would never be repaid.[101] The humiliations France suffered in war were exacerbated in the peace treaty. The old guard was castigated in a way that ensured a new generation of reformers would have influence at the Versailles court. Postwar military reforms were inevitable and significant.

The French military organization at the end of the Seven Years' War was, on paper, essentially identical to the one left by Louis XIV. But the army that was the scourge of Europe at the end of the seventeenth century had been humbled by decades of abuse and misuse, and was completely ill suited to the demands of late eighteenth-century warfare. The field army was battered. Its components were disparate and even antagonistic.[102] Peak army strength in the Seven Years' War was 330,000 in the line units, approximately 60,000 less than Louis XIV had generated some 75 years earlier, though the population of France was notably higher.[103] The annual levies were also much higher under Louis XIV than under Louis XV, about 50,000 as compared to 39,000 in the latter period.[104] Voluntary recruitment did not meet projected goals, and early in the war some 13,000 militiamen were called to line service, a practice allowed for in the Sun King's previous round of reforms but never implemented as it was considered decidedly "dangerous" to the monarchy.[105]

The militias had been created as a necessary response to the rise of mass gunpowder armies. They represented an unwanted incursion to the previous monopoly on legal violence enjoyed by the feudal nobility, and as such had never been fully accepted by them. Still, they were the only practical counter to the firearm militaries of Europe, and so the regional French militias had been organized along the same principles as those adopted by most contemporary continental states. Service was in theory compulsory for all adult males, but massive exemptions meant that only a minority was truly liable. Militias were expected to train several days annually, but pay and incentives were minimal or nonexistent, and so most were encouraged not to meet. Training and adequate arming of the militias might skip whole generations. The nobility encouraged such dishevelment wherever possible, whose innate if not learned knowledge of the political ramifications of activating and relying on such groups were well known to them. The militias had thus become an evil necessity to the state and aristocracy. The rhetorical logic generated from wartime exigencies that had established them could not be repudiated after the crisis to disband the militias. The next best option, for the aristocracy (in the absence of a strong king to enforce training requirements), was to limit training and employment of the mass militia so as to keep its members politically inert.

Hence, the most unintentionally liberalizing reforms of Louis XVI were mitigated by apathy and abandonment. But a recruiting crisis in the face of the global Seven Year's War meant that militia activations were once again needed after decades of neglect. There were not enough soldiers and sailors in the regular forces. Faced with the first real possibility of foreign invasion in decades, Louis XV called on the militias to defend his rule.

The manpower problem, endemic throughout the Seven Year's War, was in part blamed on the conviction that the regular army competed with the local militias for routine recruitment. Inactive service in the militias was distinctly preferable to a middle-class Frenchman of means than full-time service in the regular army. By joining the local levy, service in the state's national forces could be easily avoided. When a threat of an Anglo-German invasion in the early years of the war caused the government to activate more than 100,000 militia for provincial defense (1756–58), many individuals liable for military service still preferred to fulfill their active duty obligations close to home. Recruitment into the regular army was so poor in both number and quality that after 1758, no more levies into the local militia were requested, in order to ensure all newly activated troops went into national service.[106]

Service in the regular armed forces had always been voluntary, and effective recruiting had always been the bane of the French military. If any option other than the army was available, most individuals tended to jump at it, for service was not only occasionally deadly and routinely miserable, it was normally destitute. After expenses for uniforms and equipment, the soldier's pay was barely enough on which to survive. Shortfalls were made up in bonuses paid for service in out-of-country campaigns and in loot or booty after combat. Thus, recruiting and reenlistment bonuses offered by the state were the only valid monetary incentives to join, with the possible exception of pensions available for a lifetime (40 years) of loyal service. Both bonuses and pensions were offered at market rates, depending on the need of the state for troops. Of course, press gangs were common, and a drunk might find himself waking up to nurse a particularly painful hangover on the floor of a barracks or in the belly of a ship, contract for enlistment dutifully marked and filed. Prevailing practice and incentives thus drew a significant share of the dregs of society, impoverished men for whom the army and navy were salvation by comparison, or who found themselves with no other alternative.

But not all soldiers and sailors were drawn from the social margin. Remarkably, a number of men still served for the adventure, skills, and honor associated with military campaigning. This latter impetus should not be accorded to some nascent French patriotism that would rise fully formed from later revolutions. The contemporary Prussian fanaticism in combat was in fact "puzzling" to French soldiers, who could not so much as comprehend its nationalistic source.[107] A final identifiable group of men came forward to enlist, induced by far different considerations. Since the reforms of Louis XIV, service in the army or navy was seen by some as a path toward limited social advancement. It became quite possible for good service to be rewarded with a promotion to NCO, and occasionally to officer. In parallel, enlistment could also be used as a preventative for social devolution—as enlistment was routinely used as an alternative to imprisonment.[108]

All of this proved inadequate. Wartime shortfalls caused the government to suspend the old practice of command recruitment and to replace it with a nationalized system.[109] Before 1760, military units were individually responsible for their own recruiting needs, and for the most part could establish their own entrance standards and bounties. Under the national system, army and navy bureaucrats would recruit regionally, and new soldiers were placed in regiments where needed. The change, though more expensive because of the expanded bureaucracy (despite the fact that many officers paid additional bounties from their own pockets to induce the best recruits), was considerably more efficient and effective. In 1763, recruitment was permanently taken out of the hands of unit commanders. Soldier's bounties were set nationally, though the amount fluctuated according to current military demands, and to the age and height of the recruit. Tall (over 5' 6') and young (18–25) soldiers were prized in all regiments, because stature and age were two of the few objective measures of physical strength and robustness.

An increasing value assigned to ordinary citizens was instrumental in breaking down the old class distinctions in France, but it was not enough to usher in a new era of individual freedom. A crisis in the form of external threats had to catalyze the process. The battlefield failures of the French armed forces in the Seven Years' War provided precisely that means. The humiliating Treaty of Paris saw France surrender its most lucrative North American and South Asian colonies to the British. For the first time in two centuries, France was not the recognized first power of Europe, and the realization spurred a flurry of reactionary reforms. These organizational correctives can be usefully grouped into three distinct phases. The first two influenced decentralization in accordance with the hypotheses presented here, and the last was a mixture of decentralizing and centralizing reforms. The latter were implemented in a desperate attempt to reverse the liberalizing affects of the earlier reforms and to return to monarchical and aristocratic authority.

The first phase occurred under the duke of Choiseul (Étienne-François de Choiseul), Minister of War from 1761 to 1770. Although Louis XIV's regime created by fiat the standardization of recruitment and training, in practice the old methods persisted. It was Choiseul who completed the practical transfer of all recruitment to the state bureaucracy. As an additional measure creating in fact what the revered King Louis XIV envisioned, Choiseul reformed the enlarged military bureaucracy so it could pay soldiers directly, rather than through the lump-sum payments to commanders that had become the prevailing procedure. With this change, *all* soldiers also were required to take their loyalty oaths to the king of France, and not to their commanding officer or regional lord.[110] Officers, still for the most part coincident with the French aristocracy, had zealously guarded their privileged positions as intermediary between the state and its soldiers, in hope of retaining influence in the state. Under Choiseul's iron hand, that artificial layer was being systematically removed. As a result, officers feared their soldiers would be disloyal in a crisis, less willing to obey orders from their commander to combat their own people. And so they were. The noble-born officers became increasingly reluctant to rely on them in quelling regional rebellions and in other local police actions.

Choiseul then fixed the number of regiments in the line army and transferred to the king the right to determine all field-grade officer appointments (major through colonel) within and across regiments. This greatly reduced the practice of promotions and appointments based on nepotism and bribes to commanders, and engendered a tremendous amount of animosity toward Choiseul. Traditional officers of the aristocracy were in fact enraged at Choiseul's reforms, but because of their overall poor performance in the Seven Year's War, they were unable to argue that reforms of this type were not needed.[111] Humiliated by the war and now by Choiseul, the military aristocrats stewed in their bitterness, and waited for their chance to turn the tables.

The reforms of Choiseul were aimed directly at curbing the negative impacts of the practice of venality, considered by most progressives as an insidious cancer on the efficiency and capacity of the French army. As a source of revenue for the nobility, and as an assurance that the wealthier classes of society would retain leadership of the military, the sale of military commissions was common throughout Europe. The process in France was simple. Company or regiment commands could be purchased from the crown with the price varying and dependant on the prestige of the unit. Company commands cost about 7,000 livres and regiments about 70,000 livres. Cavalry regiments were more expensive, one such being sold for 100,000 livres in 1762.[112] General officer positions for field command were not venal, but were normally awarded on seniority and occasionally for exceptional service. Generalships for commissary service and other provisioning appointments remained venal, however, and astoundingly expensive. They were also enormously lucrative. In 1759, the appointments of *commisaire général* and *maestre-de-camp général* were sold for 266,000 and 332,000 livres, respectively.[113] In France, other ranks were officially not for sale, but unit commanders wishing to recoup their venal investment would frequently allot positions and promotions for monetary consideration. Although the practice was illegal, bribery was the standard method for securing initial officer appointment and most promotions.[114]

Most officers accepted venality as a reasonable means of securing a viable return on the initial venal investment. Most reformers viewed it as *the* source of inefficiency in the military. Though pay now went directly to soldiers and sailors, officers were still paid lump sums to outfit and maintain their units, and a standard method of turning a profit was to cut corners on supplies. Some less wealthy officers, dependent on their commissions to make a living, would recruit soldiers willing to kickback a percentage of their wage. Such recruits were usually deficient in some manner, merely looking for a means of survival. The most effective way to realize a profit after Louis XVI's reforms was to simply collect the pay of nonexistent soldiers. With Choiseul, corruption adapted. The commander would submit a full roster of names to the king's treasury, and would receive a full unit's provisioning fee for arms and supplies. As before, the most common illusions for deceiving the king's inspectors were to bring in local peasants as needed to fill the ranks, paying short-term wages for the service, or better yet, borrow soldiers from another regiment for the day as needed. Soldiers from a neighboring unit were superior to the locals for this particular ruse as they already had uniforms and equipment, and were drilled to a degree that they could withstand inspection by the king's representatives. Soldiers could be swapped from regiment to regiment between collaborating officers, giving the appearance of a full order of battle but in fact allowing for extreme deficiencies in combat readiness.[115]

Despite its inefficiencies, venality was an important source of income for the government, and this factor alone probably accounts for its longevity. Beyond the initial income benefits from the sale of a unit command, there were some continuing returns. Officers rich enough to purchase a command could subsist on lower salaries than those promoted on merit. Those officers lacking in outside sources of income to supplement their military pay could extract necessary personal revenue through the cost-cutting and internal promotion practices, again a saving for the king's treasury. Soldier's pay as well as that of officer's could in this way be artificially suppressed. The economic advantage to the crown was, of course, abrogated by inferior military capacity. The Seven Years' War proved the return was not worth the royal cost, and venality was systematically dismantled thereafter.

Choiseul was an able minister. In addition to army reforms, he greatly expanded the French navy. Britain had risen to a preeminent position in Europe and the world by virtue of its sea empire, and Choiseul would not have France lag significantly. But the forces of Austria-Hungary and the rising power of Prussia meant land defenses had to be paramount, and a strained budget could only do so much. "The navy," he said, "will achieve either the salvation or the downfall of France."[116] Ultimately, Choiseul would lose favor with Louis XV. He was sympathetic to the growing power of *parlements*, and against the King's wishes allowed the *Parlement* of Paris to disband the Jesuit Society in 1762.[117] His reformist preferences would undermine his political power, and Louis dismissed Choiseul in 1770.

The second postwar military reform period occurred under the War Ministry of Claude Louis, Compte de Saint-Germain, 1775–77. Pro-aristocratic conservatism did nothing to restore the fading glory of France, and the appointment of Saint-Germain represented a return to Choiseul's antiaristocracy revisions. Saint-Germain went well beyond just reforming venality, however. He sought to eliminate the practice through an innovative series of graduated reductions. Purchased commissions were to be phased out by reducing the price of a company or regiment by 25 percent on the death or replacement of its commanding officer. In this manner, after four command generations, commanding officer positions would be free and awarded entirely on merit. The phased suppression of venality managed to hold on, even though an angry aristocracy intent on reasserting its hereditary privilege plotted incessantly at court to have him removed. The unforgivable sin of Saint-Germain, one of only a handful of France's successful generals, was to attempt to install the severe Prussian code of discipline into the French army. He was chased from office in only two years. Nonetheless, when venality was officially abolished by the revolutionary government in 1790, it had already been effectively eliminated from the army.[118]

Saint-Germain went well beyond Choiseul's reforms in his attempt to correct the top-heavy nature of the military command structure. The number of officers in the military had been steadily rising through the century despite an absolute decrease in the number of soldiers since the Wars of the Spanish Succession. Hans Delbrück estimates that in 1740 the French had one officer for every eleven soldiers, at a time the Prussian army counted one officer for every 29.[119] In 1758, there were 16 field marshals and 737 generals for an army that had only 163 regiments.[120] That there were more generals than colonels was bad enough, especially when there were four times as many colonels (over 600 on active duty) as needed for regimental command requirements. This kind of bloated military structure is woefully inefficient, if for no other reason than that it forces an inordinate awareness of military protocol demanded by the myriad rank structure. Pomp and protocol, as was shown in the hypotheses, are seeds in the fertile ground of antidemocratic militarism. Little able to affect the higher rank structure, Saint-Germain was able to quickly reduce the number of company and field-grade officers required in regiments by simply reducing the number of battalions per regiment from seventeen to six.[121] This action immediately slashed the number of necessary low- to mid-ranking officers by more than two-thirds. Partly as a reflection of the growing animosity of the old guard, the reduction did not include a mass deactivation of upper-level officers corresponding to the demobilization of lower-ranking ones. By not deactivating the upper ranks, however, Saint-Germain was able to highlight the already absurd ratio of colonels and generals to troops. The mass of generals with nothing to do but clutter up the court worked silently to Saint-Germain's advantage. Moreover, it accomplished Saint-Germain's primary objective of significantly reducing the state payroll. Saint-Germain's reforms were aimed everywhere at efficiency and cost-cutting, and on that impulse he cut the strength of the Royal Guard (the famed Musketeers and Horse Grenadiers) as well as the Gendarmes and Light Horse, all personally commanded by the king and extremely loyal to his person.[122] The loss of his personal guard would severely limit the king's autonomy in the years to come.

Saint-Germain also made the first real improvements in military education in almost hundred years. In 1751, a fledgling military academy, the *École Militaire*, was established in Paris to educate young sons of the court nobility in preparation for a military career. In 1776, Saint-Germain helped establish 12 provincial military schools similar to the Parisien academy to broaden the prospective pool of military candidates to lesser nobility and upper-class merchants and artisans, a widely derided antiauthoritarian move.[123] Before the academies, the only officers that received any formal military training were artillerists and engineers, whose legacy of direct military education extended to the reforms of Louis XIV's Jean-Baptiste Colbert, who in 1666 founded the *Académie Royale des Sciences* to research and teach navigation and cartography, chemistry, ballistics, artillery, fortification, and naval engineering for army and navy officers.[124] For these highly technical branches of service, Saint-Germain created additional instruction centers. Unfortunately, these military schools were not open long enough to have a sustained pro-democratization organizational effect. The radical reformers and revolutionaries incorrectly perceived the provincial academies as aristocratic finishing schools. Rather than rehabilitate them into democratic classrooms, by allowing a broader segment of the population to attend, they were summarily closed. The École Militaire was shut down in 1787, the rest by 1791. The technical schools remained open throughout the revolutionary and Napoleonic eras, however, and continued to cull students from those with the most aptitude, regardless of their social stations.[125]

With the post–Seven Years' War increase in both size and egalitarianism of the armed forces, demands for both social reform and counterreform were rising. The period after Saint-Germain's ministerial tenure represents the third period of military reorganization influencing the French Revolution. It was a reactionary period, however, a reckless attempt to rein in the antiauthoritarian impetus now rampant in the military. The aristocracy, who rightly feared the social leveling effects of the Choiseul/Saint-Germain reforms, convinced Louis XV to repeal many of them. Moreover, the aristocracy deeply resented the cuts in active-duty officerships over the previous decade. Since there were fewer officer positions to be had, the nobility insisted they be filled with aristocrats, and successfully lobbied the crown to limit appointments to only the most-noble aspirants. On May 22, 1781, the Ségur decree allowed for *new* officer appointments only if the candidate could prove four generations of noble heritage.[126] This requirement satisfied the aristocracy, but was not as detrimental to the armed forces or to its impetus for liberalization as one might surmise. The new requirement applied only to nonmilitary personnel entering into the army. Promotions would still be based on merit, and accessions could still come from the ranks (e.g., it did not apply to field or within-ranks promotions and appointments). To do otherwise would severely restrict the overall quality of the new armed forces, especially in the technical fields. The limiting of only new military appointments to the aristocracy clearly shows a change in the prevailing French attitude. The older view held that only the nobility had been bred to the task of leading men into battle, and the lower classes were only fit to follow. That the lower classes could enter the officer ranks via performance in enlistment, and that all promotions were based on merit, represents a major change in belief structure.

The effective increase in nonaristocratic appointments to the officer, despite the Ségur decree, caused additional though not unexpected financial burdens for the state. The relative wealth of the aristocracy often allowed them to shoulder additional burdens for the units of which they were placed in charge. If pay or appropriation funds were late, the nobility might take monies from their own pocket to make up the shortfalls. Especially as regulations squeezed the ability of officers to supplement their incomes from corruption, men of lesser means could be discouraged from seeking a commission. To satisfy officers who could no longer enhance their incomes directly from their commands, a new pay scale was introduced, giving raises to all ranks but especially rewarding the higher grades. The new pay scales allowed a soldier of inferior birth to appear, in dress and living standards at least, of equal bearing to the nobility.

The retrograde counterreforms were not producing satisfactory results in either military efficiency or in reducing popular anti-crown antagonisms, and so in 1787 the king called a War Council to implement a series of new [counter-counter-] reforms in the spirit of Choiseul and Saint-Germain. To satisfy growing discontent with the ranks of soldiers, reforms included the abolition of punishments not expressly provided for in the regulations, with soldiers having recourse to official complaints in the event they felt punishment had been too harsh or incorrectly inflicted. In an interesting deferment to the recognition of the growing rights of the soldier, officers were forbidden to use the second-person singular form of address with their subordinates, as it was found to be degrading.[127] The War Council also reduced the total number of officers and set limits on future aristocratic commissions. In 1787 and 1788, the royal bodyguards were reduced substantially from Saint-Germain's reformed numbers, and the Gendarmie was eliminated.[128]

By 1789, the standing army had dwindled to about 156,000 troops, slightly less than its authorized peacetime strength.[129] A profile of the soldiers and officers of that army highlights the organizational impact of the military on the major political changes about to take place. Soldiers were now recruited for six to eight years, instead of the prevailing 20–30-year enlistments common before the reforms.[130] The shorter enlistment exposed more citizens to military service, and returned them to their homes while still politically active. In addition, soldiers received a bonus for each campaign (as an inducement to *esprit*), tempting them to volunteer for combat duty. In this way about 15 percent of active duty French soldiers had combat experience, gathered mostly in the American War of Independence and the Corsican Rebellions.[131] Thus, they had the sense of fighting on behalf of their state, the highest level of personal sacrifice, and they had exposure to patriots fighting for their national independence. This would prove a deadly combination for the *ancién regime.*

Military demographics provide fascinating insight into the nature of the pre-Revolution French military. André Corvisier has noted the propensity for troops to come from the north and east of France, a phenomenon he equates with a frontier spirit. Frenchmen from the coastal areas of west (and for Mediterranean service south) France tended to favor naval service to that of the army, and sent a large proportion of their young men to sea. These frontier regions also heavily supported a naval militia, which formed the basis for French recruitment in war.[132] Samuel Scott prefers to credit the bulk of the discrepancy to the fact that the heaviest concentration of French army garrisons were on the northern and eastern borders, thus recruiting was more concentrated in these areas, and people were naturally more inclined to participate in defense where the threat to their homes and family was most apparent.[133] Scott also observes that the military height requirement may have also been a factor. Peasants from south and west France tended to be shorter than those of the north and east.

Even so, the important factor for the coming revolution in this regional distribution of active soldiers was the markedly urban cast of the enlisted force, especially considering a general preference for rural soldiers by the aristocratic officer corps (they were more accustomed to obeying the feudal lord, the thinking went). Although just 19 percent of the French population was urban from 1763 to 1789, a full 35 percent of the foot army was urban. Not only was the infantry overrepresented by urbanites, half the urban soldiers came from the major metropolitan areas and an overrepresented proportion of them came from Paris. A full 40 percent of the infantry noncommissioned officers were from urban areas.[134] From the end of Louis XIV's reign until 1789, the percentage of artisans and shopkeepers continuously rose. By 1789, these groups were equal to those from the peasantry (about 35–40 percent each).[135] On the other hand, the nobility had almost dropped out of the enlisted ranks by 1789, to less than two per thousand soldiers.[136] The non-noble wealthier classes were also conspicuously absent, since the chances of merging socially with the aristocracy through military service, a common practice in Prussia, Russia, and England, were quite unlikely in France. The importance of the high urban concentration is that it allows for increased interaction after service. Brethren of war, dissatisfied with domestic situations after service, would be concentrated in the urban areas where they could more effectively organize, and from there, rebel. The limited social interaction of rural areas had always made it more difficult to spread ideas or to concentrate force for successful rebellion, and so it is worth stressing the high concentrations of urbanites in the military and its influence on the coming social revolution.[137]

As for the officer corps, it too had undergone serious demographic change since the first part of the century. The great reduction of officer positions after the Seven Years' War made competition for remaining commissions intense. The approximately 5–10 percent of the officer corps that was non-noble at the century's midpoint was effectively eliminated by 1789.[138] Before the bloodless purge of the Ségur decree, especially competent soldiers could be promoted to sub-lieutenant through captain.

These men were called *officiers de fortune* and performed the most thankless troop-oriented tasks, including training and discipline. In the eyes of the aristocratic officers, these men were little more than ranking noncommissioned officers.[139] In many respects, they were the equivalent of modern warrant officers—highly accomplished noncommissioned officers with command authority. Where technical competence and experience were valued, *officiers de fortune* were more prevalent. Indeed, an absolute preponderance of lower-ranking officers in the artillery and engineering branches were *officiers de fortune*, and one such commoner managed to attain the rank of brigadier in the artillery during the Seven Years' War.[140]

Hence, all non-noble officers were constrained professionally and socially by the titled aristocrats in service who had the advantages of access and occasionally kinship with the king. The nobility clung fiercely to its domination of the officer corps, especially at the higher ranks. In 1758, the 181 highest-ranking general officers were all titled (3 royal princes, 5 other princes, 11 dukes, 44 counts, 38 marquis, 14 chevaliers, and six barons).[141] The Seven Years' War brought a number of field commissions, and non-nobles climbed the ranks. Two officers of commoner origin, Bourcet and Chevret, actually made lieutenant general.[142] Their success was looked upon with great distress, and after a 1760 royal decree, only the upper aristocracy, the *noblesse presentée*, could legally advance beyond the grade of colonel.[143] The decree was not entirely effective, however, as once again it cut into the competency of the armed forces. Non-nobles of extreme skill (those promoted on merit) were still needed to provide the military with technical expertise, but the numbers were small. In 1789, of "eleven field marshals, five were dukes, four were marquis, one a prince, and one a count. Only nine of the 196 lieutenant generals were non-titled. Of more than 950 lesser generals, only one-fifth were aristocrats without titles."[144] Despite the aristocratic stranglehold on the officer corps, and the antidemocratic influence such a structure entailed, the gross scale of militarism in pre-Revolutionary France was quite low relative to its contemporaries. The bourgeoisie and upper middle class could see no reasonable route to enhanced social standing through military service, and so tended to disdain military emulation. Even for the upper classes, military trappings and associations were not highly visible. It was, for example, a serious breach of court etiquette to appear at Versailles in uniform.[145]

Reliance on mercenaries, always a heavy practice in French armies, had also been also dwindling with the absolute decrease in troops. In the Seven Years' War, there were 13 Swiss regiments, 14 German, 5 Hungarian (Hussars), 5 Irish, and 1 Scotch. In all, perhaps 20 percent of serving foot combatants counted in the strength tables as mercenaries.[146] Swiss regiments were predominantly filled with Swiss and German soldiers and officers, but not exclusively so. Most of the troops in the other foreign regiments were French, their titles being primarily honorific. By 1789, the French had standardized the number of crown regiments. Eleven were Swiss, twelve others were foreign, and 79 were in title French. Of the 91 non-Swiss infantry regiments, about 8 percent of the soldiers assigned were foreigners, though just 3 percent of cavalry and less than 1 percent of artillery regiments were foreigners.[147] Although figures are generally unavailable for officers, foreigners "were undoubtedly very numerous."[148] The foreign regiments dwindled in part because they compounded the problems of standardization and efficiency that the reformers wanted to instill. Compounding the impact of mercenary troops on liberalization, most of the foreign regiments were still paid directly by their commanders, swore loyalty to him, and maintained their own systems of military justice.[149] Still, the overall use of mercenaries was in precipitous decline before the revolution.

One more component of military organization influencing the political form of government (perhaps unique to the French experience), was the considerable role of French citizens fighting for revolution and freedom in the War of American Independence. To ease the humiliation of the disastrous Seven Years' War, France openly encouraged American rebellion as a means of balancing power with Britain. In the American War of Independence, France's naval and regular military contributions were decisive, and it went into considerable debt in order to do so at a time when it was still trying to shake off the fiscal losses of the previous conflict.[150] It is easy to presume that soldiers and sailors returning to their homes would take with them stirring tales of the egalitarian revolution taking place in America, and an understanding of the basic revolutionary ideals it embraced. They might see in themselves citizens of equal worth, and would harbor desires for similar political independence. Such notions in the commoner would be expected. What is striking, however, was how the American War of Independence proved wildly popular with aristocrats and educated classes in France, and contributed to the fashionable ongoing debates of what form good and responsible government must take.[151] Ambassador Franklin was adored at court, and Rousseau was the literary toast of the nation.

The organization of the military on the eve of the French Revolution had changed markedly since 1715, but was only slightly more liberalizing than it was at the end of the Sun King's reign. Taken together, pressures for democratic change had been consistently (if slowly rising) for almost hundred years. Rebellions had become endemic, but were still not focused. Most military reforms in the previous century contributed to an organization structure that was increasingly pro-democratic, and indirectly supportive of the popular rebellions, albeit countered by the steadily decreasing size of the armed forces both relatively and absolutely. In other words, the army was becoming more democratic in professional terms, but had less influence due to its small relative size. This suggests a straight weighting of characteristics could be usefully tweaked, but the fundamental approach is sound. The French absolutist government had managed to withstand significant reform pressures through two unspectacular monarchs, but its hold on power was slipping, and about to fall with cataclysmic force.

Revolution

On August 8, 1788, amid growing public dissension, Louis XVI promised to recall the *Estates General* for the first time in 174 years.[152] In 1614, the popular legislature had been convened at the instigation of the crown to discuss matters of political reform. The reforms suggested at that time by the Third Estate (non-noble, nonclergy; those being the First and Second Estates, respectively) were generally to reduce taxes, standardize weights and measures, and limit royal and clerical exemptions.[153] The then-radical demands of the Third Estate were unacceptable, and the body was summarily dismissed, not to be called forth again. Given the rapidly deteriorating situation in 1789, however, Louis XVI had little recourse but to call the legislative bodyand hope that in so doing, public dissent would be ameliorated. Such was his vanity that Louis probably believed that given the chance to express the logic and divine morality of his government, the representatives would be utterly swayed by his logic and would have no recourse but to enthusiastically support him.

The Estates General convened in May of 1789, and a few weeks into its session, on June 17, 1789, the delegation of the Third Estate declared itself the National Assembly and resolved to stay in session until the king formally recognized the constitutional power of the people. Louis XVI quickly annulled the resolutions, but the Assembly remained intransigent. Local soldiers refused their royal officer's commands to forcibly disband the Assembly, and on June 27, the king was forced to surrender to the demands of the National Assembly.[154]

The concessions appeared to be tactical. Louis XVI soon gathered a significant military contingent and tried to force the National Assembly to adjourn. Instead of supporting the king, however, the mostly urban foot soldiers brought in to quell the disturbance joined the rebellion and helped storm the Bastille on July 14. Their critical participation in the historic event marking French independence was so vital that it is called "the revolution of the soldiers."[155] Simon Schama reports that entire companies of the *guarde française* reinforced the crowd, and emphatically points out that many of the key military defectors had seen service in the American Revolution.[156] The revolutionaries finally had a model of democracy to mimic, and the king was now forced to make additional concessions recognizing the limited authority of the National Assembly. Serfdom, tithes, feudal dues, many aristocratic privileges, and manorial courts were abolished. The principle of equal taxation was proclaimed, the sale of public offices was banned, and all citizens, regardless of social rank, were declared eligible for any public office—*civil, military, and clerical*. On August 4, the Assembly closed with the somewhat mocking, if not outright sarcastic proclamation that Louis XVI was "the restorer of French liberty."[157]

The Assembly then moved to Paris (from Versailles), where it was thought more secure because of the strong revolutionary support of its urban inhabitants, many of who were in the military garrison. The Constitution passed in 1791, which incorporated the political reforms promised in 1789, maintained the hereditary monarchy (strictly limited by Montesquiue's "separation of powers") with a proscribed veto over some legislative actions. Suffrage was limited to citizens who paid a minimum level of taxes. These voters were dubbed "active citizens." All others, a vast majority, were declared "passive citizens," and while fully protected by the Constitution, had no vote. Military reforms included the formal abolition of venality (practically eliminated by the suppressions of Saint-Germain already), the proviso that commissions were to be open to all classes based on merit, and, in return for the critical service they had performed in the Revolution, pay for all soldiers was raised.

The French military had been undergoing drastic organizational changes in step with, and always in advance of, corresponding political upheavals. These reforms project a liberalized government equivalent to the one established by the Constitution of 1791. A more radical democracy would need correspondingly radical military restructuring. The first evidence of a purely egalitarian military influence occurs when a number of spontaneous and independent patriotic militias emerged to support the revolution in July and August of 1789, most stocked with a complement of deserting line soldiers.[158] These were all voluntarily formed, and members voted on most leadership positions. Although many of these soldiers were overcome by the patriotic swell of the revolution, many more were simply scoundrels looking for loot in the burning aftermath of urban violence. A significant number may also have been interested in advancement and power opportunities afforded in a new kind of military that did not promote based on birth or wealth. An experienced sergeant was worth a great deal to a new militia, for example, and he might instantly be made a colonel. All these self-formed militias needed to formally influence political development was state-sponsored legitimacy. And they quickly got it. One of the first acts of the National Assembly was to incorporate these disparate units into a disciplined and centrally managed national militia called the National Guard.[159] The National Guard quickly became the dominant component of the French military.

By June of 1791, prospects had become bleak for the monarchy. Louis XVI and Marie Antoinette believed their only hope of reviving the authority of the crown lay in fleeing the country and plotting its return from abroad. They were caught secreting away to the frontier and returned to Paris. In partial response, the National Assembly called for an immediate levy of 100,000 National Guard recruits to "serve along side the already existing 'line' army of France"—particularly at the border.[160] The units of the National Guard were popularly recruited, and its officers elected from local contingents, but they were drawn almost entirely from urban, upper-middle-class merchants and artisans. The rural and poorer elements of society still had not been given full participatory rights in either the government or the citizen-army, but the Guard was the most egalitarian fighting force in Europe.[161] As unrestricted and classless as the Guard had become, it was not the only avenue for upward military and social mobility. The line or regular army was also in the process of a necessary popularization. In the first year of the Revolution, over 2,000 French nobles, many of them military officers, fled the country. They were replaced by noncommissioned officers or National Guard officers, themselves generally drawn from the lower ranks. By the beginning of 1793, less than 15 percent of the regular officer corps was of the former nobility.[162] Most mercenaries, too, had been purged from the line military and, by 1793, less than 4 percent of the armed forces were of foreign birth.[163]

The revolutionary army (both National Guard and the more established line army) were glutted with new recruits, and simply could not be trained as well as Louis XIV's Colonel Martinet would have liked. To be sure, the steady influx of volunteers combined with the desertion or imprisonment of numerous experienced officers meant training was rudimentary at best, nonexistent at worst. It was enough for many units simply to issue weapons and uniforms to these raw recruits, point them to their new units, and say a prayer for their souls. The might of the new French army, which always seemed to inflict more casualties on itself than on its enemies, was based in its overwhelming numerical superiority, *esprit de corps*, and in its nationalist enthusiasm, not in its military skill.[164] Lazare Carnot, organizer of the revolutionary military forces, believed a pristine art of war had been established. The old order was founded on skill and precision with drill and weapons; the new order was based on raw numbers and boundless esprit. His infamous declaration was that in this revolutionary new age, there was no place for strategy and tactics; there were "no more manoevers [sic], no more military art but fire, steel, and patriotism."[165] The French armies would overwhelm their enemies by the sheer power of will.

This radical new military force was audacious, and terrifying to the established monarchies of Europe. The ideals of the radical new constitutional monarchy of France were a direct threat to traditional states, a type of political disease that must be quarantined then expunged. All the monarchies of Europe banded together to squash the upstart Republic before its ideology could infect them. In August 1791, Prussia and Austria ceremoniously announced that the goal of reestablishing the old French Monarchy was in the interest of all of Europe. Austria followed up by issuing the counterrevolution Declaration of Pillnitz, articulating the value of maintaining the monarchies of Europe as the best protection of individual rights, a conservative viewpoint already articulated by Burke in response to the American claims for independence. The Declaration did not appear to be a call to arms; Austria actually reduced its military forces by 25,000 before issuing it. Nonetheless, the Girondists in Paris used the declaration as a call for war, believing it might divert attention from France's internal problems and consolidate their own political positions.[166] On April 20, 1792, they had Louis request the Legislative Assembly declare war on Austria, which it did with near unanimity.

Partially in response to the declaration of war, partially in a demonstration of the personal ambition of Maximillian Robespierre and August Danton, the Jacobin-led insurrection of August 10, 1792 captured the king, suspended the legislature, and established a provisional government. The Jacobins had reason to be confident, "Senior military commanders, even those with royalist sentiments, almost unanimously concluded that the soldiers would not support a march on Paris to restore the King."[167] The democratization of the military appeared well on its way, with government then all of society bound to follow. Shortly after the August coup, instructions were given to establish a new constitution with universal suffrage to *all* adult males, *in direct recognition of the army's past service*—and perhaps in anticipation of the coming manpower needs of the defense of the state.[168] On September 20, 1792, the Jacobin-dominated National Convention convened with the goal of establishing a new, more radical constitution. At the end of the second session, the National Convention abolished the monarchy. The day after, France was declared a republic. On January 20, 1793, Louis was executed.

On December 15, 1792, the National Convention declared that its armies would establish the sovereignty of the people in every territory it occupied. The Girondist government had offended the traditional monarchies of Europe. The Jacobins, with their declaration and execution of the king, horrified them. With these actions, Republican France had formally thrown down the gauntlet to every state in Europe.[169] Representatives of the Jacobin Convention had taken a calculated risk. They believed the declaration would be a great boon to their international position by inciting an internal rebellion in every state that opposed them. France would be seen by the multitudes as a liberator, a protector of human rights. Indeed, when the

Convention delegates declared war against England on February 1, 1793, they fully expected the people there to rise up and overthrow King George unaided. They did not. One supposes the prospect of living under Revolutionary French government instead of parliament and king was less savory to the British than the French anticipated. Even if the revolutions were unsuccessful, however, they should aid the French by distracting their enemies. At any rate, the Declaration was so threatening that by the spring of 1793, France was formally at war with England, Prussia, Austria, Holland, Spain, Portugal, Sardinia, and Naples.

The declaration was more than a rhetorical tool. It would be the harbinger of a new era of war; one that would know no heretofore established bounds. The declaration meant that war would no longer be limited in aims. It could approach total war; a concept that Clausewitz would find fully formed only in theory, but nearly matched in the real world by French nationalism. From here on, war with France would not be for territorial or monetary concessions. In a stark break with the absolutist period, war with France now risked dissolution of the state.

Faced with war abroad and dissension at home, the Jacobins forcibly took control of the Convention and established a ruthless dictatorship. At its head stood the Committee of Public Safety, nine members initially, then "twelve who ruled."[170] The Committee decided to combat counterrevolution with the establishment of a single will of revolutionary democracy among the citizenry, a will to be forged by arresting and sometimes executing anyone who did not share it. Rousseau's notion that a citizen can be forced to be free was put into practice by the Committee's policy of "terror as the order of the day."[171]

The self-induced international crisis required a massive increase in military power to counter it. To increase the size and efficiency of its directly controlled military, the Committee ordered the Regular Army and National Guard to combine into a single service.[172] Both were still organized on the principle of voluntary service, and by mid-1793 the supply of spirited voluntary recruits ran out. The army was in shambles, poorly equipped and with no time for training. France was being overrun on every front. The Committee turned to Lazare Carnot, its military affairs organizer, for a solution. He obliged.

A defeated army awaited Carnot's instructions. The experts insisted it was not if, but when the seven foreign armies that were already occupying French soil would dismantle the Republic. But Carnot would not submit. He fully embraced the Jacobinist doctrine of "Audacity, more audacity, always audacity," and incorporated it into his own *agapic calculus* of the human condition.[173] He was convinced that overwhelming enthusiasm would solve what had become an impossible military dilemma. His guiding principle was "attack, attack, always attack," and for this he needed troops—a *lot* of troops.[174] "It is time to think about striking decisive blows, and for this purpose it is necessary to act *en masse*."[175] With this strategic aim, Carnot proposed to the Committee a *levée en masse*, "where every French citizen was to be mobilized against the enemy in a nonstop offensive."[176]

Under Carnot's decree, conscripts swelled the ranks. The state and military were wholly unprepared, and the vast majority had no weapons, uniforms, or even basic subsistence. But they were imbued with an extraordinary élan. They believed in the Republic and they fought with incredible courage. Their lack of baggage made them extremely maneuverable, and so Carnot ordered offensives at every point the enemy appeared weak. Within months, this ragtag army of ordinary citizens swept the invaders from France and marched into foreign territory. The *lévee* completely revolutionized war, perhaps more so than the introduction of gunpowder. The only means by which the monarchies of Europe could hope to counter the million-man army of France was to mobilize their own populations—and doing so meant that liberalization was destined to spread throughout Europe.

But more than a high population percentage engaged in the defense of the state was a factor in the continuing liberalization of France. Carnot did more than simply throw his masses of conscripts at his enemies professional soldiers. He believed deeply in the principle of the constant offensive, and that the road to victory was based on speed of maneuver and mobilization—to strike where the enemy was weak and unprepared.

The infamous *lévee en masse* of August 23, 1793, was a call for every man, woman, and child to assist in the defense of France. All unmarried men from 18 to 25 were immediately summoned to combat duty, all others to military support.[177] Scientists were enlisted to work on problems of metallurgy, explosives, ballistics, and the like. A research library was established at Meudon (which still operates) that devised the first military observation balloons.[178] The *lévee* was a desperate measure to be sure, but the new army proved itself by sheer weight of numbers and determined will to win (garnered either by elan, the terror, or a mix of both) to be an effective fighting force. The *lévee en masse* had one glaring antidemocratic flaw, however. Although every Frenchman was called to compulsory service in combat, he could purchase his deferment or discharge from duty by means of securing a *replacement* or substitution. There soon developed a "commerce in human flesh" that kept the wealthier classes from risk.[179] This perversion of the egalitarian principle of universal service was damaging to the overall spirit of the new Republic, but considering the enormous number of men who did serve, the detraction was minimal.

With its borders secured and the external crisis abated, the Convention eventually turned to the task of penning a new Constitution, but did so without including the radical modifications for which it was convened. The excesses of the Jacobins had led to their demise, and the Convention had reasserted its authority over the Committee. The 1795 Constitution was designed primarily to forestall the return of the monarchy and continue the now ensconced rule of the middle classes. Its suffrage allowances were similar to the previous Constitution. It included all men who paid a minimum tax, but in recognition of the sacrifices incurred with the *lévee en masse*, it now included any man who had served in combat at the front.[180]

The new Constitution delivered far less than was promised in 1792, and Parisians supported by renegade soldiers rose in revolt once again. The only firmly reliable military officer in the area, an experienced artillery lieutenant named Bonaparte, was tapped by the Convention to put down the insurrection. Napoleon had been made a brigadier-general in the revolutionary army by Robespierre, but after the fall of his party was imprisoned, and then demoted. Those who knew him were aware of his abilities, and believed his loyalty could be assured by playing to his ambitions.[181] As the Parisians marched on the legislature, Napoleon dispersed them with a grapeshot cannonade, and the "cannonade of Valmy" may very well have saved the revolution.[182] As a reward for his service to the Republic, Napoleon was made Commander-in-Chief of the Army of the Interior. In 1796, at his own request, he was made Commander-in-Chief of the Army of Italy. Fantastic success abroad, first in Italy, then in Germany and Egypt, cemented Napoleon's fame and popularity. He returned to France from the Orient in 1799, and completed his plans to overthrow the French government.

The levee did more than turn the French army into a citizen's militia, previous decrees had already done that. More radically, it turned the army into a *nation* of soldiers.[183] The motto of the Revolution was "liberty, equality, and fraternity." What better way to rapidly and firmly instill the ideals of all three, reasoned the Committee on Public Safety, than in the cauldron of battle? But there were inherent if not unsuspected dangers in so rapidly transforming a society of passive citizens into active warriors. The nation of soldiers so hastily removed from their monarchial and dictatorial past may have been unable or unwilling to resist the allure of one of their own, a soldier-king who promised (and delivered) military success. The rapidity of events and depth of change occurring in the revolution may have overwhelmed the capacity of citizens to adapt. Unlike the American Revolution that preceded it, the French were thrust suddenly into universal suffrage and citizenship. They may have been unable to shrug off their past experience with authority.[184]

Once in power, Napoleon began his own series of reforms. These were mostly tactical. He had no new weapon technologies to exploit, and though he manipulated the enthusiasm of the citizen-army to his own ends, he did not create it. In the aggregate, Napoleon's tactical innovations were fourfold: he standardized the French division as an autonomous unit of combined arms, giving the army greater speed, coordination, and flexibility of movement; he increased the deployment of free-firing skirmishers—the *guerre des postes*, a type of light infantry to harass the enemy's ability to maneuver; he employed a more flexible use of battlefield artillery to concentrate fire on specific points; and he emphasized the use of column attack instead of line attack, eliminating the need for a battlefield maneuver prior to engagement and emphasizing the role of shock—much as the hoplite phalanxes of free Greek warriors employed it.[185]

The new tactics were particularly suited to the new army which, for a variety of reasons already mentioned, lacked the rigorous training required for precise military tactics and the stern discipline to stand firm under withering fire, so characteristic of the armies of the ancién regime. The new volunteers may not have been disposed to accept the drill regimen of Martinet even if the army had the training cadre available to implement it. They naturally abhorred the harsh and rigorous training of the old army, and now that they had a say in it, were vociferously opposed to precise march and drill. "They were fighting as free men to defend freedom," and for them the new tactics were "the natural mode of fighting."[186]

By 1810, the Napoleonic army was stabilized, and decidedly democratic in its influence. The paradox of an emperor leading an essentially democratized people is understandable in the dramatic context of events. Democratic change had been instituted since 1789; enormous and rapid changes in fact. Many had considered France as more democratic than contemporary United States. And a democratic nation at war often proffers dictatorial power to a demagogue who promises victory.

Perhaps the test of the democracy should not be its ruling choice in crisis, but the remaining strength of dictatorship after the conflict, when peace is at hand. In the case of France, we have little to go on in this regard. What is sure is that the armed forces under Napoleon were organized in such a manner as to promote further democratic change, but the exigencies of war and the personal ambition of Napoleon combined to prevent the full realization of a truly democratic state. France, surrounded by hostile powers, did not have the luxury of time of the United States to come to terms with its sudden democratic character. The final victory of Europe over Napoleon in 1815 reversed much of the political change that had occurred over the previous 25 years, and forced a return of the old monarchy, but the impetus toward a liberalized political structure remained as well. French citizens almost continuously rebelled against political centralization, most violently in 1830, 1848, and 1871—the last date marking the final demise of the French monarchies and the beginning of permanent representative democracy.

Chapter Five

Military Organization and the Prusso-German State

Don't forget your great guns, which are the most respectable argument for the divine right of kings.

Frederick the Great (1785)

The process of political development in Prussia-Germany from 1640 to 1970 provides the soundest test of the proposition that military organization is a determining factor in the development of state-level political institutions. The transformation of this once minor principality from an unbalanced aristocracy into a model of modern liberal democracy has included intervals of absolutist despotism, constitutional monarchy, a radically progressive democratic republic, fascist dictatorship, and modern liberal democracy. Since all these governing types are evident in a distinct society over a historically short period, this case study has the advantage of holding several potentially important cultural and sociopolitical alternative intervening variables constant, thereby enhancing the focus on military factors.

A historical account of changing military organization shows that an alternating influence of military reforms inspired the development of both decentralized democratic and centralized authoritarian political structures, then back again, through several distinct periods. In historical order, requirements for ever-larger military forces assisted in breaking down feudal autocracy from the mid-seventeenth to early eighteenth century while simultaneously promoting a centralization of monarchial authority to the beginning of the nineteenth century. Military reforms in reaction to the Napoleonic invasions then triggered a period of increasing decentralization of political power evident from 1805 to 1850. Military retrenchment beginning in the 1820s ultimately promoted a strengthening of centralized absolutism from 1850 to 1914. World War I military mobilization and reorganization sharply encouraged democratization followed by an externally imposed military retrenchment after 1919 that helped set the conditions for fascist authoritarianism and centralization of government power. World War II mobilization and strategic military requirements encouraged a swing toward decentralization, followed by postwar military reorganization and augmentation that continued to promote stable representative democracy in the Federal Republic of Germany.

The Frederician State

The autonomous provinces of north Germany that comprised Brandenburg-Prussia in 1640 were decentralized, semi-constitutional feudal regimes, with a common though variably recognized heritage from both the rigidly authoritarian Teutonic Knights and the more politically permissive Republic of Nobles. Brian Downing has likened the situation to the Whig hegemony in England.[1] The entire region had been systematically plundered in the Thirty Years' War, and had suffered militarily due to its vulnerable position at the crossroads of the competing territorial ambitions of Sweden, Denmark, and Poland, and tangentially to those of France, Russia, and the Hapsburg Empire.

When Frederick William (1640–88), the "Great Elector" of Brandenburg, came to power, his small domain, which his father had maintained by diplomatic maneuvering, was on the verge of political dissolution.[2] Frederick William quickly grasped the precariousness of his situation, and astutely set about resurrecting his modest jurisdiction in a series of bold and unprecedented moves. He unilaterally extricated his country from its web of foreign entanglements, and committed to a singular reliance on his own internal resources for defense. Both moves were daring, and fraught with potential disaster. A state the size of Brandenburg-Prussia, it was thought, had no choice but to seek the protection of others. Without a mobile field army to use as leverage, the terms of any alliance would be unfavorable, and in the seventeenth century, the best field armies were augmented by contracted cohorts of professional mercenaries. Frederick William could neither afford mercenaries nor unbalanced alliances, and so he sought a fresh solution.

Frederick William immediately began to purge the misfits and undesirables from his army, including criminals and especially foreign mercenaries. This was an outlandish move at a time when military service was, for both soldier and state, an expedient alternative to imprisonment. He dismissed officers who were unfit and arrested those who had maintained their positions as an avenue to personal wealth, typically through extortion of the cities within their command. These commanders would not only demand additional revenues for billeting their troops within the city, thus protecting them from external threats, but, having done so, for keeping them from looting and pillaging. The resulting armed force amounted to just 2,500 men, a fraction of its prior strength.[3] But this was a homegrown and professional fighting force, tiny though it was, and so it was effective for Frederick William's limited aims. Through judicious fiscal and organizational management, steady subversion of the privileges of the aristocracy, and enthusiastic cooperation of the relieved populous, Frederick William assembled within eight years a small but militarily very proficient force of 8,000 men. Now, on his own terms, he reentered the ongoing Thirty Years' War just in time to win several territorial concessions in the Peace of Westphalia (1648). His astute maneuvering under duress gave Frederick William not only a loyal and now veteran military force, but also a financially viable state with significant new lands for settlement and oversight.

In peace, Frederick William proved even more effective in raising the strength of his now proficient and widely respected army. Within two years it had doubled to 16,000 men under arms, and by the end of his reign it stood at 30,000 field combatants.[4] In the new Prussian army, all individuals received uniform training by a loyal cadre. Soldiers were paid directly by the state, and their personal needs were met through the offices of the Elector, and not circuitously through the officerships of the petty nobility. The revolutionary result of these actions was to institute the first truly professional standing army in Europe, and the impact was far ranging.[5]

Key to the Elector's success was an arrangement changing the obligatory relationship between his office and the landholding aristocracy, the *Junkers*. Prior to Frederick William's military reforms, and similar to most of Europe, the Junkers operated their estates in return for military and other services in time of recognized need. With the establishment of the standing army, the old system was strained. The Elector was in effect declaring a constant external threat, but the Junkers could not be expected to maintain themselves and their retinues permanently afield. They needed time and resources to manage their estates. A negotiated agreement ensued that relieved the Junkers of their manpower responsibilities. Henceforth, they would pay taxes in lieu of service, and they further agreed to empower the Elector to maintain a permanent tax authority, so as to assess ongoing and future needs (instead of a fixed-rate plan). In this manner the *financial* capacity to build his modernized, permanent army was affirmed. In return, the Junkers were recognized as the only class eligible to own and acquire landed estates, with absolute feudal power over the peasants attached to the land. The trade-off for an increased fiscal windfall to the crown was the written recognition of the feudal institution of serfdom on the Junker estates.[6]

The new agreement meant that Frederick William could not extract recruits from the estates without compensating the Junkers for their loss. But the feudal relationship had to be maintained, in the view of the Elector, even though it cut into his authoritarian prerogative. The Junker class had a second vital role in the Elector's plans to transform the army. The landed aristocracy, especially the excess nobility produced by the firstborn rights of primogeniture, was to form the crucial basis of the new officer ranks with the rural peasantry incorporated as naturally obedient soldiers. The intention was to transform the traditional feudal relationship of lord and peasant into a new, parallel relationship of officer and soldier.[7] The absolute authority of the Junker in peace would be unquestioned in war, increasing discipline and morale. Frederick William was logically implementing in fact an idea that was widely held at the time. The aristocracy was believed to possess through birthright the traits of natural leaders. The rural peasantry, by the same hereditarily based argument, was thought to make hardier and more amenable followers—particularly more so than traditionally unruly urban subjects. The purposeful class structuring of the military reinforced aristocratic class divisions, and blunted any effect the increased military participation ratio might have had.

More than just demographic changes in the military structure occurred under Frederick William, however. Before his reforms, Prussian military supply and recruitment followed prevailing European models. When mercenary supplements to the armed forces were required, the state would negotiate a price or commission to an individual who would guarantee to deliver a military unit of determined size and armament. Rank was often conferred based on the capacity to provide soldiers; Colonel being awarded for delivered regiments of specified size, Captain for companies, and so on.[8] The excesses and inefficiencies of the contract system, described in the previous chapter, was a luxury Frederick William could ill afford. He determined to recruit and supply soldiers directly and systematically, in order to guarantee uniformity of training and capabilities.

To do so, he created the bureaucratic office of the *Generalkriegskommissariat*, and assigned to it the tasks of recruitment, supply, and administration. Frederick William's military was his most valuable possession, his guarantee of sovereignty, and so he invested the Generalkriegskommissariat with extraordinary powers. While it could not independently set its own overall budget, it had broad control over how to manage funds, and had the authority to collect taxes directly should its allotments prove slow in arriving.[9] To expedite its functions, it gradually took over the duties of the judiciary, local police, and local administration in many towns and hamlets.[10] The methods it employed were not substantially new. Press gangs were common, and desertion was endemic. What was unprecedented was the infiltration of the state bureaucracy into everyday life. Everyone knew of it and all were affected by it. The pervasiveness of the Generalkriegskommissariat was such that by 1760, one in four-teen Prussians were serving in some capacity in the military.[11] More critical for the future of the Prussian state, it gave the military the power to effectively control its own political destiny. Institutional checks on the growth of the military powers of the state were practically eliminated.

The establishment of the Generalkriegskommissariat fundamentally changed the way in which soldiers and officers interacted with the state. Loyalty in the old system was based on hierarchical allegiance to the next superior officer, in essence the person who recruited and paid for the soldier's services. The new method meant that all soldiers were paid by the state directly, and so their loyalty incentive was to the ruler of the state, with no intervening authority. While still quite personal, it was at a level of abstraction for most line soldiers sufficient enough to let them realize they were, in fact, sacrificing for the state. Officers of all ranks were made to take an oath to Frederick William not as their sovereign, but as their commander in chief.[12] Such destruction of the intervening layers between state and citizen has proven over and again to be a necessary precondition to the rise of patriotism and then nationalism.

In order to maintain the military character of the Generalkriegskommissariat, Frederick William began the practice of finding government positions for military retirees in the burgeoning Prussian bureaucracy, further promoting the structural militarization of civilian society.[13] Otto Hintze highlighted this insidious practice in his essays, and wrote convincingly on the ramifications of finding militarily trained veterans overrepresented in the civil services.[14] They will tend to employ the methods and techniques learned in military service, Hintze argued, thus recreating military-style bureaucracy in the civilian sector. They may prefer the company of veterans to nonveterans, and give preferential treatment in the distribution of government services accordingly. They may be predisposed to give favor to active military institutions, and to denigrate purely civilian ones. In this way, the state is militarized from the bottom up, and classic militarism takes hold.

In addition to finding jobs for veterans in the bureaucracy, Frederick William also began a policy of establishing discharged soldiers as tenant farmers on his personal estates, further circumventing the state-level power of the old aristocracy. These individuals were not subject to the feudal obligations and miserable compensation of the Junker serfs, and were undoubtedly quite grateful for it. The personal loyalty these veterans showed Frederick William, extricated from the layered feudal state into the modern one, was no doubt sincere. But the Great Elector had a different purpose in mind. The establishment of large numbers of veterans working his lands not only gave him a solid labor pool for personal enrichment, more importantly it became the core of a ready reserve subject to year-round training and available for quick mobilization in time of war.[15] Frederick William no longer had to rely on Junker support for rapid force augmentation, giving him a vastly freer hand in foreign and domestic policy.

Hoping to increase Prussia's overall economic prosperity, Frederick William established a royal navy for the protection of Baltic commerce, and a state-sponsored African trading company to extend the reach of Prussian merchants. Realizing the need for skilled artisans and merchants to build an industrial and commercial capacity, he welcomed the immigration of French Huguenots fleeing the persecution of the Edict of Nantes. The immediate value to the state was so obvious that the Elector's programs for accepting and settling skilled craftsmen and laborers from abroad continued well past his rule. By 1786, about 300,000 émigrés had taken advantage of Prussian offers of sanctuary, and they added enormously to Prussia's burgeoning economy.[16]

In a not unanticipated coincidence, many of the arriving Huguenots had been officers in Louis XIV's armies, and Frederick William wasted no time in declaring them citizens and incorporating their talents into the Prussian army. By the end of the seventeenth century, 29 percent of Prussian army officers were Huguenots.[17] Frederick William also accepted a significant number of Polish officers into his army. His naturalization and incorporation of foreign elements into state and military clearly demonstrated his approval of financial reward and officer appointments based on merit and competence, at least for field grade service. His continuing reliance on the Junker nobility to staff the highest ranks of his military, however, was founded on the belief they had been reared with a greater tenacity and courage than the bourgeoisie or peasantry, and for their ability to control the rural-based soldiery originating in the feudal relationship. Frederick William could see that not all nobles were great officers, but held to the belief that all truly great officers were noble. Still, he did not hesitate to appoint individuals of great talent into line positions in his army, regardless of their birth.

Frederick William's reforms were the prelude to an unprecedented consolidation of state power, at the expense of the landed nobility. The new bureaucracy absorbed many of the domestic and military functions of the aristocracy and its practice of venality, and removed them as an insulating layer between citizen and state. But the notion that this process sacrificed existing democratic political structures for the glorification of the absolutist state, as Brian Downing suggests, is in error. There simply were no existing *democratic* institutions in Brandenburg-Prussia. The pockets of semiautonomous constitutional authority held by the nobility can be viewed as the outline of a future representative assembly, but there were no champions of mass political participation among the Junkers. Indeed, the nobility was more than happy to transfer its traditional military service function for a financial one, in return for recognition of serf/slavery for the peasantry. By making soldiers and veterans directly obliged to the state, Frederick William's reforms began the process of dispersing political power directly to those individuals while at the same time geographically restricting the institutionalized political authority of the aristocracy.

To be fair, Downing focuses on the legal–constitutional foundations of feudalism as the basis for representative democracy—not the (nonexistent) democratic institutions of feudalism. But he does portray the destruction of the constitutional relationships the nobility held vis-à-vis the crown after 1500 as the major impediment of the democratization process. The destruction of feudalism, in other words, was responsible for retarding the natural rise of democracy that would have occurred based on feudal constitutionalism. There simply isn't enough evidence in this dog-that-didn't-bark argument. The alternative presented here is that the feudal system was inherently self-perpetuating, and had to be destroyed before democratization was possible. A clear comparison is drawn (in the preceding chapters) with the destruction of the feudal nobility in classical Greece and in early modern Europe as a prerequisite to democratic government. Both were the result of changes in military organization, and both acted as necessary if not sufficient preconditions for the eventual formation of decentralized, democratic government. The institutional differences in liberalizing trajectory from one to the other are explained in terms of prior military organization.

Frederick William was succeeded by his son, titled both Elector Frederick III and, as the first King of Prussia, Frederick I (1688–1713). Frederick I was the intellectual shadow of his father, a dim-witted buffoon universally regarded as a weak leader. He is also renowned and ridiculed for his love of ceremony, pomp, and military display.[18] His most infamous contribution was his elevation of military ceremony and parade drill to high art. Frederick I treated his real soldiers like the wooden ones he played with as a boy, and his precious treatment of his military as a toy army stunted any of the potentially positive decentralizing reforms of his father. The functions of militarism, as Alfred Vagts has shown, are predicated on the growth of military functions and regalia that have no combat purpose.[19] For Frederick I, the army was a pretty diversion, and he didn't want their uniforms spoiled with dirt and blood. Maneuvers were best if they were intricate and visually pleasing, but not expedient. His reign was too long and his reforms ludicrous. Though training increased under Frederick I, combat proficiency plummeted.

Frederick William I (1713–40), dubbed the "Soldier King" by his contemporaries, assumed the throne on his father's death and immediately made the growth, efficiency, and fighting effectiveness of the Prussian army his top priority. He understood that the army was the foundation and source of all his power, glory, and security. Without quick action, he was condemned to mediocrity—or worse. In his age, Prussia was transformed until it was viewed no longer as "a country with an army, but an army with a country which served as headquarters and food magazine."[20] As part and parcel of his vision, the Soldier King set out to systematically rid Prussia of every vestige of aristocratic independence. It was decisive for Prussia's future, he believed, to personally administer the fiscal and military affairs of the *entire* state.[21]

Like his father, Frederick William I was obsessed with uniforms, insignia, and equipment, and had a peculiar devotion to his famous Potsdam Grenadiers, a personal guard staffed by unusually tall men from all over Europe.[22] Unlike his father, Frederick William I was totally unimpressed with pomp and ceremony for its own sake, and was a remarkably able, if legendarily frugal, administrator.[23] Frederick I had managed to increase the size of the standing force to about 40,000, and Frederick William I quickly doubled it to 83,000.[24] In the process, he also created the technically most advanced military in Europe, eclipsing even the Dutch. At a time when raw numbers of soldiers were essential in the great power equation, Frederick William I made the Prussian army the fourth largest in Europe, even though it was just tenth in territory and thirteenth in population.[25] His fiscal prudence allowed him to accomplish this impressive growth while steadily increasing the national treasury, managing to leave the enormous sum of seven million thalers to his son.[26] Nonetheless, in foreign policy matters, he was generally considered a failure. Veit claims that although the Soldier King had built the finest fighting force in Europe, he had no idea how to use it. He was "forced into the torturous and only half-comical role of the dolt who is always being outwitted."[27] An able administrator, he was a dismal strategist.

It was in fact this same fiscal prudence that led Frederick William I to institute the definitive military innovation of his reign, the canton conscription system. The severity of Prussian military punishment (used to ensure discipline) encouraged mass desertion at the same time the rising size of competing European armies demanded a response in kind. For a nation the size and population of Prussia, competing with France and Hapsburg Austria was an enormous fiscal and human resources strain on Prussian capacities. Since the Great Elector first purged the Prussian army of mercenaries in 1640, foreign professionals had steadily been recruited to make up indigenous shortfalls, and their cost was rising as rival states competed for their services. By the end of the seventeenth century, foreign mercenaries made up almost half of the standing Prussian forces.[28] Frederick William I sought to economize by compelling his own subjects to serve in the army.[29]

A precedent for conscription had existed in Prussia since the Thirty Years' War. At that time, an *ad hoc* peasant's militia had been established for the purpose of repelling marauding bandits and foraging armies. By the Soldier King's reign, voluntary enrollment in the generally dormant militia was seen as a method of escaping forced induction into the harsh regular army.[30] In order to incorporate this semiautonomous local peasant's militia into the state's forces, a series of edicts (1732–35) was published establishing the Prussian canton system of regimental recruiting. The state was divided into regions (cantons) responsible for the provision of a specified manpower in the form of a military unit. Cantons were of varying size dependent on their population densities, predominant occupational specialty, and whether the extracted regiment was infantry, cavalry, or artillery.

The myth that it was the canton system that established universal conscription in Prussia is legal fiction.[31] The principles of universal service were annunciated, to be sure, but in practice no more than half the adult male Prussian population was ever truly liable for service. The nobility had been freed from militia conscription since 1717, and any middle-class subject with an income of 10,000 thalers or more had been exempted since 1726.[32] Skilled workers, entire populations of specified towns and provinces, and members of certain religious groups were all exempt. An example of the limited liability of the canton system is shown in the Napoleonic defense year of 1804, when Prussia had a civilian population approaching 10 million. About 4.9 million of these were men, and of these about 2.25 million were of the right age for service liability. Of this group, nearly half were exempted due to territorial privilege and another half million were exempted for various occupational, religious, or property criteria.[33] Of the slightly more than half a million truly eligible adult males, only about eighty thousand were actually conscripted into regular service. In fact, the continuing harshness of military life and extreme cruelty of Prussian military discipline remained an unsolved administrative problem. In order to keep subjects from actually fleeing the country to avoid military service, Frederick William I felt compelled to exempt an increasingly significant percentage of the population simply to maintain Prussia's economically crucial but relatively dwindling human resources. It was a vicious cycle, unsolved by the Soldier King.

The principle that military service functions as a foundation for political participation, a foundational principle in the contract theory of the state, is presented in a decidedly coercive light by the canton system edicts. Military service was only marginally voluntary and service gained only minor special rights and political endowments. To infuse it with the rising phenomenon of nationalism, the principle of universal conscription in Prussia was rhetorically defended as an inborn patriotic duty to the state.[34] In this formulation, the people of a region do not constitute the state freely in contract. Rather, the existence of the state precedes the idea of citizenship, and the residents find themselves obligated to that state in a condition of preexisting servitude. Still, the coercive model works. Despite the rhetoric of servitude, the goals of subservience intended by state will not always be consistent with outcomes derived from its policies. Howsoever the state justifies universal conscription; the soldiers who serve the state will eventually yearn to assert themselves politically.

Indeed, the coerced recruitment of the peasantry into military service was not accomplished without political concessions. Peasants on the king's estates who served in the military were granted hereditary tenure on the lands they worked and guaranteed a living. Care for the elderly who were no longer agriculturally productive was a burden that previously fell to the family. With this new rudimentary form of social security, veterans would be taken care of by the state—or at least with the state's assistance. For nonroyal estates, the king proclaimed himself the protector of the peasantry—his soldier base. He entertained petitions of complaint and intervened on the peasantry's behalf against perceived excesses of the Junkers.[35] To be sure, both king and nobility believed the agricultural peasantry was by nature a politically dormant class, bereft of governing ambition and desires for power, but they could become agitated and disorderly if they were not properly coddled. The Prussian elite became so assured of their own benevolence that the initial reaction of the Prussian government following the 1789 French Revolution was that its loyal peasantry was incapable of rebellion. Prussia, they were convinced, was an enlightened state that assured the proper amount of liberty to its subjects in return for their dutiful participation in the military.[36]

Frederick William I incorporated a number of other military reforms that would have a decided impact on the emergence of Prussian liberalism. He drastically reduced the existing reliance on household quartering of his troops, preferring to see them concentrated in barracks to facilitate their training regimens.[37] Following

Maurice of Orange's lead, he further established standardized weaponry and introduced a common drill manual, rigorously strict in the smallest detail. The training brought about a uniformity and precision that was unmatched in Europe. He also established a cadet training school for the sons of the Junker nobility, and in so doing began the German tradition of the professional military academy.[38]

Not all of the Soldier King's reforms promoted political liberalization. The canton system, with its myriad exemptions, put the burden of military service almost entirely on the peasant farming classes. In order to smoothly integrate the rural masses into the new conscript army, Frederick William I institutionalized his grandfather's policy of recruiting the Junker-class nobility as the officer class of the army. The internal stratification of the military hierarchy with the Junker officer as a privileged class would survive through the period of National Socialism and into World War II.[39] Still, these reforms established among the citizenry a sense of national belonging, replete with political rights that percolated into successive generations.

The Prussian canton recruiting system was a remarkable innovation, even if never fully utilized. It was meticulously studied throughout Europe, and though rarely copied—for it was universally recognized as a threat to absolutism—it promoted and dispersed the complementary notions of national service and trained reserves. In an era when military power was preeminently a function of how many muskets and canon could be brought to bear on the battlefield, multiplied by effective rate of fire, the scrutiny of any innovation that increased the number of personnel in active and trained reserve status was imperative. Still, the heightened sense of direct state liability should have (and would have if left alone) promoted a greater sense of popular liberalism. It was thwarted by one of the vagaries of its day, a sudden change of administration, and by an increasing ideological external threat.

When Frederick II ("The Great," 1740–86) assumed the crown, he had little fear of a liberalizing influence in the military, but was reluctant to rely on the canton system for quite different reasons. In the manner of the Dutch, he felt the true strength of a national population base was in its capacity to provide support as taxpayers, not as soldiers.[40] The addition of a conscripted soldier meant the loss of an income producer. It was a foregone value. Therefore, conscripted cantonists should never account for more than 3 percent of the population, even if that meant fielding an army composed primarily of mercenaries.[41] Again following the lead of Maurice, with enough money—and Frederick II had inherited a full treasury and a fledgling industrial and commercial base from his father—he believed he could *purchase* and train the best available military force.

Frederick II was a great military strategist, but not an organizational innovator like his predecessors. In his many campaigns he was far more comfortable in the company of, and in relying on, professional soldiers than he was with conscripts. His military reforms, with the exception of foregoing the canton system as his primary source of combatants, were strictly in maneuver and battle tactics.[42] His battlefield exploits, while legendary, require no further description here. He was extremely successful in the field. His victories had the result of slowing the popular pressure for change during his campaigns, as a nascent sense of Prussian patriotism helped instill a "rally round the flag" effect. Frederick II's strenuous campaigning, brilliant as it was, ended with the physical and fiscal exhaustion of the state in 1761. The remnant

Prussian army entered a period of "petrification" that his immediate successor was unable to correct.[43] Decades of labor and money would be needed to resurrect it, and after the nonstop wars of Frederick II, there was little national stomach for the task.

Hence by 1800 the Prussian military had slipped to a second-rate power, probably less due to its own internal demise than to the relative rise of French, Austrian, and Russian power in the same period. States with vastly more resources copied the Prussian bureaucracy, if not its antiauthoritarian recruitment model, and were able to expand well beyond the indigenous Prussian efforts. Training was hampered by economic deficiencies. Mercenaries could not be paid, much less well paid, and the better soldiers marched off to where they could find lucrative employ. And although the existence of the canton system made mass recruitment of the peasantry a potentially cheap recruitment option, post-1789 events in France meant no member of the nobility was willing to chance revolution for quick military power. Prussia continued to rely instead on mercenary forces and foreign alliances for its security. The resultant impetus toward authoritarianism, evident in the buildup of the massive military-subservient, state-centered bureaucracy, was canceled out by the limited rights afforded veterans and the enormous expansion of the recruitment base. The increase in professionalism was countered by a continuing reliance on Junker nobility in the officer ranks, and after 1761, by a conspicuous lack of drill and training. In all, at the time of Frederick the Great's death, organizational indicators suggest no overall pressure for liberalization, but neither do they lean toward a successful authoritarian retrenchment.

Prussian Military Reform after 1800

Complacency since 1761 caused the Prussian military to stagnate at a time when the rest of Europe's military potential was being fully realized. The successors of Frederick the Great, Frederick William II and III, did not share a passion for military affairs. Their interest in and reviews of military affairs were "perfunctory and casual" at best.[44] Impetus for change would come from their disgruntled professional officer corps. Forward-thinking reformers within the military were appalled by its decline in relative strength, and attempted to invigorate the Prussian army through reorganization along the dynamic lines of Carnot's French model, but mandate for change was lacking from the top. They petitioned both kings to call up the militia, to no avail. The primary goal of the reformers was to transform the fiction of universal conscription in the canton system into the fact of a mass citizen-army based on effective national service. But the dangers of such reorganization to traditional absolutism, especially in light of the excesses of the French Revolution, were plain. The two Frederick's were simply horrified at the potential, but they did not have to use their fears as justification. A return to conscription would constitute a major break with the means of conducting campaigns developed by Frederick the Great, a revered and legendary national military icon. Their proposals were summarily dismissed.

Foremost among these reformers were Generals Gerhard von Scharnhorst, Georg von Berenhorst, Heinrich von Bülow, and civilian Karl von Stein. Scharnhorst used his prestigious position as head of the fledgling officer's academy to establish a dialogue on revising the idea that only nobility should serve as officers. Selection and promotion, he argued, should be based strictly on ability—a kind of ability no longer presumed a singular characteristic of nobility.[45] Such qualities, he averred, could be scientifically evaluated, and even instilled if necessary through education and training. Berenhorst and Bülow argued that the strict discipline of drill and repetition that Frederick's I and II stressed to insure battlefield loyalty should be replaced by an instillation of nationalistic values and *esprit de corps*.[46] Stein insisted that national service could not be accomplished without a parallel emancipation of the serfs to fill the ranks of the new army. This would of course radically reform the structure of society, but was the first step in creating a nation of free citizens, the only recruitment base capable of stopping the French. The expected reward of enhanced military power for doing so would transcend any diminution of royal prerogative.[47] It is easy to comprehend that none of the reformers made practical headway until after 1806, when the Prussian government collapsed in the wake of its defeat to Napoleon at Jena and Auerstadt, and Frederick William III fled to Russia.

In perhaps his only decisive moment as king, Frederick William III responded to the disaster of 1806 by issuing a series of decrees aimed at reforming the army. The most immediately radical was a purge of all military officers who had surrendered their garrisons to the victorious French without resistance. Noble birth engendered no leniency. The king's next action, basing future commissions *entirely* in competence and loyalty, was unprecedented.[48] Last, and perhaps most important, Frederick William III established a military reform commission that was stacked with real reformers and charged with recommending and carrying out fundamental changes. Apparently, the experience of royal flight and exile made the potential democratizing threat of a modern army palatable. Specified revisions included the end of reliance on foreign mercenaries, the admission of qualified nonaristocrats to the officer ranks, a new method of formally educating officers, changes in tactical organization, and standardization of regulations for each branch of the service.[49] The first reform was for practical expedience, not wide-ranging social reconstruction.[50] Emancipation of the serfs was not considered. Reformers and traditionalists were simply convinced they would be unable to obtain foreign mercenaries due to Napoleon's effective control of the continent. The only place from which the new Prussian army *could* come was from native recruits.

The members of the commission understood that fundamental reform of the army was crucial to the future survival of the state, and that with it would come far-reaching social and political change. But without a revitalized military, Prussia could easily become a permanent vassal of France—an eventuality not entirely unwelcome to the Prussian peasantry. The French had pushed the notion of themselves as liberators wherever they conquered, and as champions of individual rights in their aftermath. To the astonishment and dismay of his majesty, the collapse of Frederick William III's government did not engender widespread popular distress or lamentation. Many Prussians embraced French dominance, seeing in it the opportunity for the forced implementation of liberalized political institutions on the French model.[51]

A sense of Prussian nationalism was needed to counter French nationalism. Without popular support, the new Prussian army could never hope to compete with the sheer numbers of enthusiastic French conscripts. The old Frederician reliance on harsh discipline and repetitive drill to coerce troops into battle was effective in a previous age of professional armies, but in the new age of citizen-soldiers was woefully inadequate. Discipline would have to be replaced by *elán* through an awakening of nationalism, and elán would require major military and social reform. Without question, the commission recognized that the changes they were being asked to implement would have far-reaching social and political ramifications. This posed little or no intellectual problem, however, since most of the reformers were sympathetic to the idea that military changes could spawn a progressive Prussian state with representative political institutions.[52]

The first instituted reforms concerned the selection of officer candidates based on educational requirements. Since the average Prussian could not afford the schooling necessary to pass the entrance requirement, the officer corps remained primarily aristocratic, but it was a definite step toward the perception of a merit-based de-stratification of the military.[53] Without the establishment of professional military academies and schools, however, the entrance reforms would have been meaningless, and the commission's next act was to expand the existing cadet academy into a full military education system. With the establishment of formal military education curricula and specialty schools, advancement as well as placement became based on capacity and achievement. The education process established uniform standards and helped curtail aristocratic capriciousness.[54]

The reformers also changed the military code of justice so that it resembled the civilian code in morality and punishment. Corporal punishment was abolished and replaced by confinement.[55] Physical abuse of recruits was made punishable, and a standard for expressing grievances was instituted. The idea was simply to make military service tolerable to the masses.[56] One of the more egregious expenditures of resources in the extant military was that necessary to coerce individuals to join, and then not run off when direct supervision was lacking. For true universal conscription to be possible, the masses must come forward freely and train rigorously, without undue coercion. They are more likely to do so, it was reasoned, if the hardships of their military lives were caused more by enemy actions than by their superiors.

The notion of a standardized military law is fundamental to the ideals of fairness and equality evident in a democratized society. Subjecting a soldier to discipline is normal, and necessary, but if the discipline is arbitrary it will influence authoritarian tendencies in subsequent political structures. This is because the soldier understands that the military purpose of *arbitrary* punishment is to instill blind obedience. Decrees from on high must be followed at once, or punishment is inflicted. No command is to be disputed. This is the authoritarian style. On the other hand, if discipline and punishment are codified, the soldier gains a sense of belonging in a system with fundamental rights. The soldier knows what he cannot do, and understands his punishment was for a failure to meet impartial and standardized requirements. The law applies to everyone, not just to him. If he feels unfairly or wrongly treated, the uniform code of justice has a mechanism for appeal. In other words, a subordinate can bring the commander to scrutiny for misinterpretation or misapplication of the law. The subordinate is a thinking and responsive element, not an automaton, whose interpretation of the law is occasionally more correct than that of his superior. This fosters the understanding that responsibility goes up and down the chain of command. His life has worth. Nonarbitrary obedience is an expedient

THE PRUSSO-GERMAN STATE / 133

to a common goal, not, as is the case for farm animals, the pathetic lot of a lesser being. This understanding of equality under the law can readily transfer to the soldier's civilian political life. He will listen to his political leaders, obey their legitimate dictates, and look to oppose those that are not in his best interests.

The reformers were not entirely successful in their efforts. They had hoped, for example, to make a minor change in the military oath of every soldier. At the time, enrolling soldiers expressed their loyalty to the person of the king, Frederick William III, in his role of "war leader."[57] The reformers wanted the oath to be to the king (abstractly) in his role as chief executive of the state. The reformer's belief was that the soldier should not have separate military and civilian loyalties if he was to be truly incorporated as a functioning citizen of the state through military service. Perhaps due to pride, or possibly paranoia, the king was adamant in his refusal to allow such a change.

The final reform was not entirely a military one, but it was made with the idea of future military service in mind. As a vassal state, Prussia was under the oversight of Napoleon, and he had decreed that the size of the Prussian standing army could be no more than 40,000 men and officers. The Prussian army was necessary, reasoned Napoleon, to quell domestic disturbances and more importantly to assist in defense of the eastern frontier against Russia, and so was permitted. Yet, it would not be large enough to assist meaningfully in a restorative rebellion if called upon by the king. The reformers calculated that the solution to the problem of a small active army was to create a modern inactive (ready) reserve. The reformers devised a plan that would be repeated after the military constricting requirements of the 1919 Versailles Peace Treaty. By maintaining a small but skilled cadre of veteran officers and noncommissioned officers, and rotating the bulk of the army through an intense annual training exercise for a few weeks each year, the Prussians built an *effective* army of over 150,000, with no more than the legal 40,000 on *active* duty at any given time. The ruse was called the *Krümper* system, and clearly defied the spirit, if not the letter of the Napoleonic dictate.[58]

The problem the Krümper reserve system created for the Junker aristocracy was that it relied on conscripting hereditary serfs from their estates. Most other groups still enjoyed their long-standing hereditary exemptions—the reason the Prussian army wasn't significantly larger (only 150,000 soldiers prepared and ready compared to well over a million in the French system). The Junkers were aghast that their politically inert serfs were going to be methodically armed and trained for battle. Surely they would become a more unruly and recalcitrant lot, and might even begin to see themselves worthy of personal rights. This perception presented the government with a dilemma. In their effort to mount serious resistance to French hegemony, they were creating a very real potential internal threat, and they still had not addressed the problem of building a new army based on fighting spirit. How could anyone be expected to fight with French enthusiasm for a government that considered the fighter of dubious moral worth and offered no opportunity for military or social advancement?[59] They simply could not, and there was no way out.

The reforms were initiated out of necessity. Without them Prussia could not be an independent state. And the new military forever changed the soldier. He became valued in a way he had never been before, and in so becoming, forced a response from the state. In October of 1808, well after France's dominant new military paradigm was evident to all and emphatically only after the earlier reforms had shown signs of military success, the worst fears of the Junkers were realized. The king reluctantly abolished serfdom and made full citizens of all his subjects. This was Stein's proposal, and he looked for it to have extraordinary social significance. And yet, although it was certainly a radical change, the extent of social reform in Stein's theory was tempered in action. Abolition was not accompanied by manorial reform, and peasants working on Junker estates were still subject to manorial jurisdiction in matters of law. The distinction remained until 1848, and limited manorial police powers lasted until 1872.[60] The freed peasants were no longer tied to the land by serfdom, but those who remained for economic or other reasons were still in effect the legal chattels of the Junkers for all practical purposes.

Combined, these reforms rejuvenated the Prussian military, and early in 1813, the old Frederician canton-inspired ideal of universal service came close to reality. In preparation for his War of Liberation, Frederick William III proclaimed that all able-bodied men were required to serve in some military capacity. Adults physically qualified were expected to serve in the standing army when called. Landed peasants would form a state militia separate from the regular army based on the old Prussian *landwehr* defensive militia. The new landwehr could be called into service in time of national emergency. The propertied nobility that had been exempted from the old canton recruitment system could voluntarily join semiautonomous *Jaeger* detachments. The Jaegers would serve as officer replacement pools in time of need. Any person unqualified for service in the regular army, landwehr, or Jaeger detachments, would serve emergency garrison duty in the *landsturm*.[61] With universal service in place, Prussia prepared to go to war allied with the rest of Europe for liberation from France. One final component in the awakening of Prussian nationalism was needed—a stirring call to arms. In his famous "Am Mein Volk" speech, Frederick William III defined the people of his realm as one nation, and asked them for their support. For the first time in Prussian history, a king felt compelled to tell his people why he was now asking them to go to war.[62] The old reliance on duty and discipline was replaced by an appeal for assistance. No other action could have been more indicative of the radical changes military reform had wrought.

After the first defeat of Napoleon, universal service needed some fine-tuning. A nation *in* arms is an expensive luxury in peace. A nation *ready* for arms was the real need, and a variation on the krümper system was incorporated. In 1814, the design for Prussian military participation was enacted that would last until the Franco-Prussian War.[63] All able-bodied men, upon reaching their twentieth birthday, would be enrolled in the standing army for three years. The next two years would be served in the active reserve, followed by a seven-year stint in the first levy of the landwehr, susceptible to service call-up with the regular field army as needed. The next seven years would be spent in the second levy of the landwehr, called up for garrison duty and home defense as needed. All together, it represented 19 years of active service with prescribed regular military training. After age 39, all veterans would be assigned to the inactive landsturm for emergency duty only. In this scheme, the Prussians felt they could rapidly mobilize a first-rate field army of over half a million men, but would need to support a standing army of just 130,000.

In the short term, the reforms worked, at least in a military sense. Napoleon was ultimately defeated in 1815 and Prussia was recognized as one of Europe's great powers at the Treaty of Paris.[64] With the end of the national crisis, however, Frederick William III became understandably concerned with the direction military reform had on social and political mores. His Russian counterpart, the tsar, became particularly alarmed, and warned his generals that they may soon have to come to the aid of the Prussian King against his own army.[65] Pressures from the king's advisors, including Prince Wittgenstein, were on the side of having the practice of universal service abolished as soon as possible, at the very least before popular rebellion was inevitable.[66]

The external threats posed by the French Revolution and subsequent Napoleonic dominance of Europe had forced the Prussian government to grudgingly undertake a series of decidedly liberal military reforms. In their wake, absolutist Prussian rulers were under extreme pressure, and felt compelled to rely on the military's police power to maintain themselves from the force of the rising demands of democratic liberalism triggered by those very reforms. A return to feudal serfdom was not an option; those who had served would never have accepted it. But movement toward a representative democracy could be halted at constitutional monarchy, the king believed, if a few reforms could be rolled back. He was bolstered by the relative failure of the reforms to completely reshape the officer class from an aristocratic stronghold to a mirror of society. Too many of the Junker caste were ensconced there, and this characteristic accounts for much of the subsequent history of retarded democratization in Prussia. Even where it was not strictly noble by birth, the officer class had maintained distinct privilege, and mostly maintained its loyalty to the monarchy. Overall, the military reforms did engender significant pressure for political reform, in Prussia and throughout Europe. Rebellions against autocratic rule would become endemic; each of the next two generations had a European-wide revolt to share, and in Prussia the rebellions joined the overall pattern. But they were muted in their outcomes relative to the other Western states, and a monarchy constrained by its loyal General Staff would survive into the next century. The peculiar state dualism that arose after 1815 would divide Prussia into two distinct parts—the increasingly liberal society and the traditionally conservative military hierarchy.[67]

Revolution and Counterreform 1815–50

The military reforms of 1807–13 helped enable and nurture the popular push toward political liberalism prominent in Prussia after Napoleon's defeat. But Prussia was not alone in its radical military reform as a response to the French threat. All of the European states that encountered Napoleon's armies were compelled to copy elements of the French military organization in order to resist it.[68] Demands for dispersion of political authority in the wake of the nationalization of war posed a distinct, new internal threat to nearly all of the absolutist monarchies of Europe, and all acted in varying degree to counter it. Particularly troubling were the liberal exhortations of academics and students in the many German universities and gymnasia. In 1819, representatives of the governments of Austria, Prussia, and several smaller central European states, led by the powerful presence of Austria's Metternich, met in Karlsbad to formulate a unified strategy of reaction.[69] The subsequent Karlsbad

Decrees authorized agents of the participating states to regulate schools and universities by controlling student and faculty disciplinary action, including the hiring and firing of professors, and lecture schedules. All printed matter, academic or civil, was subject to prior review and censorship and all liberal political publications, especially newspapers and pamphlets, were outlawed. As curbs on political freedom, these decrees were comparable to the British Six Acts of the same year.[70] In addition, the Black Commission, an independent political inquisition, was established to persecute secret societies. This Interstate Commission had the power to arrest, try, and convict in matters it deemed under its purview. The death penalty, commuted to life in prison, was not uncommon.[71]

Attempts to curb political agitation had mixed results. They may have staved off open rebellion for a time, but liberal pressure boiled beneath the surface of the Prussian state. In July of 1830, the French people rebelled against their monarchy, and the catalyst for the first generational revolution throughout Europe was introduced. Belgium declared independence from Holland and established a constitutional state. Belgian Luxembourg defected from the German Confederation, and dozens of minor German states forced their monarchs to grant constitutional assemblies. Even England, generally immune to the 1789 French Revolution and associated liberalization pressures, was compelled into initiating serious parliamentary reform. Poland, on the most vulnerable border of Prussia, rebelled against Russia. Prussia avoided an open rebellion of its own only when Frederick William III reissued his promises (first made in grateful appreciation after the success of the War of Liberation) to establish a written constitution and a national representative assembly—promises he did not keep.[72]

Secret societies and liberal political reformers continued to agitate in Prussia after 1830, but they were systematically and ruthlessly repressed by the state. An effective state police and a loyal aristocratic upper class in the German General Staff mitigated in practice what should have been a more liberalizing impact of major military reforms. Moreover, the experience of the postwar years had hardened Frederick William III against liberalization. Appreciation for his benevolent concern was absent; the more he felt he bent to accommodate the reformers, the more they demanded of him. He became so intractable that the best hope of both the political and military reformers was the natural demise of the doddering old monarch and the ascension of the likeable crown prince. Popular perception of the monarch-in-waiting as a man of the people and a liberal reformer was probably misplaced, however. He was certainly more intellectual and widely read than his father. He outwardly embraced the liberal arts and sciences, and professed to be a man of letters, and so a broad assumption as to his embrace of liberal ideals was incorrectly made. Instead, he was likely more receptive to the idea of conservative political authoritarianism as expressed by Julius Stahl and Leopold von Ranke.[73]

Shortly after his coronation in 1840, in keeping with his public image, Frederick William IV did indeed abolish the bulk of the Karlsbad Decrees and allowed uncensored distribution of political ideas for the first time in a generation. He also consented to the establishment of a popular assembly (for advising the king only, never for approval), elected on the principle of universal suffrage. Frederick William IV boasted of his enlightenment, and expected nothing but admiration from his subjects. The Prussian Diet was constructed and seated in 1847, and in its first year sent numerous petitions for political reform. The king was astonished, had he not done more than enough to earn the people's praise? Where were his commendations, his popular declarations of affection?

Among the most emphatic petitions was one from *Oberpräsident* von Schön, who argued that fulfillment of the previous king's promise (under duress) for a written constitution *would be the logical conclusion of the military reforms of 1807–13.*[74] Von Schön's position was countered by young delegate Otto von Bismarck, who denounced the liberal interpretation that soldiers who fought the wars of 1813–15 were struggling for liberation from Prussian absolutism.[75] It was pure patriotism that guided them, he passionately opined. The only liberation they desired, Bismarck concluded, was for their Fatherland and their king, from the yoke of French Empire. While Bismarck's retort was no doubt partially accurate, for political awakening often occurs after combat, the eloquence of his speech caught the receptive ear of the king.

At any rate, all this political wrangling annoyed Frederick William IV no end. He genuinely expected nothing but gratitude from the Diet, expressions of their appreciation and of their loyalty, not these petty petitions of grievance. His dalliance with liberalism was over. He quickly developed an absolute loathing for the National Assembly, and made it known that he would call on it as infrequently as possible.

But it would not be so easy for Frederick William IV to suppress the reforms he had allowed. The newly freed press published the proceedings of the Diet and fanned political passions on both sides of the ongoing debate, one for liberal constitutionalism, and the other for monarchial absolutism. In February of 1848, following an insurrection in Italy, a major revolution broke out in France that toppled the government of Louis Phillipe. The second generational rebellion from the European-wide military reforms was on. Throughout the German states, revolutionary fervor was released, and the military was called out to suppress public demonstrations. But in the larger cities, mobilizations could not come quickly enough to suppress the popular fervor. What the people demanded was a federated German state with a constitutional government similar to that of the United States.[76] The uprising became a revolt, and in March of 1848 Frederick William IV was forced to flee Berlin and give up control of the Prussian Capitol to revolutionaries. The king was obligated to negotiate with the leaders of the reform movement from this attenuated position of weakness, and so within two months the first Prussian Parliament with real political power was elected on the basis of equal and universal adult manhood suffrage.[77]

The new Parliament immediately attempted to reform military, the source of the king's remaining power, by disbanding the regular army and replacing it with a people's militia loyal to the legislature.[78] The officer corps, still dominated by the Junker class, could have no clearer statement of the real intent of the popular assembly. The nobility was to be completely eviscerated. Not only was it dismantling aristocratic privilege politically; it planned to eliminate what they believed was the strength of the Prussian military, its hereditary leadership caste. This opening act served only to harden the officer's resolve to restore the king. In November, the regular army under the leadership of General Wrangel retook Berlin and ceremoniously offered it to back to Frederick William IV. In December, backed by the regular army, the National Assembly was dissolved.

Even with the now unbending loyalty of the officer class, Frederick William IV was in a poor position to clamp down on the revolutionaries. Prussia was in a struggle with Austria for domination of Germany, and too harsh a retrenchment might instigate opposition in the other German states, especially the growing number who had already instituted constitutional reforms. Frederick William IV thus compromised and upon return to power permitted a written constitution establishing Prussia as a constitutional monarchy and not an absolutist one. With the new constitution in place and rebellion pacified, Frederick William IV offered the services of his military to those German states still beset with disorder and went about quietly restoring prerevolutionary governments. Ironically, because of its class-stratified structure, the Prussian army, whose reforms ignited the liberal passions of the post-Napoleonic era, was now being used as an instrument of authoritarian control.

The events of 1848 completed the transformation of the military from its liberalizing peak in 1813 into a now-reactionary and fully independent power, parallel to the bureaucratic government and separate from the mass of civilians. This military held no loyalty to the state. It was bound to the monarch by the dual ties of feudal loyalty and obedience to the commander in chief, "a relationship from which the ordinary citizen was excluded."[79] The reformed military of 1815 should have prompted significant democratization, and it certainly was culpable for the ongoing agitation for political change, but that agitation was fragmented and undirected. The rebellions were uncoordinated and unskilled. The Prussian king, blaming the 1806–13 military reforms for his current woes, quickly reacted to eliminate those reforms thought most dangerous, and to mitigate supporting pressure for the revolutionaries by placing the army in a position of police suppression. Despite all their efforts, the nobility could not prevent the rebellions triggered by the French-inspired military reforms that occurred throughout Europe in 1830 and 1848—but they could be curtailed with counter reforms.

The army, despite having undergone no significant organizational changes since 1815, had not maintained its Waterloo era profile. The Prussian army had not been engaged in war in 33 years, training was appreciably down, and Prussia's external military capacity could be charitably described as inept. With the exception of its size relative to the population, and a purge of mercenaries, all of the factors contributing to authoritarianism were enhanced. When the call came to attack Denmark in the first Schleswig-Holstein War (1848), the army was embarrassed. Sweden had sent a few troops to support the Danes, England threatened a naval action, and Austria and Russia applied diplomatic pressure on Prussia to withdraw, but the Prussians still should easily have defeated Denmark. Instead, Prussia was forced to accept a humiliating armistice. The Treaty of Malmö (1848) created an uneasy peace that was at best "inglorious."[80] Preparation for war was made potentially more efficient after 1815, due to increased modernization and standardization of equipment, but the rigor and frequency of active training declined sharply. Professionalism was bottoming out. After such an extended period of peace, the ranking officers of the General Staff were reluctant to risk their comfortable positions and livelihoods in the uncertain business of war, and instead began to regard their primary duties to be peacetime garrison and social repression through internal police actions.[81] Field training was crude and harsh in comparison to garrison duty, and incrementally it disappeared. The landwehr was practically and functionally disbanded.

The period 1819–33 was also marked by a decided backslide in the promise of sound military education, despite the efforts of brilliant military strategists like Clausewitz and the reorganization of the General Staff and academic training program in 1821. The War Ministry entered a reactionary period in which education was thought superfluous to officership, entirely subordinate to the noble qualities of inborn aristocratic bearing and command.[82] More disturbing for the remaining military reformers, the War Ministry came under the sway of theorists who felt the notion of a politically realized citizen-soldier was not only dangerous, but also socially foolish. The Ministry believed the role of soldier was a special calling, distinct from the rest of society. It was the essence of militarism to glorify the military virtues above all others, but the opponents of the aristocracy seemed to confirm the reactionary military philosophy. Those who wanted liberal government in Prussia now saw military only in its current configuration, an augmenter of monarchial power. Political efforts to rein in its power were overdone, looking to eliminate it altogether. In this self-confirming spiral of distrust, the army progressively—and willingly—accepted the functions of a police constabulary.

All together, from 1819 to 1840 "everything that [the reformers] had done to reconcile their military establishment with society had been destroyed."[83] The changes in military organization after 1815, affected gradually through misuse and disuse, served to cut the army off from the rest of society, and began recasting the citizenry as the "enemy within."[84] The "chasm between the Army and liberalism that opened up after 1815 [even managed to turn liberal reformer and intellectual] Clausewitz into a conservative."[85] With the military pressure now firmly swung back toward authoritarian influence, the government became increasingly despotic.

Prusso-German Military and Political Reforms, 1848–1900

The Constitution of 1848 was structurally modeled after the 1830 Belgian Constitution, but had no ideological similarity to that or other liberal Western constitutions of the late eighteenth and early nineteenth centuries. The democratizing Enlightenment in the West was overwhelmed in Prussia by German Romanticism. Heinrich von Treitsche sourly noted, "[we] did very nearly adopt the Belgian Constitution in 1848, and a great many of its clauses were incorporated into ours, [including] its accursed mixture of Radicalism and Clericalism[, which] was to be infused into our noble Prussia. But the chief clause was left out; [therefore] in Prussia, despite the constitution, the monarch is still the King."[86] The Constitution allowed the monarchy an absolute right of veto over all legislation. The king also had the right to call and dissolve the legislature at will.[87] After the fervor of the 1848 Revolution was muted, constitutional revisions repealed the system of universal suffrage in elections to the Lower House, and replaced it with a three-tiered system of granting electorships dependent on tax rates and upon total taxes paid. In this manner, the conservative aristocracy and other middle-class wealthy were provided with representation equal to or greater than the poorer masses.[88] The "revised" Constitution of 1850 also affected a repeal of all freedom of the press guarantees of the 1848 document. Moreover, the legislative structure of the upper house was changed to a royal house of peers on the English model, effectively giving the entire legislature over to the nobility.[89] In 1850, Frederick William IV, recognizing he could do no better, reluctantly took an oath to the revised, reactionary constitution.[90]

The king's oath was critically important. It settled the decisive debate on reorganization of the army from 1848 to 1850, which focused on the precise point of loyalty in the military service oath. Liberal reformers had wanted the armed forces to swear allegiance to the (1848 version) Constitution, while conservatives continued to call for an oath of loyalty directly to the king. The logic was the same for both reformers and conservatives, and centered on the army's willingness to intervene on behalf of the king during the revolution. Both knew that had the military not remained loyal to the king in 1848, the liberals might have completely swept away the royal office. Conservative leaders warned Frederick William IV that should another round of revolutionary activity erupt, an oath of loyalty to the Constitution would render the king "helpless in the face of future attacks by democracy."[91] The king was easily won over with this appeal, and the revised Constitution of 1850 specifically stated an oath to the Constitution would not be allowed by any member of the military. This decision efficiently separated the military from legislative control, creating a monarchial bulwark against future legislative encroachment. After 1850, the king would swear to uphold the Constitution and the military would swear to uphold the king.

The long transformation of the military's primary function from instrument of war (external power) to defender of the monarchy (internal power) appears to have contributed to the general decline in military skill and breadth of recruitment after 1815. Although the Prussian population had almost doubled from 1813 to 1860, the number of new recruits annually inducted had remained steady at about 40,000.[92] A growing segment of the population was not receiving military training, and Prussian reliance on an aging landwehr for external defense was by necessity increasing.

The possibility of having to rely on the landwehr, a relatively independent militia (and therefore perceived as a bastion of liberalism), was disconcerting to the pro-absolutist conservatives. Having taken care of immediate needs, the counterreformers could now properly tweak the militia. In 1860, conservatives proposed the annual levy be increased to 63,000 men, and that the individual commitment in the active reserve, fully controlled by the active military, be similarly increased from two to five years. Soldiers would then be liable to serve 11 years in the landwehr, but landwehr units would be attached to regular line units for training and administration (and watching over). In time of emergency or war, the landwehr would join up with and be incorporated into its active cadre, rather than operating as separate regiments as had been the prior practice. Liberal legislators recognized the potential threat such a military reorganization might have on hoped-for political restructuring, and tried to pass a compromise bill that would simply reduce the initial term of active service to two years, with no changes in the landwehr service commitment or its independent regimental status.[93] The reduction in active service time would raise the number of trained soldiers almost to levels requested by the loyalists, but would sift citizens through the training process faster (saving money), and more quickly fill the ranks of the pro-democracy landwehr. The liberal effort was narrowly defeated, and the conservative reforms were adopted instead. With this reorganization, the positive liberalizing influence of the landwehr was effectively destroyed.[94]

The liberals were in the minority in the government, but they had the backing of the majority of citizens and so retained significant power and autonomy. Much of the liberal legislative antagonism toward the military as an institution stemmed from its effective role as an augmenter of police authority in the state, and they were not keen to give it any more power than it already had. Their worries were legitimate. General von Moltke "took especial comfort in the thought that the Prussian police state had remained fundamentally unshaken by the revolution."[95] While the army's police power had expanded greatly, to the distress of the liberals, its capacity as an instrument of diplomatic power had degenerated to the point that it was more hindrance to Prussian political goals than help. Since 1815, Prussian forces had been used against only the Danes in an equivocal interstate struggle. Training was down and the military was woefully prepared to back the king's external aspirations. The loyalist counterreformers were wary of making changes that would instigate the kind of revolutionary fervor that occurred in the aftermath of the 1806–13 reforms, but had to have a larger and better-trained military to achieve their aims. The leader of these loyalists was Otto von Bismarck, the fiery orator who had so passionately defended the king's prerogative in the wake of the 1830 rebellions.

Chancellor Bismarck was ambitious. He wanted a united Germany under Prussian leadership and he knew he could never achieve it with the army's current malaise. Bismarck was quite well aware that much of the current liberal opposition to military reform stemmed from the belief that recent reforms were a barely disguised method for increasing the state's internal repression/policing capacity—a position that was undeniably correct. He suggested to the king that should he publicly announce the object of reform was to strengthen the army for an eventual offensive against Austria, as a prelude to German unification, nationalist unity would overcome liberal opposition and all objections to an expansion of the military and its power would disappear.[96] The king agreed, and Bismarck began to push serious training, equipping, and manpower corrections. In fact, Bismarck was prescient in his designs. When war with Austria came in 1866, the primary focus of the military did change from an internal to an outward view, and with it political opposition to military strengthening declined. But it did not disappear. The liberals were not so blinded by patriotic nationalism that they could not see that when the war ended, and the old focus returned, the military would have been strengthened—and by extension, so too the king and his supporters. In an effort to deprive the liberal reformers of their lower and middle-class support, and because he believed the new German nationalism would overcome any lingering liberalism among them, Bismarck next proclaimed that his goal was the unification of all Germany. He immediately proclaimed that in this new German nation, Prussia would champion the establishment of a united German Parliament elected via universal and direct suffrage—on the condition that *all* Germans would be liable for military service on the Prussian design.[97]

The subsequent Parliament of the North German Confederation made consideration of military affairs one of its earliest orders of business. A pan-German reorganization of common military conscription along Prussian models, calling on three-year service for all inductees followed by successive reserve and landwehr obligations, was quickly enacted. Parliament then acceded to the Prussian practice of providing enough military funding to maintain a standing force equal to 1 percent of the population. But Bismarck needed a larger armed force to forge a new Germany, and he was astute enough to realize his dreams were moot without a further dispersion of political authority. Gordon Craig relates: "Partly because of the requirement of his foreign policy, partly because he had desired a counterweight to middle-class liberalism, Bismarck had become the champion of universal suffrage."[98] It was a fair price to pay, Bismarck reasoned, for the power of militant and military German nationalism to be concentrated in his capable hands.

In the period of its unification, Germany led by Prussia would fight and win three wars (with Denmark, Austria, and France). Spectacular battlefield success emboldened and popularized the General Staff. Military leaders engaged Bismarck on a rhetorical battleground on the issues of military leadership and the proper subordination of the military in civilian society. The majority of military leaders believed the army was the guarantor of the king's sovereignty, and therefore should never be subject to parliamentary control.[99] Bismarck, who had read and understood Clausewitz, knew that the military without civilian leadership would degenerate into an absurdity. On this issue, however, the king had personal experience. The military would retain its position as guarantor of the sovereign and not the sovereignty of the state. The new Germany was born with its military as an autonomous organization within the state, but not an integral component of it.

Coincident with the political upheavals of 1848–70, the General Staff was able to impose a measure of real authority over its subordinates for the first time since the Napoleonic Wars. The humiliating truce granted to Denmark after the first Schelswig-Holstein War showed the weakness and complacency of a Prussian officer corps that had rotted from misuse and apathy. The General Staff, under the leadership of Helmuth von Moltke, instituted a rigorous training and coordination program that culminated in a Prussian military that was man for man second to none. The Prussian soldier was once again the embodiment of military virtues. A new popularity, bordering on reverence, was accorded the army. Praise was not limited to the people of new Germany. Its enemies as well as its allies showed great respect and envy. Prussian militarism was the rage in aristocratic circles. England's King William I thought it a model to be followed, especially the parts following von Moltke's insistence that the army could not and should never be fully subordinate to the state. In direct contravention of Clausewitz's famous dictum that war is an extension of policy by violent means, Moltke's argument was that in time of war the military needed to be unencumbered by political constraints. He paid lip service to the notion that the army should not determine who to fight, that was indeed a political decision, but once war commenced, the army must have free reign to conduct all operations up to and including the negotiation and acceptance of peace terms. The authority of the civilian politicians ended at the beginning of armed hostility, Moltke insisted, and resumed after its conclusion.[100]

This position set Moltke at odds with Bismarck. Clausewitz had insisted that war is an extension of politics. Accordingly, war can never be separated from political intercourse. Clausewitz admits that the absence of political influence over war could be reasonable, but only if one could conceive of the notion of total war, an eventuality he thought unlikely. It is on this point that Moltke developed his own misshapen doctrine on Clauswitzian foundations. Throughout the three Wars of the Liberation, the military under Moltke strove for more control in and of the realm of war. The final war with France ended in Moltke's resignation (which was not accepted by the king) over what he perceived as Bismarck's undue interference in the peace negotiations. Moltke wanted harsh territorial and monetary compensation from the French, and as the general in charge of the campaign, felt it was his right to demand it. Bismarck ultimately convinced the king of his own claim to primacy in foreign affairs, but Moltke had carved inroads on the concept of civilian authority. "By the eve of the First World War, military dominance over the political prerogatives of war was complete."[101]

In 1871, William I crowned himself first emperor of Germany. His brother, Frederick William IV, had once refused the imperial crown (in 1848) because it had been offered by the legislature—the people—and thus was not divinely inspired.[102] With consolidation of Germany following the war with France, William, in the style of Napoleon, laid the crown on his own head. The long-desired federation of German states was now the Second Reich. Restructuring of the military to ensure its insulation from civilian control continued. From 1871 to 1914, the General Staff pursued two primary policies that were counter to liberal democratic goals. First, through direct influence in the national legislature and with the Kaiser, they oversaw the progressive reorganization of military administration in such a way as to transfer most military matters from the Ministry of War (responsible to Parliament and swearing an oath to the constitution) and into their own hands (responsible to the emperor and swearing their loyalty oaths to him). For its part, the various War Ministers of the period tended to side with the General Staff, making the transfer of authority often unopposed and occasionally unknown to the Parliament. In 1883, the Chief of the General Staff was granted permanent, direct access to the Kaiser, a privilege formerly allowed only during the Wars of Liberation, and the personnel department of the War Ministry was abolished.[103] Henceforth, all personnel decisions, including recruiting and staffing at the highest levels, were to be decided by the General Staff.[104]

Second, the General Staff tightened the process of officer selection to include only those citizens whose loyalties to conservative and absolutist ideals were assured.[105] Still taking the events of 1848 as a paradigm, military conservatives held on to the belief that the aristocratic officer corps was the only reliable bulwark against democracy. Of more than 2,500 cadets who passed the officer examinations from 1862 to 1866, just under half (49 percent) were of the nobility while the rest were of upper middle class or bourgeoisie extraction.[106] Of these successful candidates, one-third were sons of military officers, 26 percent sons of upper echelon civil servants, and 20 percent sons of Junker owners of landed estates.[107]

The immediate problem for the General Staff was that the rapidly increasing size of the active military due to the 1860 reforms was diluting the aristocratic base of the officer class. In 1865, just over half of the officer corps were members of the nobility, and 80 percent of the top ranks (colonel and above) claimed noble birth.[108] Rapid growth of the military from 1865 to 1913 far outpaced the nobility's capacity to fill the burgeoning officer ranks. After unification in 1872, the General Staff itself was compromised. Out of 135 officers, a third "were untitled. One was even a

Jew."[109] The super-mobilization in preparation for World War I accelerated the demand for officers even more. By 1913, the nobility accounted for less than 30 percent of the officer corps, and top-rank officers with noble lineage formed a bare majority of just 52 percent.[110] The rest of the officer corps had to be drawn from the ranks of the middle class. Still, the nobility had their preference of positions. In 1906, the most prestigious branch of service was the cavalry, and the Junker class held 87 percent of the officer positions there.[111] Following the cavalry, in order of prestige, the preferred branches were: infantry (with 48 percent of officer positions held by the nobility), field artillery (41 percent), supply services (31 percent), and foot artillery and technical troops (6 percent each).[112]

The solution, for the military and the Kaiser, was to instill in the bourgeoisie and middle-class officers the same sense of loyalty and social superiority believed to come naturally to the Junker class.[113] The new officers had to be "socially adapted to the aristocratic and monarchical character of the military state."[114] A process of political training that had nothing to do with the development of battlefield skills was instituted in the military education system, and set the tone for developing a new form of peculiarly German militarism.

While all new officers were required to pass an initial examination, not everyone who passed qualified for service. Jews and other non-Christians were not allowed entrance, nor were "social misfits or young men with unorthodox political views."[115] Social Democrats were even more rigidly excluded than Jews, not so stated because of their revolutionary ideas but because of their "moral deficiencies."[116] In the Franco-Prussian War of 1870–71, six Jews served as Prussian officers, but their sons were not allowed admission. The one Jew on the General Staff in 1872 was undoubtedly inherited from a non-Prussian state in the new Germany, and was quickly retired.[117] By 1878, there were no Jewish officers at all.[118] The General Staff had an unanticipated ally in its efforts to purify the officer corps. With the founding of the empire, the image of the officer as the battling symbol of the new Reich became popularly ingrained, and more than enough applications for a military commission were processed. If not nobility, at least these young Aryan applicants were noble. Enormously popular public figures, such as von Treitschke, History Chair at Berlin University, glorified the military state and the officer as ideals of aspiration.[119] The wealthier middle class sought military commissions as a way to surmount extant social barriers.[120] The indoctrination was so complete that entrance into the officer corps became the foundation for rapid upward social mobility. Indeed, so well revered was this Prusso-German form of militarism that reserve officer commissions became an accepted enhancement for most civilian career paths.[121]

To complement the rising prestige of the officer corps and to demonstrate a profound sense of nationalism, the late 1800s saw a number of voluntary civilian patriotic associations formed to influence national policy. The first of these was the Colonial Society, founded in 1882 and dedicated to expansion of an overseas empire. Its peak membership was 42,000. Other associations quickly followed, including the Pan-German League (founded 1882, dedicated to solidifying national unification, top membership 18,000) and the Imperial League Against Social Democracy (an antidemocratic, pro monarchical association founded in 1904, peak membership 221,000).[122] The most influential of these groups, however, was the Navy League, founded in 1898 and dedicated to the passage of naval armaments legislation, peak membership 331,000. A splinter group of the Navy League was the Army League, formed by some of the more radical members of the Navy League who wanted to ensure that the land power of the nation would not be hurt by the hoped for massive buildup of the navy. In other words, the Army League was founded not to counter the Navy League, but to make sure that army expansion kept pace. The Army League was founded in 1912 and had a peak membership of 90,000.[123] The latter leagues were ostensibly formed for the purpose of demonstrating a nationalist populism and to press military spending for economic prosperity. The Navy League, in particular, equated the massive shipbuilding programs of Admiral Tirpitz to industrial growth in the Baltic port cities. Moreover, the new societies were a conduit of access for outsiders with political aspirations. Membership conferred a certain association to the military without having to serve full- or part-time and without having to give up business interests.

The Patriotic Leagues had political agendas before the legislature, and as such were pluralist agitators, but a large number of popular nationalist military clubs called Warrior's Associations (*Kriegervereine*) sprang up as well. These voluntary associations had no specific political agenda. They simply wanted to show support for, and a belief in, the values of the military state. They more than any other mani- festation of the new Germany, illustrate the level to which militarism was pervading the Reich. By 1909, as many as three million German citizens were members of one or more Warrior's Associations, not including the 750,000-member paramilitary Young German's League.[124] Consistent with definitions provided earlier, the problem for political liberalization was that these associations affected the trappings of military institutions without accepting liability for the actions of the state. While military in form, they had no direct influence or liability on the battlefield, and were clear exam- ples of Vagts's distinction between the military way and militarism.[125] The influence of the associations was without question toward continued authoritarianism.

This combination of political separation from legitimate legislative control and elitist social separation of the officer corps from the masses contributed to the German military tradition of a state within the state. The military claimed the right to define what was in the national interest, and to pursue its own policies based on that definition.[126] A form of corporatism masquerading as professionalism, it claimed the right to determine its own membership and to define nonmilitary missions for itself. The officer corps consciously molded itself into the Kaiser's Praetorian Guard. With the Kaiser's blessing, and the popular support of the civilian leagues and associations, it was easy for the military hierarchy to believe what was good for the military was good for the state. Coincident with that belief was that the military should be the *sole* judge of its own best interests.

The period after national unification also saw the rise of the German Fleet as a significant, and in many ways competing, military state within the state. The tiny Prussian fleet was drastically enlarged with the incorporation of Baltic and North Sea coastal states into the empire, and a German Admiralty was established in 1871 to oversee and coordinate the integration of these assets into a coherent national force. Still, the fleet was seen initially as an important but not vital element in Germany's overall security needs. Land warfare dominated the General Staff, and the navy was not made a parallel service until Cabinet orders of 1889 and 1899 established the Reich Naval Office as the supreme naval authority in Germany.[127]

After 1890, the navy transcended pure military intention, and came to symbolize the power and reach of the new German Militarist State. Having secured Germany's position as the dominant continental power, the Kaiser aspired to world-power status. In the popular contemporary view, forcefully espoused by American naval officer Alfred Thayer Mahan and British historian Sir Halford Mackinder, in order to be a world power Germany must establish a world-class navy and acquire an overseas colonial empire. Resources from abroad were necessary to fuel the industrial expansion of the great states, it was reasoned. In order to acquire, maintain, and protect this overseas empire, Germany must build a naval force capable of challenging the existing world powers at any point on the globe.[128] From 1889 to 1913, an astonishing 90 percent of Germany's federal budget went to the military, and from 1898, the largest portion of these expenditure went to the navy.[129]

Thus its navy symbolized the power and prestige of the new Germany. The technical and educational requirements of the modern navy meant that it had to incorporate a high proportion of middle-class origin officers in its highest ranks. Proficiency in technical seamanship was desired, and the new engines needed men with mechanical skill. This was not necessarily a boon for liberalization, however. To combat the perceived nobility deficiency vis-à-vis the army, the Kaiser knighted 22 of the highest-ranking naval officers from 1898 to 1913, and established a standardized procedure by which retired admirals could apply for promotion to the nobility.[130] Indeed, the naval officer corps was considered a personal creation of the Kaiser, and its officers displayed a remarkable loyalty to him.[131]

National consensus over Germany's coming role as a global naval power was infectious, and even the liberal element of German politics was co-opted. Parliamentary opposition to the massive naval expenditures was nonexistent.[132] The expansion of the fleet was consciously designed to be a visible manifestation of a successful and expansive foreign policy, and nationalism was directly tied to it. It was further intended to stabilize the internal political and social position of the monarchy against the encroachment of social democracy.[133] The Chief of Naval Operations, Admiral von Tirpitz, used his office as a propaganda center to rally the nonmilitary population to support of the navy.[134] Heavy industry was especially eager to back the naval expansion, as it would account for enormous new contracts. The growing German labor movement saw naval expansion as an opportunity for jobs. From its very inception, the new fleet was integrated into the economic system of the Reich.[135]

The influence of the military on political institutions during this period was significant, though mostly antiliberal and anti-inclusionary. The carefully crafted policies of the General Staff amounted to a de facto *coup d'etat* over the liberal legislature, and ensured the traditional feudal relationship between the officer corps and the crown would persist well into the twentieth century. The liberalizing influences of the reforms of 1806–15, which culminated in the 1848 revolution, were not allowed to run their course. Retrenchment in military organization influenced the political structures of the state in a way that denied further liberal democratization. Still, several components of military organization lent themselves to democratic influences. Growing size of the military, a renewed emphasis on offensive strategy, and increasing preparation for war helped spur an intense accumulation of socialist labor movements within Germany.[136]

World War I and the Weimar Republic

Following its smashing success in the Franco Prussian War (1871), the General Staff looked for methods not only to win a future war, but also to conduct it on its own terms, with limited interference from civilian politicians. Partially with this idea in mind, Army Chief of the General Staff Alfred von Schlieffen (1891–1906) devised a plan for a two-front war that was totally dependent on mobilization schedules and railroad timetables.[137] The Schlieffen plan was updated annually and revised as needed, but it was centered on the need to follow a precise sequence of events. Political considerations of neutrality and hostility were not taken into account, nor were potential diplomatic efforts by statesmen. Schlieffen's successor, Helmuth von Moltke (Chief of the General Staff from 1906 to 1914), the elder Moltke's nephew, stayed true to the Schlieffen plan and "interpreted it in such a way as to impose grave limitations on his country's freedom of diplomatic action."[138] Once begun, the elder Moltke's dream of war without civilian interference could now be realized. It was a system of interlocking mobilization schedules that simply overawed the political process. The plan had the dual effect of limiting diplomatic flexibility and prompting a military dominant government to implement it before conditions made it impractical.[139]

The German generals of World War I completely accepted the principle that matters of operations in war were the sole prerogative of the military. After tremendous early success in 1914, Generals Ludendorff and Hindenberg were able to effectively take over the German government, even forcing the dismissal of the German chancellor.[140] In crisis, the Constitution allowed the Kaiser dictatorial power, and Ludendorff especially used his privileged access to the despondent and withdrawn William to effectively govern the country. So complete was the coup that not only Parliament, but the Kaiser himself, received notice of some of the weightiest decisions of the war only after the fact.[141]

When war finally came, the attitude in Germany was "a curious compound of uncomplicated patriotism, romantic joy [and] great adventure."[142] Patriotism ruled the day. Even the radical Social Democratic Party voted to fund the War effort, claiming that "in the hour of danger, we will not abandon our Fatherland."[143] Rhetoric not withstanding, the socialists and trade unions were convinced their support of the war would "be rewarded" with "significant progress toward democratic government and social reforms."[144] Early German successes were intoxicating, but it soon became clear the boys would not be home for Christmas, as determined French and Russian forces abandoned the offensive and dug in for the long haul.[145]

The hope that social and political reform would ensue from a glorious winning campaign never materialized, but reforms were inevitable nonetheless. The massive mobilization of World War I required that soldiers be drawn from *all* social strata. Even Jews, who had been systematically purged from the officer ranks (and completely disappeared by 1878), were once again allowed to shed their blood for the fatherland as officers.[146] Religious and politically marginalized elements of the population were allowed to polish their credentials for citizenship by offering their lives in support of the state. Out of a prewar population of 60,000,000, 13,250,000 men, were mobilized for war. Around 7,209,000 were declared casualties, and 1,808,500 of those lost their lives. No state could have denied such a sacrifice by failing to reward the combatants with political rights, and survived. The instrument of power that once could have put down a popular political uprising was no longer available: "The standing army of prewar days, which had been a pliable instrument in the hands of the Supreme Military Commander, had changed into a citizen's army, which was useless for internal political action."[147]

By 1916, the Kaiser's advisors, at least, were well aware that their political situation was precarious, and their prospects for retaining power rested on the shoulders of the army in the field. Two years of trench warfare stalemate caused the nation to become war-weary. The combatants on the front line, disenchanted with the decisions being made that so ludicrously risked their lives, began to *demand* political representation. In order to maintain the war spirit of the nation, the Kaiser's military government issued public promises that if the army could prevail, future military and political reforms would be forthcoming, but that crisis was not the time for change.[148] The promises assuaged the public for only a short time. On Easter of 1917, the Kaiser (who by then had been effectively deposed by the military and was speaking on their insistence) personally and specifically promised that the end of the war would see the implementation of truly equal and direct suffrage by repeal of the three-tier electoral system and reform of the upper chamber of the Parliament. In addition, he immediately established a special committee to examine the question of postwar constitutional reform.[149]

Success in battle can only ignite passions and forestall reform for a short while. The massive mobilization of all sectors of the German state *required* that the government respond with political decentralization. The army had become professionalized in the sinkhole of slaughter, not because it desired it, but because there was no other way to prevail. Promotions were based on merit, as the capacity for devouring human life this brutal war displayed emptied the elitist force pools from which the officers had been drawn. Constant battle training is absolute training. Loyalty is to one's peers, and only patriotism can sustain an offensive in such miserable conditions, and the reality of war always diminishes the glorification of it. Though the state became wholly militarized, militarism dropped significantly. Not all the military characteristics moved toward democratization. The offensives stalled and defense became the norm (though the *stösstruppen* tactics of 1918 would restore the offensive mind-set for a time). The navy remained effectively bottled up in port. The great decisive battle of the seas that Tirpitz envisioned never happened, and the massive amounts of money spent on naval armaments were wasted.[150] The Allied blockade was never broken.

The rapid and significant rise in military pressures toward broad participation portends a major change in subsequent political structures. Accordingly, the postwar Weimar government was a model of liberal democratic modernism. The origins of democratic government in Germany transcend a strictly military explanation, of course. Its specific form was due to a host of social, political, economic, technological, and military causes. But the fact that the military influence from 1915 to 1918 so clearly indicates a change toward decentralized government should not be overlooked.

The pressures to achieve democratic reform were heightened by American President Wilson's position that he would not negotiate peace with any nation that was not at least in the *process* of democratization.[151] In October of 1918, the old Parliament began military reforms designed to curb its autonomy and place it firmly under civilian control. The chancellor was made primarily responsible to the Parliament, and not to the Kaiser. All military appointments had to be approved and signed by the chancellor, and the General Staff was made subordinate to the War Ministry.[152] Had the reforms of the old Parliament held, in concert with the positive changes wrought by wartime exigencies, the organizational impact on subsequent political structures may have remained decidedly pro-democratic. History could well have been changed.

Within a week of the parliamentary reforms, naval forces stationed at Kiel mutinied, and Germany became embroiled in civil rebellion. In November of 1918, Germany collapsed into open revolt. Kaiser William was forced to abdicate, and a provisional republican government was established. In early 1919, the revolutionary National Assembly at Weimar adopted a new national constitution. The Weimar Constitution made Germany a truly modern Liberal Democratic state.

The changes for the military were far-reaching. The president of the Assembly was *ex-officio* commander in chief of the military, but any order signed by the president had to be countersigned by the Minister of War.[153] The Minister of War also represented the military and its interests before the Assembly. The president was to nominate and dismiss all general officers (with the concurrence of the Minister of War), but routine administration of the military would be in the hands of the Ministry of War (appointed by and directly responsible to the Assembly). Finally, all members of the military had to take an oath of loyalty to the new Constitution.[154]

The Assembly had a specific goal in mind as it engineered the new military. The law creating a new provisional army (passed March 6, 1919) called for an armed force "built on a democratic basis."[155] One of the linchpins of its strategy was that the officer corps was to be selected from among the ablest candidates who applied, regardless of origin. In this way, the Assembly hoped to break the aristocratic dominance of the officer corps and better integrate the armed forces into society. Unfortunately for their design, they overlooked one major procedural point. Candidates gained entry into the military on merit, but once commissioned, the decision of who should be promoted was left entirely to commanding officers. The military leadership manipulated this prerogative so deftly that they completely thwarted the integrating process. The percentage of officers claiming noble birth was actually higher in 1921 than it was before the war.[156]

The most devastating antidemocratic military reforms were not imposed by the Weimar government, but by the victorious Entente coalition. In their genuine concern to foster democracy in Germany and create a stable peace, they made a series of blunders. Veit posits four major errors: the creation of a German speaking, culturally German Republic of Austria; demands for the surrender and judgment of so-called war criminals; failure to fix the amount of reparations; and the refusal of

German admission into the League of Nations.[157] Clearly these contributed to the isolation of Germany and fostered the rise of National Socialism. A fifth error, more damaging than any single one of those above, should be included—the systematic disarmament of an unoccupied Germany. By international decree, the victors saddled the fledgling Weimar democracy, a model of modern liberalism, with an almost perfectly authoritarian military structure.

The Armistice Treaty of Versailles dictated that Germany reduce its military strength to 100,000 volunteers with no more than 4,000 officers. The army was to be a border guard and policing formation intended to maintain internal order only.[158] The old conscription and landwehr militia systems were to be abolished. Enlisted men would serve 12 years and officers 25. With these stipulations, it was thought the Germans could not circumvent the Treaty by having high numbers of citizens serving for very short terms, creating an operational reserve in fact if not in name. Clearly the framers of the Treaty were attempting to preempt a repetition of the Prussian *Krümper* system. Because the new army from the start was unable to establish any militia-like qualities, it both retained and attracted the most absolutist elements of the prewar military, career officers and men.[159] In addition, the German military was to be deprived of all offensive capabilities. All aircraft, tanks, submarines, and seagoing vessels over 10,000 tons were to be eliminated, reinforcing the police or internal-only role of the army. Finally, the General Staff and all professional military academies were to be dissolved. Down the line, the dictates of the Versailles Treaty read like a formula for influencing subsequent political structures along centralized, authoritarian lines.

The military hierarchy, for its part, did not impassively accept the diminished role it had been handed. Versailles attempted to destroy military careerism in Germany. Military careerists knew no response but to fight back. The remnants of the General Staff immediately developed a program to regain its former power and station. In 1920, the senior military officer, General Hans von Seekt, notified the War Minister that henceforth all matters of training, selection of officers, personnel administration, and operational planning would be handled through his office.[160] The very notion of a commanding general was against the provision of the Treaty, and Seekt was manifestly and immediately overstepping his authority. The Assembly was in such a state of disorganization that his memo went unanswered, a lack of response Seekt accepted as implicit approval.[161]

Shortly after Seekt's now infamous note, the Assembly selected a new War Minister. Otto Gessler proved to be a virtual puppet for Seekt, acting as his political conduit in government. The fact that Gessler was an affable and unflappable politician was a great boon to Seekt, who was able to carry out his plans of counterreform relatively undisturbed by political constraints.[162] Seekt's first acts were to squelch the divisiveness in the officer ranks that had occurred in the last years of the War.[163] These officers were, in Seekt's view, troublemakers unfit for loyal service. He immediately set about incorporating or forcibly disbanding the independent military formations that sprang up during the revolution, and purging those officers who did not show loyalty to the old guard. Those officers that remained were forbidden to participate individually in political activity, but were required as a group to support Seekt's program.[164] The army and navy as institutions had a perfect right, again in

Seekt's view, to determine the national interest and to act both independently and in concert with the government to secure that interest. Thus, divisiveness in the officer ranks could only lead to a diminution of the total power of the state. Seekt never lost sight of his belief that "the army serves the state, only the state, for it is the state."[165]

Although the Versailles conditions proved disastrous to the establishment of a permanent democracy in Germany, they were not entirely antithetical to Seekt's attempts at counterreform. For one thing, the reduction to 100,000 troops meant that Seekt could keep only the very able and very loyal in the active force. Wartime mobilization had opened the military to millions of political undesirables, and the Versailles restrictions gave the perfect opportunity for a purifying purge of the ranks. The resulting *elite* core would become the cadre of the new German army. Man for man, the German army would again be widely regarded as the finest in the world— due entirely to the fact that it could be so selective in trimming its ranks.[166] The Assembly had decreed that any able-bodied citizen over age 17 could volunteer for service, but the military retained the ability to review applicants by means of soldier and officer "proofing."[167] This process allowed the officer corps to systematically exclude Jews, most urbanites, socialists, communists, and outspoken democrats, while at the same time dramatically raising the physical and educational standards of the entire force. Seekt knew the army must eventually expand, and he demanded that every officer be capable of assuming upper-command ranks, every noncommissioned officer be qualified and capable of becoming a junior officer, and every soldier be qualified and capable of becoming a noncommissioned officer.[168] In addition to required upward-mobility preparation, every member of the armed forces was multiply trained. All members of the transportation corps, for example, were unofficially trained as artillerymen.[169] Preparation of the advance cadre was obvious by 1922. Of 96,000 enlisted men allowed under the Treaty of Versailles, 76,000 were noncommissioned officers.[170]

Seekt also understood that the General Staff and the military academies would have to be retained in some form if the military were to regain its once-dominant position within the state. Retention was accomplished by having corps staffs meet regularly, formally and informally, performing to a large degree the functions of the old General Staff without calling undue attention to their activities. Each major military unit was also responsible for establishing a standardized training regimen that approximated the curriculum of the old military academies.[171] By 1932, the pretense for junior officer schooling was all but eliminated with the establishment of an "Officer's Course" in Berlin that was plainly a centralized staff college.[172] Seekt was further able to circumvent many of the manpower restrictions by conspiring with Gessler to vastly increase the size of the two major police establishments. The National Police for example, allowed by Treaty to own and train with heavy machine guns, increased in size from just under 100,000 personnel in 1919 to over 220,000 by 1925.[173] These paramilitary forces were intended to augment the regular military, were functionally integrated, and often trained with them.

It was during this period that the third arm of the German military, the *Luftwaffe*, gained prominence, though its rise was much more covert than that of the army, which circumvented most Treaty restrictions fairly openly. The Entente did not intend that an air force should even remain possible. The Versailles Treaty specifically ordered the destruction of all German aircraft, with the intent of permanently grounding its air capacity. The German authorities were unwilling to relinquish *all* aviation competence, however, and so of the 4,000 officers allowed, 180 were former aviators.[174] In 1923, 100 first-class Fokker aircraft were covertly purchased from the Dutch and moved to a secret training base in Russia, where over 220 German pilots and observers were trained in air operations.[175] In 1933, the Luftwaffe was officially recognized as an independent force, and was from then on equal in stature with ground and naval forces.

Despite the attempts to retain a high degree of professionalism in the period, drastic limits in both scope and scale of recruitment and retention severely restricted the potential of these reforms to provide a liberal influence. Any scoring of the organizational scoring characteristics would reflect a tremendous authoritarian turn after 1919. The size and rapidity of the drop suggests a strong military organizational influence toward centralized authoritarianism in subsequent political structures. Setting for war, composition of forces, and professionalism drop precipitously. Perhaps only strategy and tactics factors rise in favor of democratization, but only slightly, and not enough to challenge the drops in other areas. The military has been completely restructured by 1924, and the negative effect on liberal political institutions should be evident within a decade.

The German Military and National Socialism

In 1927, Gessler was forced from office due to a scandal resulting from allegations of misuse of public funds.[176] Wilhelm Groener, a former lieutenant-general, replaced him as War Minister. Seekt had already established himself as the *de facto* military leader, and Groener did not attempt to revoke his usurped authority. He did, however, endeavor to invigorate a positive liberal political spirit into the military to counter what he perceived as the "twin dangers of communism and national-socialism."[177] Groener was an elected member of the Democratic Party absolutely opposed to what he foresaw as the rising menace of Adolf Hitler, and he appeared fully prepared to use his powers to smash Hitler's organization if Hindenberg would have supported him.[178] Hindenburg did not, and Groener's efforts were limited to public and private oratory against the brown shirts and their leader.

In 1930, in recognition of his liberal credentials, Groener was given the additional post of Minister of the Interior. He was now officially responsible for the maintenance of internal law and order, and as head of the military and national police, should have had the power to act decisively.[179] The appointment was more problematic in the long term, however, as it established the precedent of official military control of domestic social and political activity. Groener would not use the power arbitrarily, it was thought, but there was no way of guaranteeing that future dual-ministers would act with equal restraint. With this new authority, it is conceivable that Groener could have eliminated the rising Nazi threat with force. As a political liberal, Groener rightly saw that an antidemocratic use of military-police force to suppress a popular political movement could have produced a severe anti-Weimar, pro-Nazi backlash. So he did not, and Hitler's movement gained ground.

An unintended consequence of the Armistice agreement limiting the size of the German army to just 100,000 was that the government was forced to accept, and may even have encouraged, the rise of private armies and paramilitary formations, especially in the post-1926 era of crippling unemployment.[180] Hitler had his own private army, the *Sturm Abteilungen* (SA) or "brown-shirts," that were seemingly omnipresent. In 1931, the SA had over a million and a half members, dwarfing the regular army.[181] The SA's commander, Ernst Röhm, made no attempt to hide his aspiration for the brown-shirts to *become* the regular army of Germany.[182] He wanted the standing army to be replaced by a militia of Nazi Party faithful (specifically the SA), with himself in the dual roles of commander in chief and Minister of War.[183]

The problem of *ad hoc* militias and private armies goes counter to democratizing ideals by restricting participation to specific ideologues and by professing fealty to an organization other than the legitimate government. By 1931, the SA was recognized as a threat to both the state, as violent disrupters of the electoral political process, and to the regular military, as a potential rival for the legitimate monopoly of violence that is so integral to the legitimacy of the state. To counter the threat, the army sought to have its official strength doubled, to 200,000, in order to offset the growing popularity of the SA among the German youth.[184] It would not be enough. Young Germans, eager for a stronger political voice, were effectively shut out of the traditional military path to enhanced political power by the Versailles manpower restrictions. They could not polish their citizenship credentials through sanctioned means. Moreover, the global economic slump had caused massive unemployment, and the military was not in a position to alleviate the social pressure with short-term recruitment. Traditional military service as a resort for fiscal solvency was denied. In addition, institutional pressures *within* the legitimate military were exacerbated by Nazi propaganda. Hitler was steadily gaining favor among the young army officers who supported his call for a vastly expanded military force.

The great tragedy of the Weimar state is that Adolf Hitler was *elected* to a position of national power. Representative democracy, the greatest form of self-government yet devised by humanity, is not without its flaws. Hitler's rise to full power was meteoric. After the death of Hindenburg, in 1933, he immediately sought to reassure the military of its continuing importance to the Third Reich, promising massive monetary and manpower support.[185] He abolished the jurisdiction of the civil courts over the military and eliminated the elected soldier's councils that permitted public airing of grievances from the lower ranks.[186] Röhm was incensed by Hitler's apparent abandonment of the SA and his embrace of the traditional military, and began to scheme for his own elevation to power. Hitler, getting word of Röhm's treachery, acted quickly to consolidate his hold on power through the institution of a domestic terror policy. The "night of the long knives" (1934) claimed Röhm, dozens of high-level SA officers, and a variety of other political opponents as Hitler unleashed Himmler's *Schützstaffeln* (the notorious SS, Hitler's private Praetorian Guard) in a murderous cross-country blood purge.[187] The regular army officers looked the other way, assuming perhaps that Hitler was cleansing his party of the unwanted refuse of his early days as a revolutionary and readying himself to rely fully on them. To a great extent, he was. Within a few weeks, every member of the armed forces was made to take a *personal* oath of allegiance to Hitler as Fürher of the German Reich, an oath that superseded the constitutional oath each had taken previously.[188]

One year later, in March 1935, Hitler announced the unilateral repudiation of the military clauses of the Versailles Treaty. Within two months the German government publicly announced the existence of the Berlin War Academy and the Luftwaffe.[189] Hitler immediately reinstituted the practice of universal conscription and increased the authorized size of the active military to over 500,000 personnel. No group of mythically Aryan men was to be overlooked in the recruitment and training of the new German Wehrmacht. This included the so-called white groups born from 1901 to 1913—too young for service in World War I but who were now beyond the normal age of conscription. This lost generation was placed into a special training category that received limited and regular instruction, and formed a supplementary reserve.[190] To rapidly augment the regular forces and better organize the population, the landwehr and landsturm were revived. Most men from ages 35 to 50 had been thoroughly trained for service in the world war, so the transition to a full reserve system was expedient. Men aged 35–45 were quickly organized into regiments and placed into the landwehr for garrison and emergency reserve duty. Men over 45 were assigned to the landsturm for future emergency garrison duty.[191]

The rapid growth of the military meant that officers and soldiers were needed in great numbers, and so the rigid post-Treaty requirements for admission and commission were drastically lowered. The officer corps quickly split into three competitive groups: the senior officers of aristocratic or upper-bourgeoisie lineage that remained true to the elder Moltke's vision of the army as autonomous guardians of the state; a large mass of Nazi Party cronies who perceived career advancement as a function of political maneuvering; and a large group of common citizens who tried to remain politically neutral. Gordon Craig cites Fabian von Schlabendorff, who claimed the neutrals through lack of character were worse than the Nazis, whose brutality was a constant source of irritation to the old guard; and General Hans Speidel, who divided the officer corps into "thinking soldiers," "party soldiers," and "just soldiers."[192] Hitler also revived the old liberal idea of universal two-year active service commitments in order to train a maximum number of citizens in the shortest possible time. With an invigorated and vastly expanded army now in his control, three battalions of infantry marched into the demilitarized Rhineland on March 7, 1936.

In 1937, Hitler publicly announced the reintroduction of offensive strategy to the military forces, couching the move in geopolitical terms of living space, or *lebensraum*. Hitler had been enormously influenced by General Professor Karl Haushofer's academic school of *Geopolitik*, from which the concept of lebensraum was taken. The geopoliticians claimed they were espousing natural principles of social-evolutionary theory. Every region on Earth had a natural center of power, and Europe's was Germany. It was geographically determined destiny that a dynamic German state should someday conquer the lands around it, and morally just that German peoples should rule over the lesser ethnic groups in those territories. The geopoliticians offered a pseudo-scientific rationale for Hitler's megalomaniac dreams, and it was systematically perverted into a "master plan" of German military resurgence.[193] Haushofer's influence was undoubtedly enhanced through one of his pupil's, Nazi party crony Rudolf Hess, whose geopolitik master's thesis was titled, "How Must the Man be Constituted Who Will Lead Germany Back to Her Old Heights."[194] Hitler was the model of that man.

Lebensraum policies, of course, dictated that the Germans must permanently occupy the territory that they would inevitably gain through military force, a decidedly undemocratic organizational principle. The rest of the strictly military reforms under Hitler began the process of changing the organizational structure of the military to a generally pro-democratic stance, however. Were it not for the effective use of public terror that the Nazis ingeniously and generously applied, the regime might have collapsed through counterrevolutionary action instead of foreign military occupation. Several organizational reasons why it did not are important.

The SS developed within the SA as Hitler's elite personal guard, a small force of 200 men in 1929 that swelled to over a quarter million members by 1939.[195] In 1935, following his renunciation of the SA and embrace of the traditional military, Hitler reorganized the SS into a fully armed and independent standing body of autonomous troops—a personal army politically superior to the regular army forces. In 1937, Hitler appointed Heinrich Himmler as *Reichsführer* of the SS and as the Ministry of the Interior's Chief of the German Police.[196] Precedence for such a duality of functions had been established with War Minister Groener's appointment as Interior Minister in 1930, but the combination in Himmler's sadistic hands proved internally ruthless. The terrorist state police, the *Geheime Staatspolizei* (Gestapo), had the authority to imprison and execute "enemies of the state," a term that had broad definitions, but included Jews, homosexuals, communists, Marxists, freemasons, political agitators, physically handicapped individuals, and anyone resisting their authority.[197] Of interest, the reorganization was generally welcomed in the military. The regular military generals for the most part despised their duties as internal police officers, and preferred to devote their time to the duties of external defense.[198]

In 1938, Hitler took direct personal control of the armed forces and transformed the War Ministry into a consolidated high command (the OKW, or *Oberkommando der Wehrmacht*). The General Staff was then bloodlessly purged through the retirement of 13 suspect general officers and the transfer of 44 others.[199] The new OKW was either slavishly loyal to Hitler or too intimidated to offer any dissent. In a stroke, the General Staff had been politically outmaneuvered. It was no longer the independent guardian of conservative German values. It no longer had its political basis to act as a state within a state.[200]

Hitler's conscious destruction of the old guard, combined with an enormous gain in the size of the armed forces, should have had—in the absence of state terrorism a tremendous democratizing impact on political structures. German mobilization in World War II was greater than in any previous war, absolutely and proportionately. Of a prewar population of 69,500,000 million, 17,900,000 soldiers, sailors, and airmen were inducted into the active armed services creating an astonishing military participation ration of 25.8 percent. Of this number, almost 7 million died; an enormous and unjustifiable sacrifice.[201]

The movement from pro-authoritarian to pro-democratic military organizational influence was unmistakably evident by 1942. Had the allies not completely destroyed Hitler's Germany, it seems likely that a liberalization of political structures would have been inevitable after the War—at least for ethnic Germans, those who served in the military.

Postwar Germany and the Bundeswehr

In 1945, the German state was shattered. The victorious Allies would settle for nothing less than unconditional surrender. Germany's military was completely disbanded and its weapons confiscated. Its territory was occupied, and effectively split into spheres of influence and control. German political and military leaders were placed on trial for war crimes. For the next decade, Germany ceased to exist as a sovereign nation-state.

When it became apparent to the Western Allies that Eastern Germany would be under the permanent political control of the Soviet Union, steps were taken to establish a democratic Western Germany under allied control. The 1948 Basic Law, established May 23, 1949, set up a working framework for representational government. On September 21, 1949, the Federal Republic of Germany (FRG) was officially established by the provisional German government under the direction of the occupying forces. Two years later, the United States, France, and the United Kingdom officially terminated the state of war against Germany (the Soviet Union did not officially terminate until 1955).

Although the FRG was instituted without any form of military organization, the United States had since inception been secretly negotiating the guidelines for a future integrated German military force to counter the perceived Soviet threat.[202] The new German army was to be organized following the American model, and to expedite the process, in 1950 the United States formally requested that the FRG contribute a military contingent for the defense of Europe.[203] Five years later, the FRG was released from official occupation status and became a sovereign state. The Paris Treaties (May 1955) provided for a German contribution to the defense of Europe through NATO and the Western European Union (WEU).

The new German army was designed from its inception as an integrated component of a NATO security force. The authorized strength of the *Bundeswehr* was set at 495,000 troops, all dedicated to the defense of German territory in case of a Soviet–East European attack. Mobilization proved difficult, however. Antiwar sentiments ran high in the West, and NATO requests for support were temporarily curtailed. In 1957, the FRG's military strength was approximately 100,000 troops, divided among 5 under-strength army divisions, a one-destroyer navy, four air squadrons, and an 11,000-person Border Guard. By 1963, total military strength was 402,000, not including the inauguration of a national reserve force. By 1970, the German ready reserve numbered over 800,000 men and women.

Despite the perceived threat of a Soviet invasion of Europe, the foremost concern in the organization of its armed force was not military competence. Politicians had learned their lessons well, and the threat from the East was less menacing than the seeming threat from within—the traditional hazard to democratic society that the military (as a state within the state) seemed to pose ever since the Karlsbad Decrees countered the genuine liberal reforms of 1806–15. The creators of the new military took it as their task to "reconstruct from the nation's past" an army "with new institutions and practices that would ensure its loyalty to the Bonn democracy."[204] The architects sought nothing less than social engineering, and keenly perceived military service as the foundation of that process.

With this primary goal in mind, Parliament (the *Bundestag*) enacted a series of constitutional reforms that unified command authority over the newly created Bundeswehr. The Minister of Defense would be responsible for the military in peace, and the chancellor, as Commander in Chief, would control the military directly in time of war. The Bundestag further established a standing Defense Committee to oversee the Bundeswehr at all times, and created an office of military ombudsman to act as a liaison between civil authorities and all service ranks so as to guarantee civil liberties within the armed forces.[205] Also created was an armed forces administration that separated the administrative functions of the military into a civilian-staffed bureaucracy.

Adjunct activities included the establishment of a personnel committee to review the political qualifications of the first volunteers for the new military's officer positions. All had to demonstrate military skills, but senior officer candidates additionally had to demonstrate a commitment to liberal democratic political ideals. Because they were in most cases recruiting former Wehrmacht officers, the committee assessed political tendencies on questions of personal views regarding the assassination attempt of Hitler in 1944.[206] Within a relatively short period of time, given the extremely egalitarian recruitment and advancement policies put consciously in place, German officer ranks closely resembled extant social distributions.

The twin notions of the citizen-soldier and *Innere Führung*, a conscious exercise of political rights, quickly characterized this new German army. Innere Führung is an attempt to balance the citizen's "demand for freedom in a liberal democracy" with the soldier's duty to obey the chain of command for the purpose of military efficiency.[207] The notion is not new with the post-war FRG. It has its roots in nineteenth-century German liberalism. The concepts combine to form the maxim: "Military service shall not lead to any basic break with the soldier's life as a citizen."[208] The fundamental idea is taken from recommendations of the 1806–08 military reform commission, which argued soldiers who experience civil rights in uniform will be more motivated to defend the state from its external enemies.[209]

By 1963, the German armed forces had become a model for other Western liberal states. Its external focus is clear, despite its defensive stance. Preparation is high for a nation not actively engaged in war, while composition of forces, strategy, and tactics are all soundly democratic in their influence. Any deficiencies are offset by extraordinary professionalism. For the first time in Germany, military and sociopolitical values are compatible, and this concurrence bodes well for the future stability of the German state.

Final Comments

Throughout the period reviewed, Prusso-German military organization has had a distinct if perverse influence on the tenor and direction of state political structures. When the government became more liberal, it tended to promote a more conservative military structure. When the government became more authoritarian, it tended to promote (usually through international pressure) prodemocratic military structure. Thus, Prusso-Germany's history is a seesaw of political change in which military reforms accurately presaged political change. It also demonstrates a wide range of potential influences over time. Perhaps most useful is the example of the Weimar Republic, when the misguided solution to antiauthoritarian influences was the virtual emasculation of the state's military capacity. The pro-democratizing capacities of the military were thus eliminated, and pro-authoritarian influences were magnified. The alternative solution emplaced after World War II, possible because of the continued existence of an outside threat to the NATO coalition, was to rearm the state and provide it with a significant military capacity that promoted egalitarian values.

CHAPTER SIX
POST–COLD WAR IMPLICATIONS AND THE AMERICAN MILITARY

This work provides too selective a history to lay any claim to comprehensive accuracy. It culls from the whole of Western experience enough supporting details to make a comprehensive *argument*, however, one that with a few modifications and corrections might stand the test of time in its broad interpretation. And that argument is simple; military organization in response to external threats shapes and helps determine the form and structure of government. When we combine this assertion with the moral opinion that liberal democracy is the most desirable form of governing, then a blueprint for action ensues. Specific organization and reorganization of extant military forces will promote and help maintain liberal democracy.

Domestically and as a plan for foreign policy, a proper military organization is a relatively inexpensive and potentially high payout option. The issue has salience as the world moves closer to universal democracy, or at least as the United States pushes democratization as a pillar of its foreign policy. As American liberal democracy is the world's oldest and most stable, it has become a model for others, a beacon of hope for many. Its military is at present the world's strongest, and the most emulated. The interplay between military organization and political institutions here becomes critical. Where goes the United States, goes the world.

The Past as Prologue

The American experience on the road to liberal democracy was considerably different from those of the states previously chronicled, but not so dissimilar as to defy comparison. Americans were not abruptly removed from their sociopolitical expectations by their Revolution. Indeed, the American democratization experience at the end of the eighteenth century was probably more restorative than revolutionary. Americans generally fought for freedoms and liberties they believed they already possessed, and at least on the frontiers already exercised. Many had come specifically to find respite from religious and political persecution, others for economic independence. They brought with them neither the trappings nor heritage of feudalism and an ensconced aristocracy with which to contend, and what limited government managed to intrude on the American colonist was local and politically decentralized. These colonials, faced with the daily rigors of life on the frontier, were ruggedly independent in their personal and public lives. The key difference with their European forebears was that the entire colonial population was participating in or liable to a continuous military service.

The Indian Wars that so definitively shaped the character of the early American proto-military forces were not waged on the European model. Daniel Boorstin points out that the Native Americans who engaged the earliest settlers had not read Grotius.[1] Rules and conventions had their place in the limited combat of the old aristocracies of Europe, but not here. Native peoples were faced with a campaign of annihilation instigated by the diseases of the white invaders as much as by their arms, and they responded with raids, ambushes, and occasionally, massacres.[2] There were no innocents, no disinterested civilians in these wars of survival, and the colonists responded with systematic destruction of the native tribes. Total war was institutionalized on the American frontier long before it made an appearance in Europe.

The organizational characteristics of the New World militaries *had* to be different than those of contemporary European armies. Even if the Europeans had wanted to transplant their style of warfare intact to North America, the effort would have proven futile. "Armor, pikes, swords, and heavy cavalry were not much use against the Indian enemy, and such European carry-overs were gradually discarded."[3] The military guidelines of the Old World were replaced with those of the New. Forest tactics of ambush, quick strike, sharp shooting, and skirmish were adopted and perfected by the colonials. Combat was an engagement of surprise, not maneuver; precision fire from protected positions, not face-to-face contests of will and fortitude. Stockades were common on the frontier and generally invulnerable. With the exception of Pontiac's attack on Detroit, there is no evidence of a sustained Indian siege.[4] This is not to suggest that either the Indians or the Colonials relied on a strategy of defense. The Indian Wars were a highly mobile series of attacks on the enemies' territory, fortifications being employed for stockpiling supplies and primarily as a useful deterrent to large armed movements from French and Spanish forces. Expedience and experience formed the basis for the American military character.

The colonists came first as military units. They responded to the conditions they found with the model they had known in England. The indisputable heritage of the military establishment of the United States is that of the British tradition of a voluntary militia. The home-defense militia in England was developed in response to the succession of raids by Angles, Saxons, Scots, Celts, Normans, and Vikings. Although generally in disuse in England following the reforms of Cromwell's New Model Army, the perpetual threat from them was analogous to the perceived danger from Native Americans and other European colonizers (the French and Spanish in particular). When the threat of raids diminished in England, the militia became less a military organization and more a social one. But there was no corresponding abatement in the colonies. The frontier dangers inherent in colonial life meant that all able-bodied men were required to carry arms and make themselves available for various military operations and expeditions. Because the viability of the colonial settlement required full agricultural and community participation as well, no one could be relieved of the duties of planting crops and erecting buildings for the purpose of lengthy campaigns, far less for permanent military duty. In light of the small but intrusive British military garrisons, a colonial standing army of local professionals was considered suboptimal, as it would draw away too much labor from the farms. Local militias at the ready were the logical response to specific *ad hoc* needs. After several generations of military and communal self-reliance, a society of free men emerged in America.[5]

The specifics of militia organization followed the old British system. Two distinct groups of military formations became established: the common militia, consisting of *all* able-bodied men (excluding slaves) who would be called and trained as needed; and the voluntary militia, composed of those free men willing and financially able to undertake regular training who would be the first mobilized in emergencies. The voluntary militias may have been necessitated by the establishment of extensive exemptions from service, due to chronic colonial labor shortages, granted in direct and increasing proportion the further removed the colonist became from the frontier. A lack of enthusiasm and any perceived sense of urgency mitigated the size and effectiveness of the voluntary militias until the Seven Years' War, but even in relatively exposed and independent-minded Massachusetts, the militia drilled only four days per year.[6] It was far from a professional military, and man for man against European equivalents it was quite lacking. Nonetheless, the voluntary militias were the predecessors of the colonial Minutemen, and formed the bulwark of the Colonial resistance to British occupation.[7]

At the core of the debate over the organization of American armed forces—an argument that has continued into the twenty-first century—was whether the foundation of the nation's military power should consist of professional soldiers or citizen-militias. At the heart of the matter is the desire to protect democratic institutions from the perceived threat of an independent, professional, and personally loyal military by relying instead on citizens whose loyalty is to the *idea* of the state, and who once armed and trained could protect themselves from their own government. The practical problem of such a solution was, and has always been, whether a citizen-militia of part-time training could sufficiently protect the state from external threats.

The positions put forward in *The Federalist Papers* outline the arguments for and against standing armies in most eloquent fashion.[8] The bulk of the debate was on which would be the most harmful to a budding democratic state, but Alexander Hamilton exposed the salient point in promotion of democracy when he averred "the bravest of them feel and know, that the liberty of their country could not have been established by their efforts alone, however great and valuable."[9] It takes a *unity* of effort to wrest the freedom of a nation from oppressive control, and the militias instill the sense that all who contribute are valuable, and necessary. The idea that national liberty is not won on the backs of individual heroes, but through the "perfected diligence" of coordinated "practice," would be echoed by Max Weber a century later.[10] National defense through coordinated and popular military mobilization is in this way directly linked to political mobilization and its manifestation of democracy. Whoever risks his life for the state has a stake in it as great as any other, and the state has an obligation to recognize that sacrifice with full franchise and legal equality.

The counterargument, best annunciated by U.S. Army Historian Emory Upton a century later, is that professional standing armies may be so militarily superior that the militia-reliant democratic state, impervious to destruction from within, may be vulnerable from without.[11] Although the militia strengthens the democracy, only through reliance on an independent and professional army, Upton averred, could the United States guarantee its *international* security. It is a classic trade-off of freedom for security, though this position was hardly reassuring given Upton's known "contempt [of] democracy and civilian control of the military."[12] In the end, the Americans attempted to prosecute their revolution with both a state militia *and* a national army. Either-or was not an attractive option.

The French and Indian Wars (1754–63), a relative skirmish in the context of the global Anglo-French conflict of the Seven Years' War, highlighted the shortcomings of the militia system and refined the components of the professional American army.[13] The militia system, which had served adequately in the primarily defensive and police roles of border garrison and Indian suppression, proved wholly inadequate for the task of carrying out an offensive campaign against regular French troops. In the nine years of the war, militia troops could claim only one meaningful victory over European armies, the early defeat of Braddock's troops near Fort Duquesne.[14] The European professional armies were not so superior to the colonial and Indian forces that they could learn nothing from them, however. They were extremely limited in the wild and rugged terrain of the colonies, and the British were ultimately compelled to detach elements of their regular regiments to learn techniques of woodcraft and forest fighting. A new kind of regiment was formed from these detachments under Lieutenant-Colonel Thomas Gage, and is now recognized as the first light infantry regiment in the British army.[15]

The primary problem of prosecuting an international war with a colonist militia, a problem that would continue to plague the Colonial army through the War of Independence, was the loathing that part-time militiamen felt in having to serve far from home, where the perils to family and livelihood were more abstract and the long-term advantages of participation were outweighed by short-term deprivations. This formulation of the modern version of social action in situations of public good could only be mitigated by large enlistment bonuses or other side payments. One of the more effective inducements was the practice of releasing indentured servants from their obligations in return for relatively short-term military enlistments. As many as one in five recruits in the first two years of the conflict may have been so-induced indentured servants from Pennsylvania.[16] While the practice proved extremely useful for filling the ranks of British colonial units, Americans who had paid for the indentured servants' passage were outraged when their perceived loss was not compensated. Even with increasingly lucrative enlistment bonuses, however, non-indentured Americans generally disdained service in the campaigns, and by the late 1750s the majority of Anglo-American combatants in the French and Indian Wars were British regulars. It was nonetheless from this experience that the small cadre of future American Colonial Army officers, including Colonel George Washington, interned. Their desires were straightforward: "we want nothing but commissions from his majesty" with the prospects of continuing a full career in the regular British army.[17]

Between the French and Indian and the Revolutionary Wars, the American military organization was consistent with a very strong pro-democratic influence. Its preparations were continuous and directly supported by a majority of the population. There were no limitations by ethnicity, though slaves were rarely brought into service, and it had no reliance on mercenaries. Indeed, the British use of mercenaries as occupying troops was widely despised. Operating from stockades and fortified frontiers, military operations were generally offensive, and the incorporation of Native American and a variety of local militias required a combined arms strategy. Militarism was decidedly low (military pageantry was often spoofed), but rank stratification was *de facto* based on wealth (though *de jure* open to all). Coordinated and disciplined training was relatively moderate (for the period), providing one of only a few minor impediments to a fully democratizing organization, a liability to be corrected by Baron Friedrich Wilhelm von Steuben, a Prussian military officer of largely imaginary credentials, who drilled the American troops at Valley Forge in 1778. Results were immediately felt at the successful battles of Barren Hill and Monmouth, in which von Steuben personally served with distinction. The following winter von Steuben wrote *Regulations for the Order and Discipline of the Troops of the United States*, which served as the principal American drill manual for the next 30 years.[18]

The small size of the American Continental Army belies the breadth of popular participation in the overall defense of the young republic. In 1776, approximately one man in every eight of military age served in the campaign forces or state militias.[19] This ratio is more remarkable when one considers that as many as a third of the colonists were loyalist Tories. Even though Americans somewhat begrudgingly enlisted in the regular armed forces, they massively and enthusiastically organized against and resisted the British wherever they appeared. Ragged irregulars harassed and sniped British troops in the streets of the largest cities and from behind stone fences on country roads. It must have been incredibly demoralizing for them. For the first time in military action against European peoples, the British were exposed to combat against the mass of the population.[20]

Add to this total number the formal and informal combatants active in the maritime forces, and the ratio of citizen participation soars. The Continental Navy was an agglomeration of the militia navies of 11 of the 13 states. At its height in 1779, it had 34 ships and almost five thousand men.[21] The American Navy was pitted against the British North American Station, which claimed 50 superior vessels and 7,460 men, just under one-third of the entire Royal Navy.[22] More numerous than the Continental Navy, and more troublesome for the British, were the swarms of American privateers that operated independently. Except for 1776, American privateers working against British shipping represented more combatants than were in the Continental Army and state militias combined.[23] "Of the more than 800 vessels captured by the Americans during the War, only 198 were taken by the Continental Navy," the rest by privateers.[24] If there is an inherently democratizing effect from navies, due to the factors described in chapter two, then the colonists were very well served.

Periodic military mobilizations would positively presage the incremental rises of political inclusion throughout the history of the United States. In the early republic, political franchise was limited to free European male property owners, the heroes of the Revolutionary War. State power dominated and it was widely perceived as more prestigious to be governor of Virginia than President. Mobilization for the War of 1812 changed much of that perception, however. It had the effect of catalyzing the nation and instilling in it a greater sense of community across state boundaries. As in the Revolutionary War, militiamen were loath to leave their home states, severely impinging on the American's capacity to invade British Canada, and substantial congressional authorizations for federal manpower were never realized. For example, in 1812 Congress offered enlistment bounties for 50,000 recruits to augment the army and navy but barely five thousand accepted the inducement and volunteered.[25] When the British invaded the Continent, however, nationalistic sentiments were galvanized. With the exception of the Civil War, the country fielded more regular army troops than at any time until the Spanish American War of 1898.[26] By 1814, at least 70,000 Regular Army and Volunteer troops were under Federal Command, with perhaps 200,000 more active in State militias.[27]

In the aftermath of the second war with Britain, Americans became keenly interested in national politics. Political mobilization at the national level increased, and after 1824, voting in presidential elections eclipsed that in most state contests, though voting in national elections was meager even by modern standards.[28] Moreover, with the reliance on nonpropertied citizens to shoulder the burden of defense in the Second British and continuing Indian Wars, a renewed interest in universal suffrage—that is, universal for adult white males—free of property requirements emerged. The period after the War of 1812 and generally extending at least to the 1848 Mexican–American War has been called the period of Jacksonian Democracy or the Jacksonian Revolution.[29] Andrew Jackson, war hero and Indian fighter, positioned himself as champion of the people against moneyed groups, and an expansion of suffrage through the elimination of most property qualifiers occurred under his administration.

This period was further highlighted by an expanding professionalization of the Regular Army, with strict oversight and control by the civilian government. Despite career enhancements like advanced military education and relatively high pay, America was the land of financial opportunity, and able-bodied young men preferred to carve out a life in civilian society. The harsh military existence was a grim alternative to the prospects of milk and honey in private enterprise. When enlistment bounties of 40 dollars plus 3 months pay in advance, along with a promise of 160 acres of federal land, proved inadequate, the military responded by expanding its potential recruitment base.[30] Forty-seven percent of the Army's enlisted ranks were foreign immigrants in the 1840s, mostly German and Irish.[31] Although most proved worthy in the various Indian Wars, problems of desertion were rife. About a third of the regular army simply walked off the job in any given year to pursue frontier options.[32] The incorporation of newly arrived émigrés was expedient for the military, and was equally useful for the immigrants who used military service as an introduction to the culture and language of the new nation, becoming sufficiently acclimated to its then-peculiar form of capitalist liberty to join into the civilian mainstream.

Lessons Learned: Modern Military Structure for a Liberal Democracy

The American miracle, a jump from colonial monarchism to liberal democracy, was relatively peaceful—until its civil war ended the issues of slavery and whether the

Union would be a strong or weak federal design. That democracy is difficult to maintain, especially fledgling democracy, is well known. The French Revolution did not succeed in immediately establishing a permanent democratic government. It would take three more revolutions (in 1830, 1848, and 1871) before France would become a relatively stable liberal democracy. Indeed, it is difficult to find any state that transitioned to democracy without some measure of protracted violence associated with it. This is perhaps inevitable. Democratic politics moves disagreements over the most contentious issues of society from the battlefield to the ballot box, from violence to voting. The process of stabilization can be enhanced by continuing military reforms to strengthen the democratic influence of the military organization.

The seven case studies that precede this section highlight the power and influence of the propositions made in chapter two. Given the clear correlation between military organization and political inclusiveness, several preliminary lessons can be applied to the current U.S. situation and prospects for Western liberal democracy.

Preparation for War: Values and Fears in a Liberal Democracy

Continuous preparation for war, for the purpose of political liberalization, is an uneasy proposition for most Americans. Having lived under the specter of potential Cold War annihilation, and paid the enormous bill for a Cold War nuclear arsenal that was thankfully never used, any respite from continuous preparation is welcomed. And so it should be. The point is not that Americans or any other people should live in a state of perpetual fear. One of the implicit goals of this work, stated in the introduction, is to find a means to increase the probability of *peace* in a way that satisfies both realists and idealists. In this regard, I intend an *active* state of peace, not simply the absence of violence or war, but one where the threat of war is remote.

In the case studies presented, active preparation for war does appear to provide an impetus for democracy, at both the individual and state-system levels. First, it allows the people of the state to feel solidarity with other members, despite ideological and other political differences. Most importantly for emerging democracies, it allows for a sense of community in the dangerous period of change, so that potential violence can be directed outward rather than internally at other members of society. Issues under debate seem more meaningful when an external threat is present, and preparations are under way to meet it. Compromise is possible, even desirable. When there is no external threat, or at least no serious external threat, internal political dialogue can become petty and obstructionist. When a lack of internal unity does not threaten the viability of the state in the international system, its electorate has the luxury of hotly debating and contesting trivial matters. And it does.

The previous argument is based on anecdotal evidence, but it is intuitively reasonable. Of importance, the threat the state's military must be constantly preparing for does not have to be a similarly structured foreign military. The current war on terrorism suffices to draw Americans together and emphasizes the importance of meaningful political discourse. Of course, the principle could be perverted. If a war on terrorism (or on drugs, poverty, etc.) turns inward, then it violates the principles of numerous other propositions, which will be discussed in turn. In the case of terrorism, so long as the military is preparing to challenge that threat outside the borders of the state, then it should advance the cause of democratic maintenance.

The systemic level of influence is revealed with the question: how can constant preparation for war increase the probability of active interstate peace? Two schools of thought are at odds here. The first claims that preparation for a thing increases the likelihood the thing will happen. The second says that in the case of violence, the best deterrence is sound preparation (from the Latin adage, "if you want peace, prepare for war"). The problem is encapsulated in the notion that the source of one state's security is the font of another's insecurity. When one state increases its preparation for war to feel safe from others, this causes fear in the others. A vicious cycle ensues. The two views are irreconcilable unless one inserts the critical intervening variable of democratization. If certain identifiable preparations for war enhance democratization, as I have asserted throughout, does democratization promote peace? The answer appears to be that *mutual* democratization does. In other words, liberal democracies do not go to war *with each other*. If they don't, then the size and efficiency of their military forces should not cause a security dilemma.

Over the years, the American military has prepared for war quite erratically. Since 1941 however, its preparation has been intense and continuous. The Cold War ensured that an external threat of terrible proportion was evident, and a global strategy of containment necessary. In the post–Cold War era, the U.S. military has engaged in six wars (or military operations) from Iraq to Afghanistan. Given the ongoing war on terror, preparation shows no sign of easing.

Ideal Scope and Scale of Military Participation in a Liberal Democracy

The ideal is to have more than 5 percent of the population *actively* engaged in military or military-support service at any given time, and greater than 30 percent of the population *eligible* for military service. The first number is easier to maintain if preparation for war is significant, but can have a very high economic cost to the state (in foregone production capacity as well as direct payments). The latter figure can be achieved relatively inexpensively, and must be high to ensure that the military does not become dominated by one ethnicity or class. The lower the percentages of the military participation ratios, the more other factors have to be emphasized to counterbalance their negative effects.

The scale of population actively engaged for war appears more critical to the *emergence* of the democratic state than the scope of population eligible for service, which is vital to the *maintenance* of the liberal democracy. This is a crucial deficiency for the American and most Western militaries. In the United States, less than 3 percent of the population is on active duty military service or active reserve status (including the state-oriented National Guard). Given the stability of its democratic institutions, this percentage could probably go lower without a major antidemocratic impact, so long as other factors are strengthened as a counterbalance. The problem for the United States is that its scope of population eligible for military service is less than 20 percent.

Eligibility for a military draft is the most common way to increase service liability, though the draft had always been a last resort option for the United States before the

Cold War. In its first widespread implementation, during the Civil War, draft riots broke out in New York and other major cities. As soon as the war ended, the draft was repealed. The extraordinary mobilizations for World War II required a comprehensive draft, and all able-bodied males of military age were required to come forward and register. Unless deferred for education, family hardship, or critical industry; or found physically or mentally unfit, most men were inducted into the armed forces. Following World War II the draft was suspended, and then reestablished for the Korean War. From that point, the draft was selective rather than universal. All had to register, but only a percentage were culled for active service. The changes were for three dominant reasons: to rapidly augment existing forces; to obtain the best recruits possible; and to ensure fairness in induction across classes, ethnicities, and regions.

The Selective Service draft system continued until the debacle of Vietnam, where 18 and 19 year-old men were being sent off to die for their country without the basic right of franchise. In 1971, to correct the injustice, age limitations were reduced universally from 21 to 18. In addition, after 1975, Congress abolished the national draft and instituted an all-volunteer military service. For several years, no person was required to register for involuntary military service. By the end of the 1970s, however, a new draft registration system was introduced to track potential recruits in case the need for a rapid massive mobilization should arise. Grandfathered to exempt those who had not registered in the half decade after 1973, all *males* were required to register their location and draft status at their local post offices upon reaching their eighteenth birthday. This system exists today.

While it seems quite unlikely to be reinstituted in the near term, draft registration has an important symbolic effect. At the same age that a young man becomes eligible to vote, he must also declare that he is available to serve the state in war. He is supposed to see the connection between rights and obligations, between franchise and service. He should be a more thoughtful citizen for the exercise. But the weaknesses of this draft model are appalling. Fully half the population is not required to go through this rite of citizenship passage. Women are not required (indeed, not even allowed) to register, and do not share the symbolic experience. Their value as a citizen is systematically patronized. Without equal requirements for liability, women have a less valid claim to full citizenship than men. The situation ought be untenable in a modern democracy.

The solution is obvious. Require *all* citizens to register for the draft upon reaching the age of political maturity. This would be an important first step, but in practice would not suffice to enhance liberal democracy. The problem is that since draft registration was reinstated, those registering have little expectation that service might actually ensue. No one has been drafted since the Vietnam War, and there appears to be no impetus to do so. There is certainly no urgent request from the military to call up recruits, as was the case in previous conflicts. This is simply because America fights its wars differently now than it used to. The equipment it uses is highly technical, and can take years to master. A conscript service, in which a large number of variably competent and motivated short-term recruits replaces the current well-motivated professional service is going to be militarily inferior (and costly in the long term) to the extant system. America's fighting forces are the best in the world, in the aggregate and man-for-man. But military effectiveness does not have to be at odds with citizen education—both can be pursued with the proper policy. Today, because of the highly unlikely event that a registrant would actually be called to service, the symbolic act of registering has lost almost all of its meaning. A more nuanced solution is needed.

Population and National Service: Military Effectiveness and Social Equality

The selective service model of the post–World War II era is the place to begin. As previously noted, it was based on three overriding principles. These were (1) a *sufficient* supply of (2) *competent* recruits, (3) *equitably* drawn from the population at large. A draft that randomly selects the needed number of recruits fulfills requirements (1) and, to a lesser extent (3), but may not satisfy (2). This was the primary problem encountered in the old system. Birth dates were randomly selected on an annual basis and placed on a list. All those whose birth dates were at the top of the list were evaluated for a minimum level of competency, screened for legal deferment, and placed into basic training. Then the second date, the third, and so on until the needed number of recruits (1) was achieved. Deferments available to middle- and upper-class citizens who could afford to attend college meant that poorer classes and minorities shouldered an unfair burden in service to the state, but it was as equitable as any system yet tried in America.

A simple yet far-reaching modification could satisfy the needs of the military *and* maximize the citizen awareness/responsibility effects of politico-military liability. Instead of calling up the precise number of recruits needed to fill the ranks for minimum military competency, draft for maximum competency. Require *all* citizens of proper age to report to the draft board and offer themselves for military service. *Everyone* is evaluated and tested for military aptitude. The military then selects from the whole those who suit its current requirements best. The rest are sent home but cautioned to maintain their addresses on file to be called up later if needed. This simple modification would have enormous social ramifications, and would maximize military readiness.

It is not perfect, however. Potential abuses can be foreseen, most of them rather conspiratorial and far-fetched, but plausible nonetheless. Some additional modifications could be implemented to address the potential pitfalls in the system. For example, conscripts do not generally see the military as a long-term commitment. There will always be those who find themselves liking military service that might not otherwise have considered it, but it seems probable that critical shortfalls in specific high technology fields would be endemic. Moreover, by allowing the military to cull the very best of the population, it limits the traditional egalitarian military influence of providing a conduit for upward social mobility. Minorities traditionally at lower economic levels do not have equal access to quality education, and might become systematically excluded from military service over time. To remedy both problems, the conscript system must be augmented by a volunteer program. Conscripts would serve for a short period, perhaps two or three years. More than that would be onerous to the citizen who was serving as a point of civic duty, but vastly preferred to move on to the civilian worlds of business or university as soon as possible. Volunteers could sign on for four to six years, with enlistment bonuses or higher pay as inducements. These would be able to train in the higher-skilled positions, and the military could take advantage of that investment with a longer service commitment.

At this point, the draft system is beginning to look like a national service, where all citizens of a certain age are brought into the military for social engineering. To a degree it is, and at the very least cannot be separated from the arguments for and against such a system. Proponents of universal national service argue that universal short-term service to the state is the most effective means of creating vibrant, competent democratic citizens. It takes young people from their homes, separating them from the apron strings of family, and intermixes them with others from around the state. This exposure is thought to instill a wider sense of community awareness, and sensitizes the individual to other cultures, attitudes, and beliefs—all of which is desirable in the good democratic citizen. One supposes all this is possible, perhaps even probable, but attempts to put theory into practice in many states has failed to meet these objectives. The major problem, it seems, is that no distinction is made between the qualities of an individual (variations in physical, intellectual, and emotional attributes) and the qualities of a citizen (equal before the law). All are placed into military service; all receive basic training; and most are shunted off to complete busy work at the direction of bored and bitter supervisors. Not all persons are suited for military service, much less basic training. Many 18-year-olds are emotionally or physically ill equipped for such rigors, and some are permanently scarred from the experience. Most report a distinctly unfavorable impression of their service, and attempts to avoid it are rampant.

Again, it does not have to be this way. Imagine the modified system described above where everyone presents him or herself to the draft board. All are tested and evaluated, but instead of selecting only a few, *all* must serve in some form. Those with military aptitude who fit the needs of the services will be sent there. Others will be selected for service duty such as the Peace Corps or Vista. Many will go to hospitals and nursing homes to aid and assist there, while others are sent to help recover from natural and manmade calamities, or to build or refurbish roads and waterways. Some would be clerks and interns. *Everyone*, no matter her or his ability, could serve the state in some capacity—the key factor is that service would be determined by the needs of the state. Individuals could request an assignment preference, to be taken into consideration, but the overriding factor is an unqualified offering of *ultimate* service to the state—exceptions made for legitimate religious or ideological exemptions from military *combat* service. With this proviso in place, it would be to the advantage of all to do their best on placement exams and evaluations. Moreover, no one would need a deferment (except for severe family hardship); since everyone would serve and all would then be equally competitive with their peers for jobs, university or technical training, or any other opportunities at the end of their service. Social leveling would be maximized. Some would have gained valuable training and skills. Others would have traveled to parts of the state (or world) that gave them new or unknown opportunities. No minority would shoulder an unfair burden for the state, as all were liable for military service, and all contributed to the health and vitality of the state in a meaningful way. The military would not have to babysit the unmotivated, would not have to accept the minimally qualified, and would not have to waste its valuable training time in busy work.

A few caveats are warranted. Some members of society may choose not to serve in the military, for religious or personal reasons, and others may not be able to serve in the military, usually for medical reasons. This should be allowed and accounted for. Conscientious objectors could still be required to complete military-style training, though perhaps a type of training undertaken by combat medics or chaplains to account for their profound convictions. This would not involve weapons training or other killing exercises, but would be rigorous, demanding, and intense. If their convictions allowed it, and they were competent, some would indeed go on to serve in the military as medics or chaplains. Others would be sent off to service duties that were congruent with their beliefs and desires. A more difficult problem, but one that is eminently solvable, is what to do with the medically disqualified?

While some people have used legitimate as well as fabricated medical and other disqualification to avoid military service, many have been kept from service despite their intense desire to serve. Malingerers will be with us forever, but what place is there for those who wish to serve but cannot perform military duties because of physical or mental limitations? In the modern high-tech military, there are fewer of the traditional infantry-type jobs that require robust physical health. Many positions are behind desks, computers, microscopes, and video screens. More are in research and development, procurement, and other support functions. It does not take a leap of genius to understand that the vast majority of previously disqualifying ailments (flat feet, poor vision or hearing, too tall or too short, etc.) can be accommodated in the new military. If they cannot, then the citizen can still perform other duties outside of the military, as do the majority of their civilian peers who would not be selected for military service, and so the symbolic offering of one's life in service is not abridged. The initial training period will need modification, but precedence has already been set for conscientious objectors. The only problem might be for the profoundly disabled, but then only for training. Accommodations can and must be made. Only those individuals who are for their own welfare institutionalized should be exempted from evaluation and placement, for obvious reasons.

Such a model maximizes the democratizing influence of military service, especially for the healthy maintenance of the state. It also allows the citizen active participation ratio to remain high even as the spread of democracy around the world lessens the likelihood of war, and progressively limits the number of citizens selected for military service each year. Of critical importance, the scope of eligibility remains optimum throughout.

Ultimately, such a program would reform the society of any state that undertakes it, especially one as individually oriented as the United States. It may even be politically impossible in the near-term. But the minor change in the current American draft system advocated at the beginning of this section could and should be made immediately. *Everyone*, regardless of gender, must register for the draft. It is not necessary for everyone in the liberal state to participate directly in war or war preparation for liberal democracy to maintain itself (though this is the group that will receive political benefits soonest). But it may be necessary that everyone in the state be personally liable for the decisions of policy makers to inspire a more participatory structure.

Population and National Service: Minority Challenges

The national service argument cannot be manipulated, as it was with the Napoleonic *levée en masse*, to argue for the emergence of a superior combat force. In an age of technology and hyper-destructive power, mass armies are vulnerable and inefficient. *The purpose of national service is not to strengthen the state militarily, but to strengthen it politically.* Organization and application decisions must be made first on that requirement. Popular contentions that women are not as good at soldiering as men, or that men do not fight as effectively with women in their ranks are debatable, but even if they are true are moot. National service (indeed, all of the policy recommendations in this chapter) is undertaken for the good of the state. If an organizing principle for national service that enhances participatory government can be made compatible with military prowess, so much the better. But the sociopolitical argument is primary.

In a liberal democracy, all citizens should be equal before the law and the state. For this simple constitutive principle to have meaning, no one should be denied the *opportunity* to serve the state due to a factor of birth or sociopolitical preference. In this regard, women face a particularly insidious impediment to full citizenship in the United States. Although they are admitted into military service, they are denied the traditional avenue of polishing their individual and group citizenship credentials through particularly valorous service. They are not allowed to serve in combat-designated specialties. With the exception of some flying duties, they remain overrepresented in support services. Again, I am not going to argue the merits of women-as-soldiers. I have already agreed that men are socially and culturally more likely to be attracted to military service, and that men are in the aggregate more physically suited to military service, but that certainly does not mean that *all* men are better soldiers, sailors, or airmen than *any* woman. To deny the *opportunity* to serve the state in its most hallowed capacity, regardless of capacities or aptitudes, is fundamentally wrong.

It is not necessary (nor desirable) to argue that women must be given equality of numbers or condition to state categorically that some women would make brilliant combatants and that some men would not. But I would argue for quotas before I would argue for exclusions based on gender. This is not a military efficiency argument, though to deny half the population the opportunity to enter combat service because of preconceived notions of the failures of femininity is ludicrous, and wasteful. The bottom line is that until women are equally able to offer their lives in service to their country, in so doing demonstrating the ultimate patriotism, they will not be equal in society.

The exclusion of homosexuals in the American military is another blatant (and wasteful) violation of classic liberalism. The debate over whether homosexuality is a factor of birth or a lifestyle choice is in this issue irrelevant. If we assume for the sake of the argument that it is the latter, then it is no different than for any other lifestyle choice. The service member subordinates his or her preferences while on duty, in certain military areas, and in uniform. Religion is a lifestyle choice, for example, and both accommodations and proscriptions on the free practice of religion are routinely made for military service. Satanists are not barred from military service, but they cannot display the symbols of their beliefs while in uniform or while acting on behalf of the military, and they cannot perform human sacrifices or any other illegal act at any time. There are rules of dress for men and women, and these must be abided regardless of sexual preference. The argument here is that whatever a military person's personal preferences, there are standards of conduct that must be adhered to. Even presuming the most flagrant stereotypes, men cannot wear makeup or earrings while in uniform, and women cannot have flamboyant hairstyles or other personal visual eccentricities. Military bearing and professionalism has no distinction for sexual preference, and no changes must be made to accommodate even the most biased misperceptions of homosexuals. As long as these standards are applied in a fair and uniform manner, and this is understood at the time of enrollment, then sexual preference is a trivial and tangential detail.

Proponents of social prudence argue that homosexuals might engage in same-gender sexual relations while in service. One supposes they probably will, on their off-duty time. Young adult men and women are prone to rampant sexual activity, be they hetero- or homosexual. And so long as such actions are legal, then they should not be standing grounds for disbarment. Again, all service members should be treated equally and fairly. Sexual relations are not allowed between heterosexuals while on duty, in barracks, or within chains of command; there need be no exception for same-sex interaction. If training and discipline are maintained—and the job of military trainers is to make discipline problems disappear—problems of unauthorized sexual relations for homosexuals will be no greater than current similar problems for heterosexuals. If the drill instructors and training officers cannot control themselves or their subordinates, then they ought to be dismissed.

The arguments that allowing homosexuals to serve in the military would cause irreparable discipline and morale problems, or that homosexuals would be poor soldiers, are completely specious. Similar arguments were made in opposition to the integration of black Americans into the armed forces, and were quickly proven totally without merit. As to the latter case, there is no valid support for the assertion. Ample historical evidence points to individual instances of homosexual soldiers and sailors serving with extraordinary military prowess. As a group, systematic exclusion of homosexuals has denied them the opportunity to prove their worth as soldiers, and I argue here, as full citizens. And of course, this is the fundamental problem. Full acceptance of homosexuals in military service, without restriction, would be viewed as social acceptance of the lifestyle choice. It is well known, and obvious from the examples given in this work, that long-standing prejudice can be quickly disrupted in military service. The real fear among those who pre-reject homosexuals from military service may be that as a group they might become politically and morally accepted in society at large.

The only military effectiveness argument against homosexual participation in the armed forces that carries *any* weight is that it might cause heterosexuals to rebel or somehow lose competence in their irrational desire to avoid association. Some service members would quit or leave the service in protest. Others might become preoccupied with separating themselves from comrades they know to be homosexual, suborning mission effectiveness to personal bias. Similar to the problems of racial integration in the 1950s, when several ranking officers tendered their resignation rather than serve equally with their fellow citizens, it is not hard to predict a repeat episode should the military be sexually integrated. But just as the country and the military were better off in the long run with the self-inflicted purge of racism in the 1950s, so will they be better off with a similar purge of homophobia in the first decade of the twenty-first century. The only intolerance the military can allow is for incompetence. If a few competent military officers are lost over the issue, it is a small price to pay.

These military reform arguments are targeted at political change or maintenance, and not at military effectiveness. But even if readiness or efficiency would suffer (even though it is impossible to find empirical support for the notion that widespread inefficiencies in military prowess would occur with the open admission of homosexuals), that argument is irrelevant. The important factor is simply this. Whether one wants homosexuals to be legally and politically equal in society or not, the proscription of homosexuals from offering their lives in support of the state creates an unequal playing field in society and courts. And that is wrong. One may choose not to associate with homosexuals in private life. One may choose not to go to bars or restaurants where they gather, or to attend churches that allow homosexual marriage or sanction homosexual ministers. One may even choose not to purchase products from businesses that hire them, or boycott television programs that accept their lifestyles. Those are rights of individual citizens. But the state cannot deny equal rights of franchise and protection under the law, nor deny the opportunity to serve the state in any capacity for which the individual is otherwise qualified.

In short, no person should be *a priori* barred from military service, and all persons should serve the state in some capacity.

Military Professionalism and the All-Volunteer Armed Force

The debate of mercenary versus citizen-conscript is over in the West, though not yet in the developing world. Today's more salient argument for liberalization and maintenance of the democratic state is found in the careerist versus conscript debate. At what point does the military professional have such a stake in his or her career that personal interests outweigh those of society? Does professionalism include the requirement to advance the best interests of the military institution over those of other government agencies or groups, or over other military services? Does the conscript, expecting to return to civilian society at the end of his or her duty, have a broader understanding of the military as service to the state than the voluntary careerist, who is more likely to see her or his service as a self-interested life pursuit? Which is more likely to see the personal benefit of going to war? In terms of promotion potential and advancement, it is clearly the professional careerist.

An all-volunteer structure *potentially* diminishes the liberalizing effects of large military forces through artificialities of force composition. When the bulk of military forces are composed of draftees selected randomly from a broad citizenry pool, its political ideology and cultural norms will reflect those of society. Over time, however, an all-volunteer force will tend to attract certain personality types and concentrate ideological factions. Individuals drawn to military service presumably share characteristics that are less apparent or possibly absent in their fellow citizens. These could include an increased sense of patriotism or nationalism, greater personal risk acceptance, higher group identification needs, and the like. Exacerbating and compounding this tendency for trait-concentration is the propensity for volunteering military personnel to have a family tradition of military service. Children *tend* to follow their parent's lifestyle choices, and additional social assimilation can occur in close-knit groups that spend generations together. This reinforces commonly held characteristics and limits the capacity of alternative ideas and preferences to be introduced. Moreover, military professionals and their families spend an average of three years at one location, limiting their ability to form close associations with nonmilitary localized or geographically constrained groups. Major religious affiliation, available at most duty stations, is reinforced as one that can be transported from tour to tour. Thus, volunteer American military professionals, and especially multigenerational military families, tend to be socially and politically conservative, intensely patriotic, personally loyal, more religiously fundamental, highly trained and educated, and worldly in outlook.

These are all fine traits, and some might argue appropriate ones for military service. I do not intend to debate their relative merits. The importance of this observation is that incrementally the military force structure may be separating itself from society as a whole. There is no conspiracy here, or any conscious effort on the part of the state or military to mold itself. It is a natural process, evolving over the course of time. When this happens, the potential for militarism—an elevation of military symbols and pageantry above mission effectiveness—is nurtured. More dangerous to the liberal democracy, should military members overidentify themselves as members of an elite group, one that is most deserving of political preferences based on their sacrifices for the state, a military elitism could be structurally emplaced in the state. The full ramification of this phenomenon is unclear, but it seems plausible that militarism or military-elitism could find fertile ground in such a distinct group. If the liberalizing effect of military forces is maximized in a non-stratified force structure, and absent when dominated by an identifiable segment of the population, the pro-democratization impact of the United States military could be expected to wane, even if that stratification is not legally mandated.

There is certainly no reason to think that America's armed forces are poised for a takeover of the government. Such an idea is absurd. But the changeover to a smaller, careerist, and less diverse structure is potentially worrisome.

Military Professionalism: Nation Building and Peacekeeping

The purpose of armed force, in the pithy words of a colleague, is to "kill people and blows things up." Such a bloodthirsty definition is troubling to some, but it has some merit. It forces decision makers who would employ military force not to do so casually. People can and will be hurt. Lives may be lost. Property will be damaged. The use of military force is—and should be—for the application or threat of the application of violence. Wherever military force is used for nonviolent operations (such as delivery of humanitarian aid or support in disaster relief), the specific value of using military assets over civilian ones is to have the *latent threat* of violence available to expedite the process. There is another rather weak reason for choosing military volunteers over civilian ones to perform risky operations. They are subordinate to a hierarchical command system that allows disobedience only for illegal commands—not deadly ones. Civilians may refuse to risk their lives at any point, generally without recrimination. Military members cannot.

Because they have formally accepted personal liability in support of state policy, there is a general acceptance of the notion that military members are *expendable*. Wherever there is risk to life or limb, there is an implicit understanding (especially in an all-volunteer force) that the soldier, sailor, or airman has offered her or his life in service should the needs of the state so dictate. Civilians make no such compact, implicit or otherwise. If soldiers are killed in the performance of their duties, it is a sad and lamentable thing, but it is not unanticipated.

This highlights a perverse aspect of peacekeeping duties. Military forces are placed in harms way not because it is risky, but specifically *so that they can be killed*. They are placed in highly visible and vulnerable locations, usually outnumbered. They are not expected to be able to defend themselves. This is a crucial point. When a peace has been brokered and a cease-fire is in effect, third-party military force is placed between the formerly combating sides. The purpose of these forces is not to *actively* prevent the two sides from resuming hostilities. This is usually obvious to the peacekeepers. Moreover, they are not there to determine which side commences new hostilities, in effect, which side has been wronged. They are usually not authorized to assist one side over the other, and sometimes not allowed to use deadly force to prevent incursions. They are not there as a deterring force in the sense that if hostilities begin, they will engage in any form of combat to stop them. No, they are there to be killed. Both sides know that if either begins hostilities, operations will have to go *through* the peacekeeping force. If Americans or other states' forces are collaterally damaged, the likelihood that the aggrieved state will enter into the fray with all its military capacity to maximize violence is increased. Therefore, peace is maintained by the inherent threat that hostilities cannot be resumed without dragging the peacekeeping nation into it. The peacekeeping force, however, must take its licks.

The political ramifications of peacekeeping forces are important, and they have little to do with military efficiency. They have everything to do with political strategy, however. Ideally, a pro-democratization military organization serves the political liberalization of society *and* the effectiveness needs of the military. While the latter is subordinate, I address it here first to make a point. If military forces must be trained and prepared to *maximize* violence in a specific area, to kill and destroy, and to be prepared to die in the process, then one must question the increasingly assigned roles of nation building and peacekeeping to the military. Both require the military to *minimize* violence. How can one efficiently train to maximize violence, and then in practice be expected to minimize it? Worse, imagine a military force that had been trained specifically for nation-building tasks (infrastructure construction, police augmentation, monitoring voting, etc.) and peacekeeping functions. Then imagine that this force, trained to minimize violence, had to be mobilized for war against a determined, well-armed opponent. The result would be suboptimal.

Why then, do liberal states like the United States insist on sending their military forces to other states to enforce civil peace and construct political institutions? What nation-building functions can a properly trained military force execute efficiently? Their latent violence capacity may be helpful in enforcing laws, curfews, and the like, but this is not the primary reason for using military forces in such a manner. More important, military forces are quickly mobilized, are prepared to take casualties, and may even have some experience in doing so. When the state is threatened internally by natural disaster, or when martial law has been declared, military reserves are appropriately called in to support rebuilding, protect individuals and property, and so defend the law of the state. The period of power application is expected to be short, either with abatement of the emergency or replacement with regular police or internal security forces. This is not the case for troops sent overseas to perform the same duties. In the authoritarian state, emergencies never end and martial law is never repealed. Using military forces for internal police augmentation, as has been argued, is one of the primary characteristics of military power that directly supports authoritarian government, and should have no routine place in liberal society.

The military efficiency argument is directly assaulted by this improper use of force, however. Again, in both peacekeeping and nation-building operations, warriors are told not to maximize violence, but to minimize it. Rules of engagement are stringent. Soldiers are sent on patrol but not allowed to carry ammunition for their weapons, to avoid the possibility of *accidentally* applying military force. Base camps and checkpoints are set up in stunningly vulnerable locations. UN peacekeepers wear powder blue helmets, and paint their vehicles in similar fashion so they are difficult to conceal. What this does to training and discipline is speculative, of course, but potentially disastrous. Instead of making quick engagement decisions, soldiers learn to hesitate. Instead of taking cover and concealment, soldiers strive for vulnerability and visibility. The dynamic is similar for nation-building efforts. Soldiers are sent into countries to assist in establishing free and fair elections, for example. How does this enhance military prowess?

Presumably, the decisive justification for using military forces in nation-building projects is due to the tremendously positive examples of Germany and Japan after World War II. Occupied by Allied forces, these two governments had liberal democracy forcibly imposed (making use of a great deal of historical and cultural symbols and heritage to facilitate the process). After ten years, the occupying forces were essentially withdrawn and the governments allowed full sovereignty. Today, these nations are two of the most robust liberal democracies in the world. But anything can be proved by analogy, and the fact is the analogy does not hold in most areas of nation building today. In none of these states have the leaders of the people surrendered unconditionally to the occupying forces. In none of them has martial law under the control of the occupying forces been declared. The transformation model is not applicable, and I most certainly *do not* recommend destroying a country before sending in the military to rebuild it.

So far, the argument against pursuing such missions with military forces is that they are inherently nonmilitary tasks. These are at best policing functions, and not strictly military ones. Though the argument is made that occupying and pacifying territory is a legitimate army role, the analogy runs false here as well. Occupation and pacification in war has far fewer restraints on it than these missions. The army moves in, destroying any resistance, sets up control infrastructure and its own martial law, and enforces its dictates ruthlessly. In peacekeeping operations, military forces move in carefully, along specific routes. They employ regular military law for themselves and allow the local population to continue under their own domestic laws and enforcement, and avoid confrontation. None of this can enhance the capacity of the military to wage war.

Of note, I do not exclude humanitarian aid missions from proper military operations. These can be very much in keeping with military force use and training. Flying in supplies to refugees, for example, is good training for pilots who will be doing the same for their own troops in war. Building roads, dams, communications systems, and other infrastructure by army engineers is invaluable practical training. Any nontraditional function that enhances training for wartime operations is useful. Tracking and monitoring drug smugglers, for example, might be an especially appropriate training for military intelligence units, especially for gaining skills in preventing terrorists with weapons of mass destruction across borders.

I also cannot aver that the American military does its peacekeeping and nation-building duties poorly. I have been genuinely impressed with its abilities to adapt to changing missions and requirements to complete its assigned missions. Indeed, it is precisely their success I find so worrisome. Imagine this case. The American military becomes well known for establishing and promoting good government in formerly adversary or perceived failed states. Within a reasonable period, military nation-building activities install a government that respects individual liberties, fosters efficient markets leading to economic prosperity, and maintains foreign policies compatible with American interests. After many years of remarkable transitions around the globe, a sizable number of nation-building veterans have been returned to civilian life in the United States.

Now imagine that an economic downturn, perhaps caused by a severe drought or a successful cartel action raising the price of oil, raises unemployment levels to 15 percent and inflation to about 20 percent. The American government is unwilling or unable to control the situation, and appeals to the American people for calm patience. In this milieu, a populist call spontaneously emerges: "let the military take over." They have the experience and the knowledge of how to get things done. They have the tools. They have worked miracles in foreign lands that were in far worse shape than America; they should do the same for us.

In nations whose democratic institutions are as mature and stable as America, this is the only remotely plausible scenario that allows for a military coup. In Pakistan and Nigeria, the democratic governments have had a pattern of devolving into corrupt ineptitude. Military forces have routinely intervened, for the stated purpose of fixing political problems and setting up the state for a return to democratic rule at a future date. In these states, the populous rarely laments the military's action. In some cases, people celebrate the military coup openly. The military has great respect in these countries, and a reputation for bringing the state to order. When disputes in policy inevitably arise, no sense of compromise has been instilled in these countries. If an opponent does not agree, or a political official acts egregiously, the first resort is to call for military intervention. And there is a sympathetic ear in the military that practices nation building. We know that experience gained in military service translate to political attitudes. The veterans who have built viable states in other lands may feel that they alone have the capacity to do so in America. This is not an attitude that serves the liberal democratic state.

Final Observation

The potential pitfalls described in the current American military organization are real, and bear close monitoring. For the most part, however, the American military as it is currently designed has a strong liberalizing effect within the state, and is a bulwark of democracy domestically and democratization abroad. Some reorganization must be made to counter what will become increasingly deleterious effects of a manpower draw down, and the increasing separation of the all-volunteer force from the rest of society. But there is as yet no crisis. The most effective means to curbing the potential problems just described would be to institute a national draft along the radical lines outlined above. With such a national service requirement, individuals disposed to conflict management could be sent to specific peacekeeping training, and a professional international peacekeeping force could be created along paramilitary organizational lines. Some of the concerns broached here are context-specific, a function of time and place. Some will prove endemic. Some will challenge the political will of the state; others will simply fade away. All can be fixed.

CHAPTER SEVEN

CONCLUSION

This examination began as an inquiry into the role of war in the development of individual political values. It quickly became apparent that war is a wild card, its meaning indeterminate. The key factor is preparation for war. Assessments were made concerning the reaction of rational, self-maximizing individuals to changes in the organizational structure of the military. Change could be stimulated by a variety of social, political, technological, cultural, and geographic inputs, but all instances in this study were brokered by military factors. Clear associations were observed and isolated. Changes that tended to increase or broaden the scope and scale of military participation tended to broaden political participation. Changes that maintained an outward or external bias, envisioning the threat as an interstate vice domestic problem, tended to limit direct military intervention in the political process, increasing the stability of extant democratic governing arrangements and undermining authoritarian ones.

I further relied on contract approaches to state development. Much of the analysis of military impact was shaped by the twin notions of the *authoritarian bargain* and the *democratic moment*. The first was not necessarily a contract openly discussed and ratified by all concerned in a single action; it was more likely an implicit social division of labor that evolved over time, perhaps many generations. But the logic remains. The authoritarian bargain was a comfortable and profitable working and living arrangement that maximized society's potential for wealth accumulation and technological progress. The democratic moment, too, did not have to be formally proposed and accepted, though increasingly in modern cases it is written into law. It represents a political upheaval of established social patterns consistent with the development of democratic inclusivity throughout the Western world.

The source of this upheaval is a sudden incursion of individual liability for state actions. Individuals under the authoritarian bargain are not held accountable for routine state decisions, and so long as they are able to manage their lives divorced from politics, they remain contentedly inert in a blissful variant of Hobbesian political ignorance. When the state can no longer protect individuals from the ravages of interstate politics—war or the threat of war—those individuals pressed into service have personal liability and political interest thrust upon them, and the authoritarian bargain is void. Military activity in this way becomes the conduit for political awakening.

The case studies show that war does not need to act directly upon the individual, that is, everyone who benefits from the democratic moment need not be a direct combatant in war (though it is more difficult to deny the fighting group than the supporting one). But it is always influenced indirectly through the individual's relationship with the government's executor or agent of war—the military. War may be an entirely abstract concept until the individual is faced with the reality of recruitment, training, and/or combat. The peasant whose king wages war in a distant province is disrupted only by an increase in taxes levied to support the royal army. The peasant whose field is overrun by the army and must quarter troops in her home is more directly drawn in. But the individual who participates in military action as a soldier has the longest and most direct contact with war, hence the more profound impact from it.

Direct contact with or participation in the military during war undoubtedly influences the future political behavior of individuals. There are exceptions to every aggregate influence, but for the most part those who serve expect some form of payment. If that recompense is political, it usually takes the form of a greater voice in the affairs of the state. The military's organizational structure then becomes the narrower subject for inquiry. Since war has been evident in every phase of state development, from primitive despotisms to the modern liberal democratic state, the military could be viewed as a constant and unchanging externality with no influence on the political form of the state. This is the null hypothesis or counterargument, that war and military participation have nothing to do whatsoever with political and state development. Under this view, the military as constant antithesis of democratic values and bulwark of tyranny is conceivable, but would be empirically valid only if domestic military forces could be shown to be passive or absent just before and at the time of democratic development. This is clearly not accurate. War and military participation have been as historically evident in democracies as in autocracies. Even if one accepts the premise that most causal relationships between arms and state show military influence to be antidemocratic, this is sufficient to invalidate the null hypothesis. The lone remaining explanation is that military influences must be multidimensional, and that in certain circumstances, they can be positively reinforcing for democratic or participatory political development.

Military participation enhances political participation through the instillation of sociopolitical values. These can run the gamut from traditional military virtues including bravery, loyalty, and honor, to the more despised characteristics of brutality and contempt for human life. Included, too, are the relatively neutral values of obedience, discipline, and group cohesion. Since not all militaries are organized in the same manner, values are not uniformly instilled. In this study I attempted to disaggregate military organization into a set of characteristics that can be shown to have both autocratic and democratic manifestations. A military that embodies a predominance of autocratic characteristics will tend to reinforce autocratic values in its members; one that embodies a predominance of democratic values will do the opposite.

The military, as the state's primary tool of applied power, has considerable direct influence on the state as well. The dynamic interaction of institutions creates a structural influence that corresponds with the agent-values influence. Military characteristics that tend to produce democratic values in individuals also tend to produce democratic structures in the government. Increasing military inclusivity, for example, initiated to meet external challenges from other states, creates a sense of self-worth and participation in the individual while at the same time forcing the state to broaden the scope of its political inclusion to compensate the newly armed citizenry. An emphasis on offensive strategy and tactics compels the state to loosen command and control of its military forces, a dispersion of power and authority that provides individuals with greater decision-making opportunities.

The powerful associations between military organizations with a high democratic quotient and the emergence and maintenance of democratic political structures suggest that the role of the military in determining governmental structure is significant. At the very least, it confirms that the data is consistent with the argument. Sophisticated definitions of modern democracy further suggest the ten constitutive arguments will require additional fine-tuning before they will be universally applicable. Nonetheless, the military contributions to instilling liberal democracy seem to meet the broad requirements of participatory institutions and political inclusivity. Modern militaries require massive government support. In return, they assist in consolidating power into a single bureaucratic authority, reducing the pockets of authority that existed in the feudal system, and most importantly, eliminating the layers of authority between the state and the individual. Then, with expansion to a government-of-scale sufficient to field large military forces, political authority reaches directly to individuals in recognition of their service to the state. Four stages of development appear necessary to this process.

The first is social leveling. Military service has an ample capacity for social equalization at both the macro level, via general impoverishment of the vanquished through wealth destruction and overall wealth enhancement for the victors through redistribution of spoils and booty, and at the micro level, through integration of service and shared risk-liability. Respect in battle comes from prowess. The mightiest Goliath can be humbled by David. The medieval knight is ignominiously dispatched by the bowman; the birthright nobleman killed by the lowly peasant musketeer. The prospect of death in battle is the great military leveler. It binds disparate social groups to the common good of preservation, and it dispels myths of invincibility.

Second, new institutions arise to take the place of the old, incorporating the latest ideals of inclusivity and the realities of the preceding social leveling. Here the military lends its bureaucracy, and the notions of appointment and promotion through merit come with it. Eventually, government bureaucracies reflect military ones, from which many of its functionaries were trained, and to which the predominant share of resources are sent. As opposing states copy the inclusion model, and grow in response to the threat, military effectiveness demands greater inputs from the state. As the military capacity of the state grows, new institutions are required to administer it. An administrative hierarchy is established that mimics the military chain of command.

Third, the democratic state requires a set of common interests be recognized and embraced by its members. Without such a perspective, the state will have little foundation on which to build, and interest groups will splinter away from the whole. Often, this common understanding can be a shared threat. Internal differences recede into manageable dialogue when a greater problem is at hand. Military training emphasizes the common basis of individuals, especially in unit-level training and coordinated drill. All individuals have responsibilities to the whole and all can expect support from the whole. Individuals learn that their contributions are valued, and perhaps more importantly, that the contributions of others are equally needed.

The fourth stage of democratic state-building is recognition that commonalities of understanding are the foundation of the stable state, but that individuals will retain differences and each will have separate and distinct capacities. These differences must be tolerated to the extent that they do not contravene the law, and this is the essence of liberal democracy—popular rule within the framework of minimum rights guaranteed and with constraints on the governors. Military training and participation in this stage is extremely useful, as proper military command authority works two ways. Where upward loyalty is expected, downward guarantees of individual rights must be ensured. Every individual in the chain of command, military and bureaucratic, is aware of and expects a minimum floor of rights and privileges. Be they rights of loot and booty (or of regular pay) or the more modern notions of right to file grievances and to be heard, freedom from arbitrary punishment, and survivor's benefits, all are stated and expected in return for service.

Designing a Military for Liberal Democracy

A breakdown of the kind of military organization that would most benefit democratic development shakes out as follows. For setting, militaries should be continuously prepared for war. This is not to say that they must be constantly engaged in war. Indeed, such perpetual conflict would lead to the overall impoverishment if not downfall of any state that attempted it, severely limiting its capacity to prosecute war. The military itself, as subset of the sociopolitical group, must be so engaged in preparation that it has little time or energy to expend on direct political or social influence, or on its own aggrandizement. It must also be continuously aware of its primary mission, protection of the state from *external* threats.

The composition of forces must be such that eligibility for military service incorporates the largest percentage of the population financially and socially viable, and also includes representation from all minority groups. This is not to say the entire population must be *actively* engaged in the military. Such a stance would again lead to general national impoverishment. It may be useful enough to the state simply to ensure that eligibility for service is encompassing. Within this category, citizens should be prepared to take on all military duties, and reliance on mercenaries should be eliminated. It is critical that this citizen's military be sanctioned and regulated by the state. Private militias are organized to ensure gains for their own members, and cannot promote broad social participation. They must be systematically removed.

Strategy should be heavily weighted toward offensive operations, retaining only so much defensive capability as may be deemed sufficient to dissuade foreign adventurism. The deterrence value of such a military force is effective so long as a credible punishment against a transgressor state can be maintained. An international system with offensively organized military components appears at first unstable. If all democratic states are so prepared then a stable balance through strength is possible (realist view). The observation that democratic states do not war with each other (neo-Kantian idealist view) makes the strength of their arms moot. If the democratic state ensures that its offensive forces are severely limited in their capacity for long-term occupation of territory, they will be less threatening internationally and domestically. Other states will not fear direct loss of sovereignty or permanent loss of territory in case of conflict. It will also limit the capacity for the military to perform internal police functions, making it an inefficient instrument for internal repression. As for tactics, the democratically influential military should be well drilled in combined arms and unit integration. In this way, individuals learn self-worth as part of a cooperative effort, learn social responsibility as they rely on and are relied upon by others, and have instilled a respect for and lasting belief in rules and social regulations. Individuals who are not well trained as a group, or who have been trained to operate as individuals in combat, do not develop the necessary respect for others foundational to a stable law-abiding democracy.

Finally, in the area of professionalism, any appearance of militarism must be purged. Militarism (as distinct from militarization or militarizing) is a social cancer to both the welfare of the political state and the efficiency of the military structure. Military members who aggrandize themselves and their functions have the power and the means to influence politics directly, and this potential for praetorianism is inconsistent with the democratic state. Within the military, there should be no distinction of social class, political preference, culture, religion, or gender in matters of recruitment, assignment, or promotion. All individuals must be assessed on merit and capacity. One last critical factor must be observed—loyalty to the state and to the legal offices (not the personalized officeholders) of that state. An oath is an important social statement, and it should not be made to a person or persons, or to an organization within the state.

Summary and Conclusion

For the military to influence political development, war itself is not a necessary or direct factor. But it is an indirect one, a catalyst for change. War has been historically prevalent in the great revolutions and major changes in political styles of individual states, but it seems to have little or no correlation with the direction of those changes. One factor that is critical, of course, is the outcome of war—who wins and who loses. The loser may be at the mercy of the winner, who can dictate changes to government that are compatible with its own. But this is not always the case. In the history of states, most wars have not been life-and-death struggles. Most have had a winner and loser, but the aims of war have been limited and the state is not at risk of dissolution. The outcome can still have a strong effect in the matter of military reform; particularly in a state that is attempting to construct a military to serve its own ends. If the state wins its war, the performance of the military is often one of the major reasons for success, and the state will be poorly motivated to—and the military will be resistant to—implement far-reaching institutional changes. Conversely, in the case of a losing war, the state may be highly motivated to restructure its military to make it more proficient in battle (and perhaps to make it more compliant and politically compatible). The military, especially if its performance can be directly linked to the lost war effort, will be in a poor position to resist political attempts at restructuring.

In newly modernizing and democratizing states, governments should not punish, ignore, prohibit, or eliminate existing military structures. Reforms should be made to bring the military in line as nearly as possible with the characteristics of a highly pro-democratic military, as quickly as is reasonable. Attempts to severely limit military power may have the opposite effect of that intended. The example of Weimar Germany is a case in point. Of note, if not all military characteristics can be made to adhere to the pro-democratic model, then as many as possible should be attempted in order to enhance the pro-democratic sway of the military and detract from its authoritarian influences. For example, if it is difficult, unnecessary, or otherwise undesirable to maintain a large military force, then the state should ensure that the existing force is entirely indigenous and that entrance to the military is open to all strata of society. Induction should be based on military-only qualifications or by lot in the case of excessive qualified volunteers. Should budget constraints make it difficult to provide intensive combat-arms training, it may be necessary to balance the deficiency with high reliance on an offensive strategy with limited occupational capacities. In all cases, professionalism should be maintained at very high pro-democratic levels in order to balance deficiencies in other areas.

The military as a legitimate public institution is not likely to disappear in the near future. States continue to perceive a need for protection from external threats, and so long as these threats remain, some military force will be retained. The question is how to reconcile the traditional security dilemma with the pervasive notion that the military is an antidemocratic force, ready and waiting to usurp legitimate governing authority for its own ends.

In this work, I have endeavored to show that the military as a unitary actor is miscast, that its true nature is dependent upon a set of organizing characteristics. There are economic, cultural, and social components to the process of democratization, to be sure, but the former have been set aside in order to focus on and evaluate the power of the military's role in that process. The military as institution has been disaggregated and studied systematically. The normative focus of the military as a purely authoritarian force has been challenged, and a more complex view of the military as a multifaceted carrier of social influences has emerged.

The role of the military in state development, particularly for the democratic state, is extensive. No argument is put forward against the widespread observation that the role of the military has been historically weighted toward the establishment and maintenance of authoritarian, antiparticipatory political structures. In every case of spontaneous democratic development examined, however, military forces have had a crucial and positive impact. At critical historical junctures, the military, through changes in its structural organization, has been a catalyst for politically inclusive change.

One cannot credibly argue that merely restructuring the military will guarantee that democracy is maintained in Western states and that it will brilliantly emerge in non-Western ones. Military reform has not been proved itself a sufficient cause for democratization. But it may be a necessary one. Just how necessary the military component is to the overall process of democratization is hard to gauge, but what is repeatedly evident from the historical cases is that it is quite often *the* critical or tipping component.

NOTES

Chapter One Military Service, Citizenship, and the International Environment

1. Much of this argument is an extension of my "War and (the Democratic) Peace: Military Service, Citizenship, and the International Environment," *Citizenship Studies* 4:2 (July 2000), 117–48.
2. David Apter, *The Politics of Modernization* (Chicago: University Press, 1965), 450. My emphasis.
3. See Brian Downing's, *Military Revolution and Political Change* (Princeton: University Press, 1992), 238–40.
4. David Singer and Melvin Small, "The War Proneness of Democratic Regimes," *Jerusalem Journal of International Relations* 1 (1976); Michael Doyle, "Kant, Liberal Legacies, and Foreign Affairs, parts 1 and 2," *Philosophy and Public Affairs* 12 (1983), 206–35 and 323–53.
5. See John Owen, "How Liberalism Produces Peace," *International Security* 19 (1994), 87–125. An excellent overview is Bruce Russet, *Grasping the Democratic Peace* (Princeton: Princeton University Press, 1993).
6. William Thompson, "Democracy and Peace: Putting the Cart Before the Horse," *International Organization* 50 (January 1996), 141–74.
7. John Mearsheimer, "Back to the Future: Instability in Europe After the Cold War," *International Security* 15 (Summer 1990), 5–56.
8. Zeev Maoz and Bruce Russett, "Normative and Structural Causes of the Democratic Peace, 1946–86," *American Political Science Review* 87 (September 1993), 624–38.
9. Jack Snyder, *Myths of Empire* (Ithaca: Cornell University Press, 1991), 9–10 and 258–59.
10. Classics include Seymour Lipset, "Some Social Requisites of Democracy: Economic Development and Political Legitimacy," *American Political Science Review* 53 (March 1959), 69–105 and *Political Man* (New York: Doubleday, 1960); Dankwart Rustow, "Transitions to Democracy: Toward a Dynamic Model," *Comparative Politics* 2 (Summer 1970), 337–64; and Robert Dahl, *Polyarchy* (New Haven: Yale University Press, 1971) and *A Preface to Economic Democracy* (Cambridge: Polity Press, 1985).
11. Otto Hintze, *The Historical Essays*, translated by Felix Gilbert (New York: Oxford University Press, 1975), 181.
12. Charles Tilly, "Reflections on the History of European State-Making," in Charles Tilly (ed.), *Formation of National States in Western Europe* (Princeton: Princeton University Press, 1975), 42.
13. Hintze, *Historical Essays*, 207. David Rappoport concurs: "in all periods of history, [states] utilized the military experience to educate the citizen to his public responsibility." See "A Comparative Theory of Military and Political Types," in Samuel Huntington (ed.), *Changing Patterns of Military Politics* (New York: Free Press, 1962), 80.
14. See Michael Howard, *War in European History* (New York: Oxford University Press, 1976), 94–96.

15. Stanislas Andreski, *Military Organization and Society* (London: Routledge & Kegan Paul, 1954), 68–70.
16. Jean-Paul Bertaud, *The Army of the French Revolution*, translated by Robert Palmer (Princeton: University Press, 1988).
17. Fisher Ames, "Conservative Forebodings," in Russel Kirk (ed.), *The Portable Conservative Reader* (New York: Viking Penguin, 1982), 92. My emphasis.
18. Ibid., 95.
19. Alfred Vagts, *A History of Militarism* (New York: W.W. Norton, 1937), 167.
20. Hintze, *Historical Essays*, 213–15; Vagts, *History of Militarism*, 13 and 356.
21. Sue Berryman, *Who Serves?* (Boulder, CO: Westview Press, 1987), 10; Dennis Segal, *Recruiting for Uncle Sam* (Lawrence: University of Kansas Press, 1989), 10.
22. Joseph Glatthaar, *Forged in Battle* (New York: Free Press, 1990), 231.
23. Charles Moskas, "Social Considerations of the All-Volunteer Force," *Military Service in the United States*. American Assembly Book (Englewood Cliffs, NJ: Prentice-Hall, 1982), 136.
24. Ibid., 150.
25. James Lacey, "The Case for Conscription," *Military Service in the United States*, 200.
26. Vagts, *History of Militarism*, 171.
27. Gunnar Myrdal, *An American Dilemma* (New York: Harper, 1944).
28. Richard Dalfume, *Desegregation of the U.S. Armed Forces* (Columbia: University of Missouri Press, 1969), 1.
29. Berryman, *Who Serves?*, 87.
30. Martin Binkim and Shirley Bach, *Women and the Military* (Washington DC: Brookings Institution, 1977), 37–38.
31. Ibid., 38.
32. Colin Cameron and Judith Blackstone, *Minorities in the Armed Forces* (Madison: University of Wisconsin Press, 1970), 1.
33. Berryman, *Who Serves?*, 82.
34. Hintze, *Historical Essays*, 211.
35. Huntington, *Soldier and the State*, 163.

Chapter Two   Arms and State

1. Stanislas Andreski, *Military Organization and Society* (London: Routledge & Kegan Paul, 1954), 1.
2. Carl von Clausewitz, *On War*, edited and translated by Michael Howard and Peter Paret (Princeton: Princeton University Press, 1976), 579.
3. Ibid., 75.
4. Ibid., 87.
5. See John Keegan, *A History of Warfare* (New York: Vintage Books, 1993); Barbara Ehrenreich, *Blood Rites* (New York: Henry Holt, 1997).
6. Douglass North, *Structure and Change in Economic History* (New York: W.W. Norton, 1981). See also Douglass North and Robert Thomas, *The Rise of the Western World* (Cambridge: University Press, 1973); and Richard Bean, "War and the Birth of the Nation-State," *Journal of Economic History* 33 (1973), 203–21. Much of the contracting logic is theoretically based in Douglass North's, "A Transaction Cost Theory of Politics," *Journal of Theoretical Politics* 2 (1990), 355–67.
7. Charles Tilly, "War Making and State Making as Organized Crime," in Evans, Rueschmayer and Skocpol (eds.), *Bringing the State Back In* (Cambridge: Cambridge University Press, 1985), 169–91.
8. Arnold Toynbee, *War and Civilization* (New York: Oxford University Press, 1950); and *A Study of History* (London: Oxford University Press, 1956).
9. Arthur Marwick, *The Deluge* (London: Bodley Head, 1965).

10. Bruce Porter, *War and the Rise of the State* (New York: Free Press, 1994), xiv.
11. Ibid., 60.
12. John Nef, *War and Human Progress* (Cambridge: Harvard Press, 1950).
13. Lewis Mumford, *Technics and Civilization* (New York: Harcourt, Brace and Co., 1934), 84; See also Raymond Aron, *War and Industrial Society* (New York: Oxford University Press, 1958).
14. Ibid., 90.
15. Werner Sombart, *The Quintessence of Capitalism*, new edition (New York: Fertig, 1967).
16. William McNeill, *The Pursuit of Power* (Chicago: University of Chicago Press, 1982).
17. J.F.C. Fuller, *The Foundations of the Science of War* (London: Hutchinson, 1926); and *Armament and History* (New York: Scribner's, 1942).
18. John Hale, *War and Society in Renaissance Europe* (New York: St. Martin's Press, 1985).
19. John Ellis, *The Social History of the Machine Gun* (Baltimore: Johns Hopkins University Press, 1975).
20. Rosa Luxembourg, *Selected Political Writings*, Translated by William Graf (New York: Grove Press, 1974).
21. Heinrich von Treitschke, *Politics* (abridged), translated by Hans Kohn (New York: Harbinger, 1963), 300.
22. Cited in Toynbee, *A Study of History*, vol 4, 644.
23. Max Weber, Max, *General Economic History*, translated by Frank Knight (Glencoe, IL: Free Press, 1927), 324.
24. Otto Hintze, *Historical Essays*, translated by Felix Gilbert (New York: Oxford University Press, 1975), 181.
25. Charles Tilly, "Reflections on the History of European State-Making," in Charles Tilly (ed.), *Formation of National States in Western Europe* (Princeton: Princeton University Press, 1975), 35–36. My emphasis.
26. Ibid., 73. My emphasis.
27. See Robert Gurr, Keith Jaggers, and Will Moore, "The Transformation of the Western State: The Growth of Democracy, Autocracy, and State Power since 1800," *Studies in Comparative International Development* 25 (1990), 73–108.
28. Harry Eckstein, "A Theory of Stable Democracy," *Research Monograph* 10 (Center for International Studies: Princeton, 1961).
29. Mancur Olson, *The Rise and Decline of Nations* (New Haven: Yale University Press, 1982).
30. Figures drawn from *Brassey's Annual*, published from 1884 (New York: Praeger), and *The Statesman's Yearbook*, published from 1864 (London: MacMillan).
31. See Edward Rhodes, *Power and MADness* (New York: Columbia University Press, 1989) and John Gaddis, *The Long Peace* (New York: Oxford University Press, 1987).
32. Frank Zagare, *The Dynamics of Deterrence* (Chicago: University Press, 1987), 93.
33. John Mearsheimer, *Conventional Deterrence* (Ithaca: Cornell Press, 1983), 29.
34. Andreski, *Military Organization*, 35.
35. Beginning in 1935 with the work of German General Erich Ludendorf, *der Totale Krieg*, cited in William Shirer's *The Rise and Fall of the Third Reich* (New York: Simon and Schuster, 1960), 259; Also useful is Arthur Marwick, *Britain in the Century of Total War* (London: Bodley Head, 1968).
36. An exception is Michael Howard, "Total War in the Twentieth Century: Participation and Consensus in the Second World War," in Brian Bond and Ian Roy (eds.) *War and Society, volume II* (New York: Holmes and Meier, 1975), 216–26.
37. Population data was extracted from Brian Mitchell, *International Historical Statistics* (New York: Stockton Press, 1992). Election data was taken from Mitchell and from Peter Flora, Franz Kraus, and Winnifred Pfenning, *State, Economy, and Society in Western Europe, 1815–1970, 2 volumes* (Chicago: St James Press, 1987). In order to assess levels of political participation, Tatu Vanhanen's indices of competition, participation, and democratization, in *The Process of Democratization* (New York: Crane Russak, 1984 and 1990) were

invaluable. Raw totals of personnel under arms, percentage of population participating in active-duty military formations, casualties, service and reserve participation, militia participation, were extracted from David Singer and Melvin Small, *The Wages of War* (New York: Wiley, 1972), and *Resort to Arms, second edition* (Beverly Hills, CA: Sage, 1982); Quincy Wright, *A Study of War*, second edition (Chicago: University Press, 1965); Michael Clodfelter, *Warfare and Armed Conflict* (Jefferson, NC: McFarland, 1992); Lewis Richardson, *Statistics of Deadly Quarrels* (Pittsburgh: Boxwood Press, 1960); Trevor Dupuy and R. Ernest Dupuy, *The Harper Encyclopedia of Military History*, fourth edition (New York: Harper Collins, 1993); and interviews with James Dunnigan and access to his data published in *How to Stop a War* (Garden City, NJ: Doubleday, 1987); and J.F.C. Fuller, *A Military History of the Western World, volume II* (New York: Funk and Wagnall's, 1955). Additional data sources were Brassey's *Armed Forces Yearbook* and MacMillan's *Statesman's Yearbook*. Specific military and mobilization data for the two world wars were derived from Randal Gray and Christopher Argyle, *Chronicle of the First World War, 2 volumes* (New York: Facts On File, 1991); and John Ellis, *World War II* (New York: Facts On File, 1993).

38. Brian Downing, *Military Revolution and Political Change* (Princeton: University Press, 1992).
39. Martin Edmonds, *Armed Services and Society* (Leicester: Leicester University Press, 1988), 59.
40. Ibid., 61.
41. Peter Riesenberg, *Citizenship in the Western Tradition* (Chapel Hill, NC: University of North Carolina Press, 1992).
42. Andreski, *Military Organization*, 69.
43. Max Weber, *General Economic History*, translated by Frank Knight (Glencoe, IL: Free Press, 1927), 324–5.
44. Everett Dolman, "Obligation and the Citizen-Soldier: Machiavellian *Virtú* versus Hobbesian Order," *Journal of Political and Military Sociology* 23 (1995), 191–212.
45. Isaiah Berlin, "The Originality of Machiavelli," in Berlin (ed.), *Against the Current: Essays in the History of Ideas* (New York: MacMillan, 1975), 35.
46. Kenneth Waltz, *Man, the State, and War* (New York: Columbia University Press, 1954), 307; Leo Strauss, *Thoughts on Machiavelli* (Seattle: University of Washington Press, 1958).
47. William Bluhm, *Theories of the Political System*, second edition (Englewood Cliffs, NJ: Prentice-Hall, 1971), 285.
48. Sheldon Wolin, *Politics and Vision* (Boston: Little-Brown, 1965), 207.
49. Niccolo Machiavelli, *Discourses on the First Ten Books of Titus Livy*, translated by Leslie Walker (New Haven: Yale University Press, 1950), chs. III, XLI.
50. See Robert Price, "*Ambizione* in Machiavelli's Thought," *History of Political Thought* 3 (1982), 193–221.
51. Thomas Hobbes, *Leviathan*, in Richard Tuck (ed.), *Cambridge Texts in the History of Political Thought* (New York: Cambridge University Press, 1991).
52. Machiavelli, *Discourses*, III.16.
53. Niccolo Machiavelli, *The Art of War*, translated by Ellis Farneworth (New York: Da Capo, 1965), 3.
54. Jean Jacques Rousseau, *La Nouvelle Heloise*, cited in Carl Friedrich, *Man and His Government* (New York: McGraw-Hill, 1963), 421.
55. Immanuel Kant, *Perpetual Peace*, translated by Ted Humphrey (Indianapolis, IN: Hacket, 1985).
56. Alexander Hamilton et al., *The Federalist Papers* (New York: Penguin, 1961), 183.
57. Ibid., 185.
58. Bluhm, *Theories of the Political System*, 249.
59. McNeill, *Pursuit of Power*, 76–78; See also Sebastian de Grazia, *Machiavelli in Hell* (Princeton: University Press, 1989), 290–91.
60. Ibid., 76.

61. Martin Van Creveld, *Technology and War* (New York: Free Press, 1989), 21.
62. Karl von Clausewitz, *War, Politics, and Power*, translated by Edward Colins (Washington: Regnery Gateway, 1962), 70.
63. Earnst Breisach, *Renaissance Europe* (New York: MacMillan, 1973), 147.
64. Machiavelli, *Art of War*, 4.
65. Thomas Hobbes, *The Collected Works of Thomas Hobbes*, 11 volumes, edited by Sir William Molesworth (London: Routledge Thoemmes, 1992), vol II, 140.
66. Donald Hanson, "Hobbes 'Highway to Peace'," *International Organization* 38 (1984), 350.
67. Andreski, *Military Organization*, 75.
68. Alfred Stepan, "The New Professionalism of Internal Warfare and the Military Role Expansionism," in Stepan (ed.), *Authoritarian Brazil* (New Haven: Yale University Press, 1973); referring to Samuel Huntington, *The Soldier and the State* (Cambridge: Harvard University Press, 1957); and Morris Janowitz, *The Professional Soldier*, revised edition (New York: Free Press, 1971).
69. John Mearsheimer, *Conventional Deterrence* (Ithaca: Cornell Press, 1983), 24–25.
70. Otto Hintze, *The Historical Essays*, translated by Felix Gilbert (New York: Oxford University Press, 1975); Alfred Vagts, *A History of Militarism* (New York: W.W. Norton, 1937).
71. Porter, *Rise of the State*, 21.
72. Roy Macredis and Bernard Brown, "Legitimacy and Consensus," in Macredis and Brown (eds.), *Comparative Politics*, fourth edition (Homewood, IL: Dorsey Press, 1972), 99–105.
73. Ibid., 100. My emphasis.
74. Ibid.
75. Weber, *General Economic History*, 324.
76. Samuel Finer, "State- and Nation-Building in Europe: The Role of the Military," in Tilly (ed.), *Formation of National States*, 89.
77. Edmonds, *Armed Services and Society*, 53.
78. See John Gillis (ed.), *The Militarization of the Western World* (New Brunswick: NJ: Rutgers University Press, 1989), 1. See also Volker Berghan, *Militarism* (Cambridge: University Press, 1984).
79. Vagts, *History of Militarism*, 11.
80. Ibid.
81. David Ralston, *Importing the European Army* (Chicago: University of Chicago Press, 1990); Samuel Finer, *The Man on Horseback*, second enlarged edition (Hammondsworth, England: Penguin, 1975).
82. Vagts, *History of Militarism*, 12.
83. Ibid., 39.
84. Tilly, "Reflections," 75.
85. Ralston, *Importing*, 175.
86. Ibid., 176.
87. Ibid., 324.
88. Huntington, *Soldier and the State*.
89. Edmonds, *Armed Services and Society*, 15.
90. Gaetano Mosca, *The Ruling Class*, translated by Hannah Kahn (New York: McGraw Hill, 1939), 229 and 245.
91. Bengt Abrahamsson, *Military Professionalism and Political Power* (Beverley Hills, CA: Sage, 1972).
92. Charles Moskos, "Institutional/Occupational Trends in Armed Forces," *Armed Forces and Society* 4 (1977), 41–50; see also "Institutional/Occupational Trends in Armed Forces: An Update," *Armed Forces and Society* 12 (1986), 377–82.
93. Moskos, "Institutional/Occupational" (1977), 42.
94. Ibid., 43.
95. Finer, *Man on Horseback*, 112.

Chapter Three   Ancient Republics and Radical Democracy:
Athens and Sparta

1. Thucydides's *History of the Peloponnesian War*, translated by Benjamin Jowett (London: Folio Society, 1994), 98.
2. Ibid., 98–99.
3. Arthur Ferrill, *The Origins of War* (London: Thames and Hudson, 1985), 91–94.
4. Frank Adcock, *The Greek and Macedonian Art of War* (Berkeley: University of California. Press, 1957), 2.
5. Hans Delbrück, *History of the Art of War*, volume 1, translated by Walter Renfroe (Westport, CN: Greenwood, 1975), 256.
6. Ferrill, *Origins of War*, 99.
7. Carrol Quigley, *Weapons Systems and Political Stability* (Washington, DC: University Press, 1983), 271.
8. Aristotle, *The Athenian Constitution*, translated by P.J. Rhodes (New York: Penguin, 1984), 4.
9. Quigley, *Weapons Systems*, 276.
10. From Delbrück's comments, *History of Warfare*, 259.
11. Josiah Ober, "Hoplites and Obstacles," in Victor Hansen (ed.), *Hoplites* (New York: Routledge, 1991), 180–88.
12. Ibid., 273.
13. Robert Littman, *Kinship and Politics in Athens 600-400 BCE* (New York: Peter Lang, 1990).
14. See William Everdell, *The End of Kings: A History of Republics and Republicans* (New York: Free Press, 1983), 31.
15. Quigley, *Weapons Systems*, 280.
16. Alfred Snodgrass, "The Hoplite Reform and History," *Journal of Hellenic Studies* 97 (1977), 84–101.
17. This observation is evident in the "uncommon superiority of the knights over bourgeois and peasant infantry before the latter are trained and accustomed to being grouped together in tactical units." Delbrück, *History*, 257.
18. John K. Anderson, *Military Theory and Practice in the Age of Xenophon* (Berkeley: University of California Press, 1970), 13.
19. Hilda Lorimer, "The Hoplite Phalanx with Special Reference to the Poems of Archilochus and Tyrtaeus," *Annual of the British School at Athens* 42 (1947), 121–24.
20. Adcock, *Greek Art of War*, 8.
21. Quigley, *Weapons Systems*, 281.
22. Yigael Yadin, *The Art of Warfare in Biblical Lands, volume 1* (New York: A. Knopf, 1963), 134–35.
23. Also called the Vulture Stele, see Trevor Watkins, "The Beginnings of Warfare," in John Hackett (ed.), *Warfare in the Ancient World* (New York: Facts on File, 1989), 20.
24. Robert O'Connell, *Of Arms and Men* (Oxford: University Press, 1989), 36.
25. Victor Anderson, "Hoplite Weapons and Offensive Arms," in Anderson (ed.), *Hoplites* (London: Routledge, 1991), 28.
26. Delbrück, *History of War*, 53.
27. Ibid., 54.
28. Ibid., 58.
29. Ibid.
30. Ibid., 61.
31. Ibid., 63.
32. Ibid., 44.
33. Ibid.
34. Aristotle, *Politics*, V:10.
35. Plutarch, *The Rise and Fall of Athens* (Baltimore: Penguin, 1962), 55–58.

36. Ibid., 59–62.
37. Ibid., 68.
38. See any translation of Thucydides's *Peloponnesian War*, Book III: Scrolls 27–28.
39. Ibid., Book III: Scrolls 37–40.
40. See John Morrison and J.F. Coates's classic, *The Athenian Trireme* (Cambridge: University Press, 1986).
41. Quigley, *Weapons Systems*, 299.
42. Xenophon, *Hellenica*, translated by Rex Warner (New York: Penguin, 1978).
43. William Forrest, *A History of Sparta 950-192 BCE* (London: Hutchinson, 1968), 31.
44. George Huxley, *Early Sparta* (London: Faber, 1962), 37–39.
45. O'Connell, *Arms and Men*, 52.
46. Anderson, *Military Theory*, 84–85.
47. *Peloponnesian War*, Book I: Scroll 6.
48. E.L. Wheeler, "The Hoplomachoi and Vegetius' Spartan Drillmasters," *Chiron* 13 (1983), 12.

Chapter Four   Early Republics: Switzerland, the Dutch, and France

1. A controversial thesis detailed by Lynn White, Jr., *Medieval Technology and Social Change* (New York: Oxford University Press, 1966).
2. Michael Roberts, *The Military Revolution, 1560–1660* (Belfast: Belfast University Press, 1956). See also Michael Duffy (ed.), *The Military Revolution and the State 1500–1800* (Exeter: University of Exeter Press, 1980).
3. See Hans Delbrück, *History of the Art of War*, volume III, translated by Walter Renfroe, Jr. (Lincoln: University of Nebraska Press, 1982), 506–17.
4. Michael Howard, *War in European History* (New York: Oxford University Press, 1976), 12.
5. Ibid., 17.
6. Delbrück, *Art of War*, volume IV, 16.
7. Ibid., volume III, 555–56.
8. Michael Drake, *Problematics of Military Power* (London: Frank Cass, 2001), 227.
9. Robert O'Connel, *Of Arms and Men* (New York: Oxford University Press, 1989), 102.
10. Martin Van Creveld, *Technology and War* (New York: Free Press, 1989), 91.
11. Delbrück, *Art of War*, volume III, 563–65.
12. Ibid., 608.
13. Ibid., 608–10.
14. An account is given in Ibid., volume IV, 16.
15. Ibid., volume III, 586.
16. Drake, *Problematics*, 233.
17. Delbrück, *Art of War*, volume III, 591.
18. Geoffrey Parker, *The Army of Flanders and the Spanish Road 1567–1659* (Cambridge: Cambridge University Press, 1972), 5.
19. Ibid.
20. Jonathan Israel, *The Dutch Republic* (Oxford: Clarendon Press, 1995), 2.
21. Hendrik Van Loon, *The Fall of the Dutch Republic*, new edition (Boston: Houghton Mifflin, 1924), 5.
22. Israel, *Dutch Republic*, 2. See also Hendrik Riemens, *The Netherlands* (New York: Eagle, 1944).
23. Israel, *Dutch Republic*, 27–29.
24. Ibid., 33.
25. Adriaan Barnouw, *The Pageant of Netherlands History* (New York: Longmans, 1952), 114.
26. Ibid., 116.
27. Ibid., 121.
28. Israel, *Dutch Republic*, 57.

29. Ibid., 130–32.
30. Parker, *Army of Flanders*, 6.
31. Israel, *Dutch Republic*, 133.
32. Cicely Wedgewood, *William the Silent* (New Haven: Yale University Press, 1944), 11.
33. William was not called "the Silent" because of passivity or quiescence. To the contrary, he was a grand speaker. The moniker comes from his ability to speak a great deal without saying anything. Israel, *Dutch Republic*, 139.
34. Wedgewood, *William the Silent*, 30.
35. Ibid., 30.
36. Adriaan Barnouw, *The Making of Modern Holland* (New York: W.W. Norton, 1944), 68.
37. Israel, *Dutch Republic*, 152–53.
38. O'Connel, *Of Arms and Men*, 132.
39. Israel, *Dutch Republic*, 156–57.
40. Barnouw, *Pageant*, 117. See also R.A. Stradling, *The Armada of Flanders* (Cambridge: Cambridge University Press, 1992).
41. Barnouw, *Pageant*, 117.
42. Howard, *War in European History*, 50; Barnouw, *Making of Modern Holland*, 76.
43. Israel, *Dutch Republic*, 156.
44. Ibid., 169–70.
45. Ibid., 171.
46. Ibid., 182.
47. Parker, *Army of Flanders*, 29.
48. Israel, *Dutch Republic*, 192–93.
49. Ibid., 185.
50. Ibid., 186.
51. Barnouw, *Pageant*, 120.
52. From Israel, *Dutch Republic*, 188–89.
53. Ibid., 198.
54. From Israel, *Dutch Republic*, 199–205.
55. Barnouw, *Making of Modern Holland*, 80.
56. Ibid., 78–79.
57. Israel, *Dutch Republic*, 211.
58. Wedgewood, *William the Silent*, 190.
59. Barnouw, *Making of Modern Holland*, 82.
60. Israel, *Dutch Republic*, 220, 293–94.
61. Barnouw, *Making of Modern Holland*, 85.
62. Israel, *Dutch Republic*, 292.
63. Barnouw, *Making of Modern Holland*, 85.
64. Garret Mattingly, *The Armada* (Boston: Houghton Mifflin, 1959), 42–45.
65. Israel, *Dutch Republic*, 237; Howard, *War in European History*, 57.
66. Howard, *War in European History*, 56.
67. Drake, *Problematics*, 288.
68. Delbrück, *Art of War*, volume IV, 156.
69. Ibid., 157.
70. See William McNeill, *The Pursuit of Power* (Chicago: University of Chicago Press, 1982), 128–29.
71. Delbrück, *Art of War*, volume IV, 159.
72. Ibid., 161.
73. McNeill, *Pursuit of Power*, 128.
74. Cited in Drake, *Problematics*, 290; Howard, *War in European History*, 55–57.
75. Gunther Rothenberg, "Maurice of Nassau, Gustavus Adolphus, Raimondo Montecuccoli, and the 'Military Revolution' of the Seventeenth Century," in Peter Paret (ed.), *Makers of Modern Strategy* (Princeton: Princeton University Press, 1986), 41.

76. Israel, *Dutch Republic*, 268.
77. Ibid., 268.
78. Ibid., 268. Also Delbrück, *Art of War*, volume IV, 163.
79. McNeil, *Pursuit of Power*, 130. See also Van Creveld, *Technology and War*, 94.
80. Israel, *Dutch Republic*, 253.
81. Van Loon, *Fall of the Dutch Republic*, 35.
82. Cited in Barnouw, *Pageant*, 154.
83. Howard, *War in European History*, 42–43.
84. Andrew Vincent, *Theories of the State* (New York: Basil Blackwell, 1987), 64–65.
85. David Kaiser, *Politics and War* (Cambridge: Harvard University Press, 1990), 142.
86. Ibid., 144.
87. John Lynn, "A Quest for Glory," in Murray Williamson, MacGreggor Knox, and Alvin Bernstein (eds), *The Making of Strategy* (Cambridge: University Press, 1994), 188–92.
88. Henry Guerlac, "Vauban: The Impact of Science on War," in E.M. Earle (ed.), *Makers of Modern Strategy* (Princeton: University Press, 1971), 26–48; See also Francis Hebbert, *Soldier of France* (New York: Lang, 1981).
89. Russel Weigley, *The Age of Battles* (Bloomington: Indiana University Press, 1991), 48–49.
90. Richard Preston, Sydney Wise, and Herman Werner, *Men in Arms*, revised edition (New York: Praeger, 1962), 113; see also Kaiser, *War and Politics*, 145–50.
91. Trevor Dupuy, Curt Johnson, and David Bongard, *Harper Encyclopedia of Military Biography* (New York: Harper Collins, 1992), 491.
92. Bruce Porter, *War and the Rise of the State* (New York: Free Press, 1994), 110.
93. Geoffrey Symcox, *The Crisis of French Seapower* (Amsterdam: Martinus Nijhoff, 1974), 26.
94. Brian Downing, *The Military Revolution and Political Change* (Princeton: University Press, 1992), 129.
95. Weigley, *Age of Battles*, 51. The militia system was based on compulsory service in case of invasion. Its role in the regular army was negligible.
96. Howard, *War in European History*, 64.
97. Ibid., 63.
98. Francis Hebbert, *Soldier of France* (New York: Lang, 1981) 235.
99. Franklin Ford, *Robe and Sword* (New York: Harper, 1965), 96–104; Bailey Stone, *The French Parlements and the Crisis of the Old Regime* (Chapel Hill, NC: University of North Carolina Press, 1986), 115–77.
100. Lee Kennet, *The French Armies in the Seven Years' War* (Durham, NC: Duke University Press, 1967), ix.
101. Preston et al., *Men in Arms*, 134–35.
102. Kennet, *French Armies*, 38.
103. Ibid., 77.
104. Ibid.
105. Ibid., 78.
106. Ibid., 80.
107. Ibid.
108. Samuel Scott, *The Response of the Royal Army to the French Revolution* (Oxford: Clarendon, 1978), 7.
109. Kennet, *French Armies*, 80.
110. Scott, *Response of the Royal Army*, 26–27.
111. Ibid., 27.
112. Kennet, *French Armies*, 55.
113. Ibid., 55 fn.
114. André Corvisier, *L'Armée Française de la Fin du XVIIᵉ Siècle au Ministére de Choiseul*, two volumes (Paris: Presses Universitaires de France, 1964), I: 309.
115. Kennet, *French Armies*, 70.

116. "Etienne-François, Duc de Choiseul," in *The Catholic Encyclopedia*, http://www.newadvent.org/cathen/03694a.htm, October 29, 2002.
117. "The Suppression of the Jesuits (1750–1773)," in *The Catholic Encyclopedia*, http://www.newadvent.org/cathen/14096a.htm, October 29, 2002.
118. Scott, *Response of the Royal Army*, 28.
119. Delbrück, *Art of War*, volume IV, 268.
120. Kennet, *French Armies*, 65–66.
121. Scott, *Response of the Royal Army*, 28.
122. Ibid.
123. Kennet, *French Armies*, 68.
124. See Guerlac, "Vauban," 32.
125. Scott, *Response of the Royal Army*, 24.
126. Ibid., 29.
127. Ibid., 31.
128. Ibid.
129. Ibid., 5.
130. The length of enlistment is in dispute. Six years according to Kennet, *French Armies*, 72; eight years claims Scott, *Response of the Royal Army*, 6.
131. Scott, *Response of the Royal Army*, 9.
132. Corvisier, *L'Armée Française*, I: 439–41.
133. Scott, *Response of the Royal Army*, 10–11.
134. Corvisier, *L'Armée Française*, I: 408.
135. Ibid., 472–80.
136. Scott, *Response of the Royal Army*, 18.
137. Marx, of course, believed rural revolution to be impossible. A sophisticated assessment of the propensity for urban over rural revolutions in the west is provided by Barrington Moore, *Social Origins of Dictatorship and Democracy* (Boston: Beacon Press, 1966) and Theda Skocpol, *States and Social Revolutions* (Cambridge: Cambridge University Press, 1979).
138. Scott, *Response of the Royal Army*, 20.
139. Ibid.
140. Kennet, *French Armies*, 58.
141. Ibid., 57.
142. Ibid., 59.
143. Scott, *Response of the Royal Army*, 22.
144. Ibid., 23.
145. Kennet, *French Armies*, 81.
146. Ibid., 74.
147. Scott, *Response of the Royal Army*, 12–13.
148. Kennet, *French Armies*, 60.
149. Ibid., 69.
150. Porter, *War and the Rise*, 127; Kennet, *French Armies*, 88–98.
151. See Liah Greenfield, *Nationalism* (Cambridge: Harvard University Press, 1992), 180–84.
152. Simon Schama, *Citizens* (New York: Alfred Knopf, 1989), 281–83 and 292.
153. Robert Ergang, *Europe: From the Rennaissance to Waterloo*, revised edition (Boston: D.C. Heath, 1954), 328–29.
154. Ibid., 652–56.
155. Scott, *Response of the Royal Army*, 59–70.
156. Schama, *Citizens*, 402.
157. Ergang, *Europe*, 659.
158. Geoffrey Best, *War and Society in Revolutionary Europe, 1770–1870* (New York: St Martin's, 1982), 71–72.

159. Peter Manicas, *War and Democracy* (New York: Basil Blackwell, 1989), 209.
160. Ibid., 210.
161. Ibid.
162. Porter, *War and the Rise*, 129–30.
163. Ibid.
164. Gunther Rothenberg, *The Art of Warfare in the Age of Napoleon* (Bloomington, IN: University of Indiana Press, 1980), 94.
165. Cited in Howard, *War in European History*, 80.
166. Porter, *War and the Rise*, 128–29; Schama, *Citizens*, 587.
167. Porter, *War and the Rise*, 127–28.
168. Manicas, *War and Democracy*, 211.
169. Ergang, *Europe*, 679.
170. Robert Palmer, *Twelve Who Ruled* (Princeton: University Press, 1942).
171. "Terror is the Order of the Day," Schama, *Citizens*, 726–92; See Skocpol, *States and Revolutions*, 201–05.
172. Scott, *Response of the Royal Army*, 2.
173. Stated by Committee-member Georges Jacques Danton in his pre-coup speech to the Legislative Assembly in 1792. Cited in Bartlett and Kaplan (eds.), *Bartlett's Familiar Quotations*, sixteenth edition (Boston: Little, Brown and Company, 1992), 364; Pierre Baudry, "Lazare Carnot: Organizer of Victory—How the 'Calculus of Enthusiasm' Saved France," *The American Almanac*, July 21, 1997.
174. See Sidney Watson, *Carnot* (London: Bodley Head, 1954).
175. Baudry, "Lazare Carnot." Original emphasis.
176. Ibid.
177. John Lynn, *Bayonets of the Republic* (Urbana: University of Illinois Press, 1984), 55–57.
178. Howard, *War in European History*, 81; Guerlac, "Impact of Science on War," 62 and 66.
179. Heinrich von Treitschke, *Politics*, abridged and edited by Hans Kohn (New York: Harcourt Brace, 1963), 253.
180. Ergang, *Europe*, 691–93.
181. Samuel Wilkenson, *The Rise of General Bonaparte* (Oxford: University Press, 1930).
182. Howard, *War in European History*, 80.
183. Porter, *War and the Rise*, 131.
184. Jean-Paul Bertrand, *The Army of the French Revolution* (Princeton: University Press, 1988).
185. Howard, *War in European History*, 76–79.
186. Ibid., 79.

Chapter Five   Military Organization and the Prusso-German State

1. Brian Downing, *The Military Revolution and Political Change* (Princeton: University Press, 1992), 84.
2. See Ferdinand Schevill, *The Great Elector* (Chicago: University Press, 1947).
3. Gordon Craig, *The Politics of the Prussian Army* (New York: Oxford, 1955), 2–3.
4. Robert Ergang, *Europe* (Boston: D.C. Heath, 1954), 490–92; See also Walter Goerlitz, *History of the German General Staff 1657–1945*, translated by Brian Battershaw (New York: Praeger, 1953), 5.
5. Hans Delbrück, *History of the Art of War*, volume IV (Westport, CT: Greenwood, 1985), 242–45.
6. Downing, *Military Revolution*, 96–98; Craig, *Prussian Army*, 3–4.
7. Walter Simon, *The Failure of the Prussian Reform Movement, 1807–1819* (Ithaca: Cornell University Press, 1955), 147.
8. Craig, *Prussian Army*, 5–6.
9. Downing, *Military Revolution*, 91–92.
10. Ibid.

11. Andre Corvisier, *Armies and Societies in Europe, 1494–1789*, translated by Abigail Siddall (Bloomington: University of Indiana Press, 1979), 113.
12. Ibid., 6–7.
13. Hans Rosenberg, *Bureaucracy, Aristocracy and Autocracy* (Boston: Beacon, 1958), 64–65.
14. Otto Hintze, *The Historical Essays*, translated and edited by Felix Gilbert (New York: Oxford University Press, 1975), 159–81.
15. Craig, *Prussian Army*, 5.
16. See Catherine Behrens, *Society, Government, and the Enlightenment* (New York: Harper, 1985), 123–25; Trevor Dupuy, Curt Johnson, and David Bongard, *The Harper Encyclopedia of Military Biography* (New York: Harper Collins, 1992), 261–62.
17. Rosenberg, *Bureaucracy*, 59.
18. Dupuy et al., *Military Biography*, 259 and 262; Craig, *Politics of the Prussian Army*, 7.
19. Alfred Vagts, *A History of Militarism* (New York: W.W. Norton, 1937), 32–35.
20. Rosenberg, *Bureaucracy*, 40.
21. Valentin Veit, *German People* (New York: Alfred Knopf, 1946), 254.
22. Ibid., 253–55; Rosenberg, *Bureaucracy*, 19–34.
23. Veit, *German People*, 253–55.
24. Robert Ergang, *The Potsdam Führer* (New York: Columbia University Press, 1941), 63.
25. Ibid., 254.; Craig, *Prussian Army*, 8.
26. Veit, *German People*, 260.
27. Ibid., 255.
28. Craig, *Prussian Army*, 23; William Shanahan, *Prussian Military Reforms 1780–1813* (New York: AMS, 1966), 56.
29. Shanahan, *Prussian Reforms*, 36.
30. Ibid.
31. Craig, *Prussian Army*, 23.
32. Shanahan, *Prussian Reforms*, 42.
33. Figures from Curt Jany, cited in Shanahan, *Prussian Reforms*, 58.
34. "The obligation to defend the state is the inborn duty of every subject who enjoys the protection of the state." From the Canton regulation of 1792, cited in Shanahan, *Prussian Reforms*, 47.
35. Ibid., 17.
36. Craig, *Prussian Army*, 20.
37. Ergang, *Potsdam Führer*, 66.
38. Ibid., 81.
39. Francis Carsten, *The Origins of Prussia* (Oxford: Clarendon, 1964), 258.
40. Robert Palmer, "Frederick the Great, Guibert, Bülow: From Dynastic to National War," in Edward Earle (ed.), *The Makers of Modern Strategy* (Princeton: University Press, 1971), 54.
41. Craig, *Prussian Army*, 22.
42. Christopher Duffy, *Frederick the Great's Army* (London: Routledge, 1974); and *Frederick the Great* (London: Routledge, 1988).
43. Goerlitz, *General Staff*, 9.
44. Shanahan, *Prussian Reforms*, 61, 86–87.
45. Craig, *Prussian Army*, 38.
46. Shanahan, *Prussian Reforms*, 66.
47. Craig, *Prussian Army*, 40–41.
48. Shanahan, *Prussian Reforms*, 94–95.
49. Ibid., 103.
50. Craig, *Prussian Army*, 46.
51. Ibid., 38; Goerlitz, *General Staff*, 28–35.
52. Ibid.
53. Shanahan, *Prussian Reforms*, 132–33.
54. Ibid., 133–35.

55. Veit, *German People*, 343.
56. Ibid., 135–40.
57. From Shanahan, *Prussian Reforms*, 38–39.
58. See Shanahan, *Prussian Reforms*, ch. 6; Veit, *German People*, 343.
59. An argument put forward by Otto Hintze in *Die Hollenzollern*, cited by Craig, *Prussian Army*, 41.
60. Veit, *German People*, 336–37.
61. Shanahan, *Prussian Reforms*, 197–213; Craig, *Prussian Army*, 60–63.
62. Hintze, *Die Hohenzollern*, 471, cited by Craig, *Prussian Army*, 60.
63. Craig, *Prussian Army*, 69.
64. Edward Gulick, *Europe's Classical Balance of Power* (New York: Norton, 1955), 4.
65. Craig, *Prussian Army*, 67.
66. Ibid., 69.
67. Eckart Kehr, *Economic Interest, Militarism, and Foreign Policy*, translated by Grete Heinz (Berkeley: University of California Press, 1965), 3.
68. Richard Preston, Sydney Wise, and Herman Werner, *Men in Arms*, revised edition (New York: Praeger, 1962), 176–92.; Michael Howard, *War in European History* (New York: Oxford University Press, 1976), 75–93.
69. Veit, *German People*, 373–76.
70. See Rene Albrecht-Carrie, *A Diplomatic History of Europe Since the Congress of Vienna* (New York: Harper & Row, 1958), 25 and 28.
71. Veit, *German People*, 376–77.
72. Ibid., 388–93; Also Alan Taylor, *Bismarck* (New York: Vintage Paperback, 1967), 23.
73. Veit, *German People*, 396.
74. Craig, *Prussian Army*, 87; Veit, *German People*, 413.
75. Taylor, *Bismarck*, 24; Craig, *Prussian Army*, 88.
76. Veit, *German People*, 419.
77. Craig, *Prussian Army*, 110.
78. Ibid., 111–12.
79. Kehr, *Economic Interest*, 5.
80. Veit, *German People*, 425.; Ernest Dupuy and Trevor Dupuy, *Harper Encyclopedia of Military History*, fourth edition (New York: Harper, 1993), 842 and 844.
81. Craig, *Prussian Army*, 83.
82. Ibid., 79.
83. Ibid., 81.
84. Martin Kitchen, *A Military History of Germany* (Bloomington: Indiana University Press, 1975), 69.
85. Goerlitz, *General Staff*, 63.
86. Heinrich von Treitschke, *Politics*, translated by Hans Kohn (New York: Harcourt Brace, 1963), 74.
87. Craig, *Prussian Army*, 121–22.
88. Veit, *German People*, 434.
89. Craig, *Prussian Army*, 122.
90. Veit, *German People*, 434.
91. *Deutsche-Wehrzeitung*, cited in Craig, *Prussian Army*, 123.
92. Craig, *Prussian Army*, 139.
93. Ibid., 147–48.; Kitchen, *Military History*, 99–102.
94. Kehr, *Economic Interest*, 101; Veit, *German People*, 454–55; Kitchen, *Military History*, 107.
95. Goerlitz, *General Staff*, 74.
96. Craig, *Prussian Army*, 167.
97. Ibid., 174–75.
98. Ibid., 178.

99. Goerlitz, *General Staff*, 89–95.
100. Helmuth von Moltke, *On the Art of War: Selected Writings*, Daniel Hughes (ed.), translated by Harry Bell (Novato, CA: Presidio, 1993), 35–36 and 39–40.
101. Gordon Craig, *Germany 1866–1945* (New York: Oxford University Press, 1978), 44.
102. Ibid.
103. Goerlitz, *General Staff*, 108.
104. Craig, *Prussian Army*, 229.
105. Ibid., 218.
106. Karl Demeter, *The German Officer Corps in Society and State, 1650–1945* (New York: Praeger, 1965), 21–22.
107. Ibid.
108. Craig, *Prussian Army*, 233.
109. Goerlitz, *General Staff*, 96.
110. Craig, *Prussian Army*, 233.
111. Gerhard Ritter, *The Sword and the Scepter* (Miami: University of Miami Press, 1970), VII: 287.
112. Ibid.
113. Ibid., 104.
114. Kehr, *Economic Interest*, 101.
115. Craig, *Prussian Army*, 236.
116. Kehr, "Prussian Reserve," 107.
117. Craig, *Prussian Army*, 167.
118. Martin Kitchen, *German Officer Corps, 1890–1914* (Oxford: Clarendon Press, 1968), 38.
119. Treitschke, *Politics*.; Craig, *Germany*, 48–49; Emilio Willems, *A Way of Life and Death* (Nashville, TN: Vanderbilt University Press, 1986), 79.
120. Willems, *Life and Death*, 82.
121. Ritter, *Sword and the Scepter*, VI: 240–45.
122. Roger Chickering, "Patriotic Societies and German Foreign Policy, 1890–1914," *International History Review* 1 (1979), 470–89. On the Colonial Society see Woodruff Smith, *The German Colonial Empire* (Chapel Hill: University of North Carolina Press, 1978). For membership figures, see Geoff Eley, *Reshaping the German Right* (New Haven: Yale University Press, 1980), 366, and Marilyn Coatzee, *The German Army League* (New York: Oxford Press, 1990), 4.
123. On the Navy League, see Geoff Eley, "Reshaping the Right: Radical Nationalism and the German Navy League, 1898–1908," *Historical Journal* 21 (1978), 327–54; and on the Army League see Coatzee, *German Army League*.
124. Kitchen, *Officer Corps*, 84.
125. Vagts, *Militarism*, 12.
126. Craig, *Prussian Army*, 252.
127. Kehr, *Economic Interest*, 7.
128. Craig, *Germany*, 302–38.
129. Volker Berghan, *Germany and the Approach of War in 1914* (London: Thames, 1973), 76.
130. Holger Herwig, *The German Naval Officer Corps* (Oxford: Clarendon, 1973), 15.
131. Willems, *Life and Death*, 90.
132. Ibid., 91.
133. Kehr, *Economic Interest*, 82.
134. Ritter, *Sword and Scepter*, VII: 137.
135. Kehr, *Economic Interest*, 7.
136. Alfred Rapp, "The Untrue Myth," in Walter Stahl (ed.), *The Politics of Postwar Germany* (Hamburg: Hafen-Druckerei, 1963), 146.
137. Goerlitz, *General Staff*, 130–34.; See also Barbara Tuchman's, *The Guns of August* (New York: Alfred Knopf, 1962).
138. Craig, *Germany*, 315.

139. Hajo Holborn, "Moltke and Schlieffen: The Prussian-German School," in *Makers of Modern Strategy*, 186–205.
140. Ritter, *Sword and Scepter*, VII: 457; Willems, *Life and Death*, 106.
141. Craig, *Prussian Army*, 328.
142. Craig, *Germany*, 339.
143. Fritz Fischer, *War of Illusions: German Policies from 1911–1914*, translated by Marian Jackson (London: Chatto, 1975), 511–12.
144. Craig, *Germany*, 340–41.
145. Stephen Van Evera, "The Cult of the Offensive and the Origins of the First World War," *International Security* 9 (1984), 58–105.
146. Kitchen, *Officer Corps*, 47.
147. Kehr, *Economic Interest*, 135.
148. Craig, *Prussian Army*, 322.
149. R.H. Lutz, *The Fall of the German Empire*, volume I (Stanford: Stanford University Press, 1932), 261.
150. Herwig, *Naval Officer Corps*, 231.
151. Craig, *Prussian Military*, 344.
152. Ibid.
153. Harold Gordon, *The Reichswehr and the German Republic, 1919–26* (Princeton: University Press, 1957), 174.
154. Craig, *Prussian Army*, 361; fn. 3.
155. Cited in Craig, *Prussian Army*, 362.
156. Francis Carsten, *The Reichswehr in Politics, 1918 to 1919* (Oxford: Clarendon, 1966), 216.
157. Veit, *German People*, 587–89.
158. Article 160. Cited in Albert Seaton, *The German Army, 1933–45* (New York: St. Martin's, 1982), 4.
159. Kehr, *Economic Interest*, 136.
160. Herbert Rosinski, *The German Army* (New York: Praeger, 1944), 158–60.
161. Goerlitz, *General Staff*, 222.
162. John Wheeler-Bennett, *The Nemesis of Power* (London: MacMillan, 1953), 89.
163. Rosinski, *German Army*, 106.
164. Seaton, *German Army*, 6.
165. Cited in Craig, *Prussian Army*, 388.
166. Seaton, *German Army*, 10; Goerlitz, *General Staff*, 223–24.
167. Craig, *Prussian Army*, 394.
168. Rosinski, *German Army*, 129.
169. Goerlitz, *General Staff*, 224.
170. Craig, *Prussian Army*, 398: fn. 1.
171. Ibid., 399.
172. Seaton, *German Army*, 34.
173. Craig, *Prussian Army*, 404–45. See also William Jordan, *Great Britain, France and the German Problem, 1918–1939* (London: Unwin & Allen, 1943), 143–44.
174. Seaton, *German Army*, 29.
175. Ibid.
176. Ibid., 16–17.
177. Ibid., 19; Goerlitz, *General Staff*, 258–59.; Craig, *Germany*, 535.
178. Dupuy et al., *Military Biography*, 298; Craig, *Germany*, 553.
179. Seaton, *German Army*, 21.
180. Ibid., 5.
181. Craig, *Prussian Army*, 474.
182. Wheeler-Bennett, *Nemesis*, 309.
183. Seaton, *German Army*, 43.
184. Craig, *Prussian Army*, 441–2.

185. Wheeler-Bennett, *Nemesis*, 291.
186. Ibid., 300; Craig, *Prussian Army*, 471.
187. Seaton, *German Army*, 48–49.
188. Craig, *Prussian Army*, 479–80; See also Robert O'Neil, *The German Army and the Nazi Party 1933–39* (London: Cassell, 1966), 54–55.
189. Seaton, *German Army*, 78.
190. Ibid., 58 and 70.
191. Ibid., 69–70.
192. Craig, *Prussian Army*, 483–84.
193. See Robert Strausz-Hupe, *Geopolitics* (New York: Putnam, 1942).
194. William Shirer, *The Rise and Fall of the Third Reich* (New York: Simon and Schuster, 1960), 48.
195. Willems, *Life and Death*, 135.
196. Seaton, *German Army*, 52–53.
197. Willems, *Life and Death*, 138.
198. Ibid., 53.
199. Craig, *Prussian Army*, 495.
200. Wheeler-Bennett, *Nemesis*, 373.
201. Figures from John Ellis, *World War II: A Statistical Survey* (New York: Facts on File, 1993).
202. Thomas Schwartz, "The 'Skeleton-Key'—American Foreign Policy, European Unity and German Rearmament, 1949–1954," *Central European History* 19 (1986), 370–71.
203. Karl Deutsch and Lewis Edinger, *Germany Rejoins the Powers* (Stanford: University Press, 1959); Hans Spier, *German Rearmament and Atomic War* (Evanston, IL: Row & Peterson, 1957); and Gordon Craig, *NATO and the New German Army* (Princeton: University Press, 1955).
204. Donald Abenheim, "The Citizen in Uniform: Reform and its Critics in the Bundeswehr," in Stephen Szabo (ed.), *The Bundeswehr and Western Security* (New York: St Martin's, 1990), 31.
205. Ibid.
206. Ibid, 9–10 and 41.
207. Abenheim, "Citizen in Uniform," 32–33.
208. From an FRG publication, "Principles of Leadership and Civic Education," cited in Abenheim, "Citizen in Uniform," 32.
209. Palmer, "Frederick, Guibert, Bülow," 71–74.

Chapter Six   Post–Cold War Implications and the American Military

1. Daniel Boorstin, *The Americans* (New York: Random House, 1958), 347.
2. See Erhard Geissler, *Biological and Toxin Weapons Today* (Oxford: University Press, 1986), 8.
3. Richard Preston, Alex Roland, and Sydney Wise, *Arms and Men*, fifth edition (New York: Harcourt Brace, 1991), 163.
4. Ibid., 164.
5. See Louis Morton, "The Origins of American Military Policy," *Military Affairs* 26 (1958), 75–82; Boorstin, *Americans*, 190.
6. Preston, *Arms and Men*, 164.
7. James Hill, *The Minute Man in Peace and War* (Harrisburg, PA: Stackpole, 1963).
8. Alexander Hamilton, James Madison, and John Jay, *The Federalist Papers* (New York: Penguin, 1961): See Nr. 4 by Jay; Nrs. 23–26, and 29 by Hamilton; and Nr. 41 by Madison.
9. Ibid., Nr 25, 166.
10. Ibid.; Also see Max Weber, *General Economic History*, translated by Frank Knight (Glencoe, IL: Free Press, 1927), 324.

11. Emory Upton, *The Military Policy of the United States from 1775* (Washington DC: U.S. Government Printing Office, 1904). Joseph Bernardo and Eugene Bacon, *American Military Policy* (Harrisburg, PA: Stackpole, 1955), expand on and update the themes of Upton's work.

12. Russell Weigley, *History of the United States Army*, enlarged edition (Bloomington: Indiana University Press, 1984), v.

13. See Stanley Pargellis, *Lord Loudoun in North America* (New Haven: Yale University Press, 1933); Howard Peckman, *The Colonial Wars, 1869–1762* (Chicago: University Press, 1964); and Edward Hamilton, *The French and Indian Wars* (Garden City, NJ: Doubleday, 1962).

14. Preston, *Arms and Men*, 168.

15. Ibid., 166.

16. Pargellis, *Lord Loudoun*, 121.

17. James Flexner, *George Washington* (Boston: Little Brown, 1965), 160–61.

18. John Palmer, *General von Steuben* (New Haven, CT: Yale University Press, 1937).

19. Preston, *Arms and Men*, 173.

20. Ibid., 174.

21. John Hattendorf, "The American Navy in the World of Franklin and Jefferson, 1775–1826," Brian Bond and Ian Roy (eds.), *War and Society*, volume 2 (New York: Holmes and Meier, 1977), 9.

22. Ibid.

23. Preston, *Arms and Men*, 173.

24. Hattendorf, "American Navy," 9–10.

25. Richard Hoffstader, William Miller, and Daniel Aaron, *The American Republic*, volume one, *Through Reconstruction*, second edition (Englewood Cliffs, NJ: Prentice-Hall, 1970), 348.

26. Marvin Kriedberg and Merton Henry, *History of Military Mobilization in the United States Army* (Washington, DC: Department of the Army, 1955).

27. Weigerly, *History*, 121

28. See William Crotty, *Political Reform and the American Experiment* (New York: Harper and Row, 1977), 46.

29. See Robert Remini, *Andrew Jackson and the Course of American Democracy, 1832–1845* (New York: Praeger, 1984); for a counterargument, see Edward Pessen, *Jacksonian America: Society, Personality, and Politics*, revised edition (Chicago: University of Illinois Press, 1985).

30. Bernardo and Bacon, *American Military Policy*, 126.

31. Ibid., 163–65.

32. Weigerly, *History*, 168.

WORKS CITED

Abenheim, Donald. "The Citizen in Uniform: Reform and Its Critics in the Bundeswehr." In Stephen Szabo (ed.), *The Bundeswehr and Western Security* (New York: St. Martin's, 1990), 31–39.

Abrahamsson, Bengt. *Military Professionalism and Political Power* (Beverley Hills, CA: Sage, 1972).

Adcock, Frank. *The Greek and Macedonian Art of War* (Berkeley: University of California Press, 1957).

Albrecht-Carrie, Rene. *A Diplomatic History of Europe Since the Congress of Vienna* (New York: Harper & Row, 1958).

Ames, Fisher. "Conservative Forebodings." In Russel Kirk (ed.), *The Portable Conservative Reader* (New York: Viking Penguin, 1982), 84–112.

Anderson, John. *Military Theory and Practice in the Age of Xenophon* (Berkeley: University of California Press, 1970).

Anderson, Victor. "Hoplite Weapons and Offensive Arms." In Anderson (ed.), *Hoplites* (London: Routledge, 1991), 15–37.

Andreski, Stanislas. *Military Organization and Society* (London: Routledge & Kegan Paul, 1954).

Apter, David. *The Politics of Modernization* (Chicago: University Press, 1965).

Aristotle. *The Politics.* Translated by T.A. Sinclair (Harvard: Harvard University Press, 1932).

———. *The Athenian Constitution.* Translated by P.J. Rhodes (New York: Penguin, 1984).

Aron, Raymond. *War and Industrial Society* (New York: Oxford University Press, 1958).

Bandry, Pierre. "Lazare Carnot: Organizer of Victory—How the 'Calculus of Enthusiasm' Saved France," *The American Almanac,* July 21, 1997.

Barnouw, Adriaan. *The Making of Modern Holland* (New York: W.W. Norton, 1944).

———. *The Pageant of Netherlands History* (New York: Longmans, 1952).

Bartlett and Kaplan (eds.), *Bartlett's Familiar Quotations,* Sixteenth edition (Boston: Little, Brown and Company, 1992), 364.

Bean, Richard. "War and the Birth of the Nation-State." *Journal of Economic History* 33 (1973), 203–221.

Behrens, Catherine. *Society, Government, and the Enlightenment* (New York: Harper, 1985).

Berghan, Volker. *Germany and the Approach of War in 1914* (London: Thames, 1973).

———. *Militarism* (Cambridge: University Press, 1984).

Berlin, Isaiah. "The Originality of Machiavelli." In Berlin (ed.), *Against the Current: Essays in the History of Ideas* (New York: MacMillan, 1975), 25–79.

Bernardo, Joseph and Eugene, Bacon. *American Military Policy* (Harrisburg, PA: Stackpole, 1955).

Berryman, Sue. *Who Serves?* (Boulder, CO: Westview Press, 1987).

Bertrand, Jean-Paul. *The Army of the French Revolution* (Princeton: University Press, 1988).

————. *The Army of the French Revolution*. Translated by Robert Palmer (Princeton: University Press, 1988).

Best, Geoffrey. *War and Society in Revolutionary Europe, 1770–1870* (New York: St. Martin's, 1982), 71–72.

Binkim, Martin and Shirley Bach. *Women and the Military* (Washington DC: Brookings Institution, 1977).

Bluhm, William. *Theories of the Political System*. Second Edition (Englewood Cliffs, NJ: Prentice-Hall, 1971).

Boorstin, Daniel. *The Americans* (New York: Random House, 1958).

Brassey's Annual, published from 1884 (New York: Praeger).

Breisach, Earnst. *Renaissance Europe* (New York: MacMillan, 1973).

Cameron, Colin and Judith Blackstone. *Minorities in the Armed Forces* (Madison: University of Wisconsin Press, 1970).

Carsten, Francis. *The Origins of Prussia* (Oxford: Clarendon, 1964).

————. *The Reichswehr in Politics, 1918 to 1919* (Oxford: Clarendon, 1966).

Chickering, Roger. "Patriotic Societies and German Foreign Policy, 1890–1914." *International History Review* 1 (1979), 470–89.

Clausewitz, Carl von. *War, Politics, and Power*. Translated by Edward Colins (Washington: Regnery Gateway, 1962).

————. *On War*. Edited and translated by Michael Howard and Peter Paret (Princeton: Princeton University Press, 1976).

Clodfelter, Michael. *Warfare and Armed Conflict* (Jefferson, NC: McFarland, 1992).

Coatzee, Marilyn. *The German Army League* (New York: Oxford Press, 1990).

Corvisier, André. *L'Armée Française de la Fin du XVIIᵉ Siècle au Ministére de Choiseul*. Two Volumes (Paris: Presses Universitaires de France, 1964).

————. *Armies and Societies in Europe, 1494–1789*. Translated by Abigail Siddall (Bloomington: University of Indiana Press, 1979), 113.

Craig, Gordon. *The Politics of the Prussian Army* (New York: Oxford, 1955).

————. *NATO and the New German Army* (Princeton: Princeton University Press, 1955).

————. *Germany 1866–1945* (New York: Oxford University Press, 1978).

Crotty, William. *Political Reform and the American Experiment* (New York: Harper and Row, 1977).

Dahl, Robert. *Polyarchy* (New Haven: Yale University Press, 1971).

————. *A Preface to Economic Democracy* (Cambridge: Polity Press, 1985).

Dalfume, Richard. *Desegregation of the U.S. Armed Forces* (Columbia: University of Missouri Press, 1969).

de Grazia, Sebastian. *Machiavelli in Hell* (Princeton: University Press, 1989).

Delbrück, Hans. *History of the Art of War*, 4 Volumes. Translated by Walter Renfroe (Westport, CN: Greenwood, 1975).

Demeter, Karl. *The German Officer Corps in Society and State, 1650–1945* (New York: Praeger, 1965).

Deutsch, Karl and Lewis Edinger. *Germany Rejoins the Powers* (Stanford: University Press, 1959).

Dolman, Everett. "Obligation and the Citizen-Soldier: Machiavellian *Virtú* versus Hobbesian Order." *Journal of Political and Military Sociology* 23 (1995), 191–212.

————. "War and (the Democratic) Peace: Military Service, Citizenship, and the International Environment." *Citizenship Studies* 4:2 (July 2000), 117–48.

Downing, Brian. *Military Revolution and Political Change* (Princeton: Princeton University Press, 1992).

Doyle, Michael. "Kant, Liberal Legacies, and Foreign Affairs, Parts 1 and 2." *Philosophy and Public Affairs* 12 (1983), 206–35 and 323–53.

Drake, Michael. *Problematics of Military Power* (London: Frank Cass, 2001).

Duffy, Christopher. *Frederick the Great's Army* (London: Routledge, 1974).

———. *Frederick the Great* (London: Routledge, 1988).

Duffy, Michael (ed.). *The Military Revolution and the State 1500–1800* (Exeter: University of Exeter Press, 1980).

Dunnigan, James. *How to Stop a War* (Garden City, NJ: Doubleday, 1987).

Dupuy, Trevor and R. Ernest Dupuy. *The Harper Encyclopedia of Military History*. Fourth Edition (New York: Harper Collins, 1993).

Dupuy, Trevor, Curt Johnson, and David Bongard. *Harper Encyclopedia of Military Biography* (New York: Harper Collins, 1992).

Eckstein, Harry. "A Theory of Stable Democracy." *Research Monograph* No. 10 (Center for International Studies: Princeton, 1961).

Edmonds, Martin. *Armed Services* (Leicester: Leicester University Press, 1988), 59.

Ehrenreich, Barbara. *Blood Rites* (New York: Henry Holt, 1997).

Eley, Geoff. "Reshaping the Right: Radical Nationalism and the German Navy League, 1898–1908." *Historical Journal* 21 (1978), 327–54.

———. *Reshaping the German Right* (New Haven: Yale University Press, 1980).

Ellis, John. *The Social History of the Machine Gun* (Baltimore: Johns Hopkins University Press, 1975).

———. *World War II: A Statistical Survey* (New York: Facts On File, 1993).

Ergang, Robert. *The Potsdam Führer* (New York: Columbia University Press, 1941).

———. *Europe* (Boston: D.C. Heath, 1954).

Everdell, William. *The End of Kings: A History of Republics and Republicans* (New York: Free Press, 1983).

Ferrill, Arthur. *The Origins of War* (London: Thames and Hudson, 1985).

Finer, Samuel. *The Man on Horseback*. Second Enlarged Edition (Hammondsworth, England: Penguin, 1975).

———. "State- and Nation-Building in Europe: The Role of the Military." In Tilly (ed.), *Formation of National States in Western Europe* (Princeton: Princeton University Press, 1975), 84–163.

Fischer, Fritz. *War of Illusions: German Policies from 1911–1914*. Translated by Marian Jackson (London: Chatto, 1975).

Flexner, James. *George Washington* (Boston: Little Brown, 1965).

Flora, Peter, Franz Kraus, and Winnifred Pfenning. *State, Economy, and Society in Western Europe, 1815–1970*, 2 Volumes (Chicago: St James Press, 1987).

Ford, Franklin. *Robe and Sword* (New York: Harper, 1965).

Forrest, William. *A History of Sparta 950–192 BCE* (London: Hutchinson, 1968).

Friedrich, Carl. *Man and His Government* (New York: McGraw-Hill, 1963).

Fuller, J.F.C. *The Foundations of the Science of War* (London: Hutchinson, 1926).

———. *Armament and History* (New York: Scribner's, 1942).

———. *A Military History of the Western World*, Volume II (New York: Funk and Wagnall's, 1955).

Gaddis, John. *The Long Peace* (New York: Oxford University Press, 1987).

Geissler, Erhard. *Biological and Toxin Weapons Today* (Oxford: University Press, 1986).

Gillis, John. (ed.). *The Militarization of the Western World* (New Brunswick, NJ: Rutgers University Press, 1989).

Glatthaar, Joseph. *Forged in Battle* (New York: Free Press, 1990).

Goerlitz, Walter. *History of the German General Staff 1657–1945*. Translated by Brian Battershaw (New York: Praeger, 1953).

Gordon, Harold. *The Reichswehr and the German Republic, 1919–26* (Princeton: University Press, 1957).

Gray, Randal and Christopher Argyle. *Chronicle of the First World War*, 2 Volumes (New York: Facts On File, 1991).

Greenfield, Liah. *Nationalists* (Cambridge: Harvard University Press, 1992), 180–84.

Guerlac, Henry. "Vauban: The Impact of Science on War." In E.M. Earle (ed.), *Makers of Modern Strategy* (Princeton: Princeton University Press, 1971), 26–48.

Gulick, Edward. *Europe's Classical Balance of Power* (New York: Norton, 1955).

Gurr, Robert, Keith Jaggers, and Will Moore, "The Transformation of the Western State: The Growth of Democracy, Autocracy, and State Power since 1800." *Studies in Comparative International Development* 25 (1990), 73–108.

Hale, John. *War and Society in Renaissance Europe* (New York: St. Martin's Press, 1985).

Hamilton, Edward. *The French and Indian Wars* (Garden City, NJ: Doubleday, 1962).

Hamilton, Alexander, James Madison, and John Jay. *The Federalist Papers* (New York: Penguin, 1961).

Hanson, Donald. "Hobbes 'Highway to Peace.'" *International Organization* 38 (1984), 329–54.

Hattendorf, John. "The American Navy in the World of Franklin and Jefferson, 1775–1826." In Brian Bond and Ian Roy (eds.), *War and Society*, Volume 2 (New York: Holmes and Meier, 1977), 7–19.

Hebbert, Francis. *Soldier of France* (New York: Lang, 1981).

Herwig, Holger. *The German Naval Officer Corps* (Oxford: Clarendon, 1973).

Hill, James. *The Minute Man in Peace and War* (Harrisburg, PA: Stackpole, 1963).

Hintze, Otto. *The Historical Essays*. Translated by Felix Gilbert (New York: Oxford University Press, 1975).

Hobbes, Thomas. *Leviathan*. In Richard Tuck (ed.), *Cambridge Texts in the History of Political Thought* (New York: Cambridge University Press, 1991).

———. *The Collected Works of Thomas Hobbes*, 11 Volumes. Edited by Sir William Molesworth (London: Routledge Thoemmes, 1992).

Hoffstader, Richard, William Miller, and Daniel Aaron. *The American Republic*, Volume One, *Through Reconstruction*. Second Edition (Englewood Cliffs, NJ: Prentice-Hall, 1970).

Holborn, Hajo. "Moltke and Schlieffen: The Prussian-German School." In Peter Paret (ed.), *Makers of Modern Strategy* (Princeton: Princeton University Press, 1986), 186–205.

Howard, Michael. "Total War in the Twentieth Century: Participation and Consensus in the Second World War." In Brian Bond and Ian Roy (eds.), *War and Society*, Volume II (New York: Holmes and Meier, 1975), 216–26.

———. *War in European History* (New York: Oxford University Press, 1976).

Huntington, Samuel. *The Soldier and the State* (Cambridge: Harvard University Press, 1957).

Huxley, George. *Early Sparta* (London: Faber, 1962).

Israel, Jonathan. *The Dutch Republic* (Oxford: Clarendon Press, 1995).

Janowitz, Morris. *The Professional Soldier*. Revised Edition (New York: Free Press, 1971).

Jordan, William. *Great Britain, France and the German Problem, 1918–1939* (London: Unwin & Allen, 1943).

Kaiser, David. *Politics and War* (Cambridge: Harvard University Press, 1990).

Kant, Immanuel. *Perpetual Peace*. Translated by Ted Humphrey (Indianapolis, IN: Hacket, 1985).

Keegan, John. *A History of Warfare* (New York: Vintage Books, 1993).

Kehr, Eckart. *Economic Interest, Militarism, and Foreign Policy*. Translated by Grete Heinz (Berkeley: University of California Press, 1965).

———. *Economic Interest, Militarism, and Foreign Policy: Essays on German History*. Translated by Grete Heinz and edited by Gordon Craig (Berkeley: University of California Press, 1965).

Kennet, Lee. *The French Armies in the Seven Years' War* (Durham, NC: Duke University Press, 1967).

Kitchen, Martin. *German Officer Corps, 1890–1914* (Oxford: Clarendon Press, 1968).

————. *A Military History of Germany* (Bloomington: Indiana University Press, 1975).

Kriedberg, Marvin and Merton Henry. *History of Military Mobilization in the United States Army* (Washington, DC: Department of the Army, 1955).

Lacey, James. "The Case for Conscription." *Military Service in the United States*. American Assembly Book (Englewood Cliffs, NJ: Prentice-Hall, 1982).

Lipset, Seymour. "Some Social Requisites of Democracy: Economic Development and Political Legitimacy." *American Political Science Review* 53 (March 1959), 69–105.

————. *Political Man* (New York: Doubleday, 1960).

Littman, Robert. *Kinship and Politics in Athens 600–400 BCE* (New York: Peter Lang, 1990).

Lorimer, Hilda. "The Hoplite Phalanx with Special Reference to the Poems of Archilochus and Tyrtaeus." *Annual of the British School at Athens* 42 (1947), 121–24.

Lutz, R.H. *The Fall of the German Empire*, Volume I (Stanford: Stanford University Press, 1932).

Luxembourg, Rosa. *Selected Political Writings.* Translated by William Graf (New York: Grove Press, 1974).

Lynn, John. *Bayonets of the Republic* (Urbana: University of Illinois Press, 1984), 55–57.

————. "A Quest for Glory." In Murray Williamson, MacGreggor Knox, and Alvin Bernstein (eds.), *The Making of Strategy* (Cambridge: Cambridge University Press, 1994), 178–204.

Machiavelli, Niccolo. *Discourses on the First Ten Books of Titus Livy*. Translated by Leslie Walker (New Haven: Yale University Press, 1950).

————. *The Art of War*. Translated by Ellis Farneworth (New York: Da Capo, 1965).

Macredis, Roy and Bernard Brown. "Legitimacy and Consensus." In Macredis and Brown (eds.), *Comparative Politics*. Fourth Edition (Homewood, IL: Dorsey Press, 1972), 99–105.

Manicas, Peter. *War and Democracy* (New York: Basil Blackwell, 1989), 209.

Maoz, Zeev and Bruce Russett, "Normative and Structural Causes of the Democratic Peace, 1946–1986." *American Political Science Review* 87 (September 1993), 624–38.

Marwick, Arthur. *The Deluge* (London: Bodley Head, 1965).

————. *Britain in the Century of Total War* (London: Bodley Head, 1968).

Mattingly, Garret. *The Armada* (Boston: Houghton Mifflin, 1959).

McNeill, William. *The Pursuit of Power* (Chicago: University of Chicago Press, 1982).

Mearsheimer, John. *Conventional Deterrence* (Ithaca: Cornell Press, 1983).

————. "Back to the Future: Instability in Europe After the Cold War." *International Security* 15 (Summer 1990), 5–56.

Mitchell, Brian. *International Historical Statistics* (New York: Stockton Press, 1992).

Moltke, Helmuth von. *On the Art of War: Selected Writings*. Daniel Hughs (Ed.) Translated by Harry Bell (Novato, CA: Presidio, 1993).

Moore, Barrington. *Social Origins of Dictatorship and Democracy* (Boston: Beacon Press, 1966).

Morrison, John and J.F. Coates. *The Athenian Trireme* (Cambridge: University Press, 1986).

Morton, Louis. "The Origins of American Military Policy." *Military Affairs* 26 (1958), 75–82.

Mosca, Gaetano. *The Ruling Class*. Translated by Hannah Kahn (New York: McGraw Hill, 1939).

Moskos, Charles. "Institutional/Occupational Trends in Armed Forces." *Armed Forces and Society* 4 (1977), 41–50.

————. "Social Considerations of the All-Volunteer Force." *Military Service in the United States*. American Assembly Book (Englewood Cliffs, NJ: Prentice-Hall, 1982), 129–50.

————. "Institutional/Occupational Trends in Armed Forces: An Update." *Armed Forces and Society* 12 (1986), 377–82.

Mumford, Lewis. *Technics and Civilization* (New York: Harcourt, Brace and Co., 1934).

Myrdal, Gunnar. *An American Dilemma* (New York: Harper, 1944).

Nef, John. *War and Human Progress* (Cambridge: Harvard Press, 1950).

North, Douglass. *Structure and Change in Economic History* (New York: W.W. Norton, 1981).
————. "A Transaction Cost Theory of Politics." *Journal of Theoretical Politics* 2 (1990), 355–67.
North, Douglass and Robert Thomas. *The Rise of the Western World* (Cambridge: University Press, 1973).
Ober, Josiah. "Hoplites and Obstacles." In Victor Hansen (ed.), *Hoplites* (New York: Routledge, 1991), 180–88.
O'Connell, Robert. *Of Arms and Men* (Oxford: University Press, 1989).
Olson, Mancur. *The Rise and Decline of Nations* (New Haven: Yale University Press, 1982).
O'Neil, Robert. *The German Army and the Nazi Party 1933–39* (London: Cassell, 1966).
Owen, John. "How Liberalism Produces Peace." *International Security* 19 (1994), 87–125.
Palmer, John. *General von Steuben* (New Haven, CT: Yale University Press, 1937).
Palmer, Robert. *Twelve Who Ruled* (Princeton: University Press, 1942).
————. "Frederick the Great, Guibert, Bülow: From Dynastic to National War." In Edward Earle (ed.), *The Makers of Modern Strategy* (Princeton: University Press, 1971), 91–119.
Pargellis, Stanley. *Lord Loudoun in North America* (New Haven: Yale University Press, 1933).
Parker, Geoffrey. *The Army of Flanders and the Spanish Road 1567–1659* (Cambridge: Cambridge University Press, 1972).
Peckman, Howard. *The Colonial Wars, 1869–1762* (Chicago: University Press, 1964).
Pessen, Edward. *Jacksonian America: Society, Personality, and Politics*. Revised Edition (Chicago: University of Illinois Press, 1985).
Plutarch. *The Rise and Fall of Athens* (Baltimore: Penguin, 1962).
Porter, Bruce. *War and the Rise of the State* (New York: Free Press, 1994).
Preston, Richard, Sydney Wise, and Herman Werner. *Men in Arms*. Revised Edition (New York: Praeger, 1962).
Price, Robert. "*Ambizione* in Machiavelli's Thought." *History of Political Thought* 3 (1982), 193–221.
Quigley, Carrol. *Weapons Systems and Political Stability* (Washington, DC: University Press, 1983).
Ralston, David. *Importing the European Army* (Chicago: University of Chicago Press, 1990).
Rapp, Alfred. "The Untrue Myth." In Walter Stahl (ed.), *The Politics of Postwar Germany* (Hamburg: Hafen-Druckerei, 1963), 146–54.
Rappoport, David. "A Comparative Theory of Military and Political Types." In Samuel Huntington (ed.), *Changing Patterns of Military Politics* (New York: Free Press, 1962), 71–101.
Remini, Robert. *Andrew Jackson and the Course of American Democracy, 1832–1845* (New York: Praeger, 1984).
Rhodes, Edward. *Power and MADness* (New York: Columbia University Press, 1989).
Richardson, Lewis. *Statistics of Deadly Quarrels* (Pittsburgh: Boxwood Press, 1960).
Riemens, Hendrik. *The Netherlands* (New York: Eagle, 1944).
Riesenberg, Peter. *Citizenship in the Western Tradition* (Chapel Hill, NC: University of North Carolina Press, 1992).
Ritter, Gerhard. *The Sword and the Scepter*, Volume VII (Miami: University of Miami Press, 1970).
Roberts, Michael. *The Military Revolution, 1560–1660* (Belfast: Belfast University Press, 1956).
Rosenberg, Hans. *Bureaucracy, Aristocracy and Autocracy* (Boston: Beacon, 1958).
Rosinski, Herbert. *The German Army* (New York: Praeger, 1944).
Rothenberg, Gunther. "Maurice of Nassau, Gustavus Adolphus, Raimondo Montecuccoli, and the 'Military Revolution' of the Seventeenth Century." In Peter Paret (ed.), *Makers of Modern Strategy* (Princeton: Princeton University Press, 1986), 32–63.

————. *The Art of Warfare in the Age of Napoleon* (Bloomington, IN: University of Indiana Press, 1980), 94.

Russet, Bruce. *Grasping the Democratic Peace* (Princeton: Princeton University Press, 1993).

Rustow, Dankwart. "Transitions to Democracy: Toward a Dynamic Model." *Comparative Politics* 2 (Summer 1970), 337–64.

Schama, Simon. *Citizens* (New York: Alfred Knopf, 1989), 281–83 and 292.

Schevill, Ferdinand. *The Great Elector* (Chicago: University Press, 1947).

Schwartz, Thomas. "The 'Skeleton-Key'—American Foreign Policy, European Unity and German Rearmament, 1949–1954." *Central European History* 19 (1986), 370–71.

Scott, Samuel. *The Response of the Royal Army to the French Revolution* (Oxford: Clarendon, 1978).

Seaton, Albert. *The German Army, 1933–45* (New York: St. Martin's, 1982).

Segal, Dennis. *Recruiting for Uncle Sam* (Lawrence: University of Kansas Press, 1989).

Shanahan, William. *Prussian Military Reforms 1780–1813* (New York: AMS, 1966).

Shirer, William. *The Rise and Fall of the Third Reich* (New York: Simon and Schuster, 1960).

Simon, Walter. *The Failure of the Prussian Reform Movement, 1807–1819* (Ithaca: Cornell University Press, 1955).

Singer David and Melvin Small. *The Wages of War* (New York: Wiley, 1972).

————. "The War Proneness of Democratic Regimes." *Jerusalem Journal of International Relations* 1 (1976), 50–69.

————. *Resort to Arms.* Second Edition (Beverly Hills, CA: Sage, 1982).

Skocpol, Theda. *States and Social Revolutions* (Cambridge: Cambridge University Press, 1979).

Smith, Woodruff. *The German Colonial Empire* (Chapel Hill: University of North Carolina Press, 1978).

Snodgrass, Alfred. "The Hoplite Reform and History." *Journal of Hellenic Studies* 97 (1977), 84–101.

Snyder, Jack. *Myths of Empire* (Ithaca: Cornell University Press, 1991).

Sombart, Werner. *The Quintessence of Capitalism.* New Edition (New York: Fertig, 1967).

Spier, Hans. *German Rearmament and Atomic War* (Evanston, IL: Row & Peterson, 1957).

Stepan, Alfred. "The New Professionalism of Internal Warfare and the Military Role Expansionism." In Stepan (ed.), *Authoritarian Brazil* (New Haven: Yale University Press, 1973), 47–65.

Stone, Bailey. *The French Parlements and the Crisis of the Old Regime* (Chapel Hill, NC: University of North Carolina Press, 1986).

Stradling, R.A. *The Armada of Flanders* (Cambridge: Cambridge University Press, 1992).

Strause-Hupe, *Geopolitics* (New York: Putnam, 1942).

Strauss, Leo. *Thoughts on Machiavelli* (Seattle: University of Washington Press, 1958).

Symcox, Geoffrey. *The Crisis of French Seapower* (Amsterdam: Martinus Nijhoff, 1974).

Taylor, Alan. *Bismarck* (New York: Vintage Paperback, 1967).

The Statesman's Yearbook, published from 1864 (London: MacMillan).

Thompson, William. "Democracy and Peace: Putting the Cart Before the Horse." *International Organization* 50 (January 1996), 141–74.

Thucydides. *History of the Peloponnesian War.* Translated by Benjamin Jowett (London: Folio Society, 1994).

Tilly, Charles. "Reflections on the History of European State-Making." In Charles Tilly (ed.), *Formation of National States in Western Europe* (Princeton: Princeton University Press, 1975), 3–83.

————. "War Making and State Making as Organized Crime." In Evans, Rueschmayer, and Skocpol (eds.), *Bringing the State Back In* (Cambridge: Cambridge University Press, 1985), 169–91.

Toynbee, Arnold. *War and Civilization* (New York: Oxford University Press, 1950).

————. *A Study of History* (London: Oxford University Press, 1956).

Treitschke, Heinrich von. *Politics* (abridged). Translated by Hans Kohn (New York: Harbinger, 1963).

Tuchman, Barbara. *The Guns of August* (New York: Alfred Knopf, 1962).

Upton, Emory. *The Military Policy of the United States from 1775* (Washington DC: US Government Printing Office, 1904).

Vagts, Alfred. *A History of Militarism* (New York: W.W. Norton, 1937).

Van Creveld, Martin. *Technology and War* (New York: Free Press, 1989).

Van Evera, Stephen. "The Cult of the Offensive and the Origins of the First World War." *International Security* 9 (1984), 58–105.

Vanhanen, Tatu. *The Process of Democratization* (New York: Crane Russak, 1984 and 1990).

Van Loon, Hendrik. *The Fall of the Dutch Republic*. New Edition (Boston: Houghton Mifflin, 1924).

Veit, Valentin. *German People* (New York: Alfred Knopf, 1946).

Vincent, Andrew. *Theories of the State* (New York: Basil Blackwell, 1987).

Waltz, Kenneth. *Man, the State, and War* (New York: Columbia University Press, 1954).

Watkins, Trevor. "The Beginnings of Warfare." In John Hackett (ed.), *Warfare in the Ancient World* (New York: Facts on File, 1989), 15–35.

Watson, Sidney. *Carton* (London: Bodley Head, 1954).

Weber, Max. *General Economic History*. Translated by Frank Knight (Glencoe, IL: Free Press, 1927).

Wedgewood, Cicely. *William the Silent* (New Haven: Yale University Press, 1944).

Weigley, Russell. *History of the United States Army*. Enlarged Edition. (Bloomington: Indiana University Press, 1984).

———. *The Age of Battles* (Bloomington: Indiana University Press, 1991).

Wheeler, E.L. "The Hoplomachoi and Vegetius' Spartan Drillmasters." *Chiron* 13 (1983), 1–20.

Wheeler-Bennett, John. *The Nemesis of Power* (London: MacMillan, 1953).

White, Jr., Lynn. *Medieval Technology and Social Change* (New York: Oxford University Press, 1966).

Wilkenson, Samuel. *The Rise of General Bonaparte* (Oxford: University Press, 1930).

Willems, Emilio. *A Way of Life and Death* (Nashville, TN: Vanderbilt University Press, 1986).

Wolin, Sheldon. *Politics and Vision* (Boston: Little-Brown, 1965).

Wright, Quincy. *A Study of War*. Second Edition (Chicago: University Press, 1965).

Xenophon. *Hellenica*. Translated by Rex Warner (New York: Penguin, 1978).

Yadin, Yigael. *The Art of Warfare in Biblical Lands*, Volume 1 (New York: A. Knopf, 1963).

Zagare, Frank. *The Dynamics of Deterrence* (Chicago: University Press, 1987).

INDEX